PARADIGM SHIFT

PARADIGM SHIFT

From the Jewish Renewal Teachings of
Reb Zalman Schachter-Shalomi

Edited by Ellen Singer

JASON ARONSON INC.
Northvale, New Jersey
London

This book was set in 10 pt. Times Roman by Lind Graphics of Upper Saddle River, New Jersey, and printed and bound by Haddon Craftsmen of Scranton, Pennsylvania.

Library of Congress Cataloging-in-Publication Data

Schachter-Shalomi, Zalman, 1924–
    Paradigm shift : from the Jewish renewal teachings of Reb Zalman
    Schachter-Shalomi / by Reb Zalman M. Schachter-Shalomi and edited by Ellen
    Singer.
        p. cm.
    Includes index.
    ISBN 0-87668-543-2
    1. Spiritual life — Judaism. 2. Judaism. 3. Prayer — Judaism.
    4. Spiritual life — New Age movement. 5. New Age movement.
    I. Title.
    BM723.S294 1993
    296.8′34 — dc20   93-8238

Manufactured in the United States of America. Jason Aronson Inc. offers books and cassettes. For information and catalog write to Jason Aronson Inc., 230 Livingston Street, Northvale, New Jersey 07647.

The Prayer of Atzilut — ׳—Yud

Dear God,

I need to pray You this writing/reading. In it may my soul pour out its content into Your being and may Your being flow into mine in full oneness and love and receive You without resistance, marveling and rejoicing to adore You in this.

Hold this intention in the will during the entire process of writing, editing, typesetting, printing, binding, shipping, selling, buying, reading, reflecting, and praying that follows.

The Prayer of B'riyah — ה — Heh

ENTER:

Cosmic Computer
>LOOP<
For the sake of the meaningful survival of life on our planet I do my part to enter this program into the consciousness of human biocomputers - >LOOP<

Enter this repeating routine as constant for aligning the mind's priority routing while scanning the system to harmonize all subsidiary programs with the resulting decrease of chaos, wrong perception, wrong concepts, attitudes, and conversely, an increase in energy and consciousness and the maximalization of probabilities for human survival.

The Prayer of Yetzirah — ו — Vav

Master of the Universe
Center of all Gravity
Full-and All-ness
Allah-ness
Wholly-ness
Divinity
Infinity
Force making for Salvation and Enlightenment
Loving Parent
Most intimate Lover
Best of all friends
Us-ness
Source and goal
O Truth! O Beauty! O Goodness!
I am Yours to use for Your process.
For Your sake,
For my very Self-ishness
I want to live out the intention You have for my
life.
Take my disposition and shape it to Your will.

משוך עבדך אל רצונך

Keeping this *kavvanah* as intermittent
heart focus

The Prayer of Assiyah−הֵ−heh

ADONAI!
I know that You want me to do this book
You gave me the time and the space,
the solitude and the equipment,
the motivation and the thoughts.
You set me to learn in life and from it.
You kneaded and shaped me,
wrenched me and fired me,
set me^up and up^set me.

You kept me alive and in functioning existence,
and made me reach this here and this now.
And You don't want me to bullshit either.

So OK, I am willing, and I can't do this by myself. I really want You to
open me to the beings of light, the souls that came before me and those that
will yet come. I want You to open me to the process of revelation,
enlightenment, holy spirit, the means You use to bring to us what we need
in order to serve You, Life of Life.

I ask You to focus the consciousness
of Angels, guides, holy masters
who can best help me in this work.
Inasmuch as You are the Other—

I address You as You.
Inasmuch as I-AM-that-I-am
dreams this flight of consciousness
that is human evolution to divine awakening,
I witness the dream—
I want this to be good,
really good,
state of the art of in-forming and re-forming
this set of selves
that will be involved with this book
and the echoes these selves will make
in other processes
of revelation—

I want it to produce
a minimum of moral pollution
and a maximum of benefits.

I don't want it to become a stumbling block
to any soul in transit to Your Presence.

I want it to help clarify what is happening to us now
so that we can participate willingly, consciously,
                    Yes,
                    ecstatically in the birth of the new
                    and not see in this birth our enemy
                    but our progeny—
Shekhinah
God-Presence
Holy Mother,
help us gently
to ride the contractions
of the birth pangs of *Mashiach*
in world events,
the labor pangs of politics,
economics,
ecological changes
with awareness,
with presence of mind and heart.

Teacher, Revealer, Healer!

Let the changes through which You have to take us to make us see and hear,
evaluate and respond intelligently, be as gradual and gentle as possible. At the
brink of planetary destruction we cannot afford madness and delirium. Please
calm our anxiety that it may not cloud our discernment. And keep us
bouyant with compassion and love, with understanding and care in real ways,
toward the real people in our lives, mates and parents and children, neighbors
and co-workers, yea, those who ride with us daily to work, to those who take
the parking places we would have, and those human beings who have to
handle sanitation and taxes.

Keep us focused with the vision and the hope; keep us prudent and caring. And those of us who serve You as instruments, keep us sane and don't let us burn out.

Help and guide me, God, to have the right readers in mind and to communicate with them clearly. Steer me to friends who will participate in shaping this book, who will read it and make suggestions to improve its effectiveness.

In all of this, God, make me appreciate the treasures of our holy traditions even when You make me aware of how, for these days, we need new forms. Allow me and the others who enter into this process, Book-Reader-Writer, to see that as we are, so others were, waves in a river of light and life, and that it is inevitable that someday this will also have to be abandoned for something that is yet to come.

May I in this way fulfill the trust of my teachers, and not betray the interest of my students.

Amen.

This book, in some way
a contribution to thinking
about the Holy *Shekhinah*,
the feminine *partzuf* of God,
is dedicated to Her daughters,
the women in my life:
my dear later mother — peace upon her —
my partner, Eve Penner-Ilsen,
my sisters Dvorah Kieffer, Ada Scharfman, peace be upon her,
my daughters Mimi Gess, Tina Duskis, Lisa, and Shalvi,
and to all the others,
my co-parents and partners of the present and the past —
may they all live and be blessed.

CONTENTS

PART II *SHOAH*

PART III THINKING ABOUT GOD, REALITY, AND LIFE

PART IV DAVVENOLOGY: THE ART AND SCIENCE OF *DAVVENEN*

AUTHOR'S PREFACE

Which one of the voices is really my voice? In truth they all are and this is why I am so delighted that I can use the typography made accessible by the computer. When I first published Fragments of a Future Scroll *I wanted to print the book in four typefaces to correspond to PaRDeS, the Four Worlds, the four letters of the Name. Then it was not yet feasible, but now my heart and right brain can use Times Roman and my left brain can use Helvetica. The traffic controller can use Courier, and all is clear. So now as the* Apter Rebbe *used to write,*

Yitgadal Hakadosh-barukh-hu
Vetukdash Hashekhinah
Avi Haneshamot Yesh Haamitti
Almighty Divine Nurthuring Yah
Shehechyanu Vekiyemanu Vehigiyanu Lazman Hazeh

In such ways did our teachers obm. begin their books with thanks and praises to God cast in initials that spelled one or a series of sacred names. Names are connected with attributes and aspects. Rabbi Yitzchak Luria describes some aspects of God as *partzufim*, masks and personae. In other, more contemporary words, we speak of these attributes and aspects as interfaces, templates and root metaphors. Our stories with God always connect us with one *partzuf* or another. We live by these stories, myths, and as afterthoughts to our experiences in these encounters we make our theologies. Covenants are made under the aegis of the *partzufim* and the *mitzvot*; action directives, the promises made in the covenanting, the accepting of the Yoke of the Kingdom and the Commandments, flow naturally from our mutuality with the *partzufim*.

There are so many ways in which I wrestled with God. As Him/Her or the One—who is androgynous both and neither, the named—the Kabbalah is so full of these—and the Nameless, the Self, the Wholly Other and both and neither I sought, found and lost and was found by the Living God, time and again.

The Hymn of Glory has this verse: "Through countless visions did their pictures run, Behold through all their visions Thou art One." There is an identity of Being despite the shifts of images that served to place us in the Presence.

My devout affirmation at one time was in the warm and accessible Person-ness of God. This was my experience of God one lonely night in the empty *bet hamidrash* of the Shomrey Shabbat Anshei Sfard in Boro Park, where we lived when we first came to the United States. In *davvenen Maariv* I was faced by God as the compassionate, helmeted Knight-Warrior, and a floodgate of tears opened for me and yes! I promised fealty and service.

On another occasion, seeing the late *rebbe* Rabbi Yosef Yitzchak of Lubavitch in heartrending weeping in the *Maariv* prayer of Rosh HaShanah 1943, I too pleaded with a vividly present God to rebuild His Majesty and please, please deign again to extend life and take on the will to reign over us. And then and there I covenanted to work for the Kingdom.

Then there were times when I knew God as the cosmic Atheist, the One in solitary confinement in Himself who has no God, alas! And then I was content to be a figure in God's dream, a bit actor in the cosmic play. Or as I knew in all sureness at another time that the God who truly and absolutely "is" as the nominative I-am-that-I-am Subject of the Universe does not "exist" as an object in the accusative. In one such moment I wrote "Beyond I and Thou." Or the time when God was for me the Power of the *Mafli'-Laasot*, the Radical Amazement that Rabbeinu A. J. Heschel spoke of and I stood transfixed for three hours in front of an old maple near the *Chabad beth hamidrash* in awe of the magnificent immanence in tree, air, and soil. All I wanted then was to glory and appreciate that I too was a *mishkan*, a sanctuary for that amazing Presence. Or once in a deep, deep meditation I "died" and dissolved in the void and only after a while did I come back into form and name and I thought I now knew what *gilgul*—the wheel of reincarnation, transformation—was all about. Each time I would have claimed that that was the only face—*partzuf*—God could have.

And then there was another time—beyond ordinary time—when the masks were on a spinning carousel of cosmologies and truths, once this, once that. Then the omnipotentiality of the interfaces came clear to me. And I gave assent: "Thou canst do anything." So my perspectives have shifted as life led me.

Some may see contradictions in these essays; so be it. As the poet David Slabotsky put it, they are not really serious, "they are only contra-*dictions*." Not worse than Pesach and Yom Kippur, to eat *matzoh* or not to eat. There is a time for everything.

This book is post-Holocaust. There are some ideas about Holocaust that need to be examined freshly as well as an understanding of our renewed relationship with the land and the state of Israel. It takes for granted that the reader wants to make sense of the present state of Jewish self-reflection and wants to follow my evolution from apologetics for *Chabad* Hasidism (in an article from 1966 I referred to myself as one of "we Orthodox" and at that time this was my proper identification) to my present state of understanding of the Jewish-Human-Global situation.

I am a survivor of the eastern European Judaism from before the *Shoah*. My roots are in the *shtibel* where I grew up as well as in the modern Dr. Rabbiner Chajes Gymnasium in Vienna. I am also deeply involved in understanding and shaping the emerging *Gaian* cosmology. There was a time when after the Holocaust I believed that all we can do is create a Noah's Ark into which to gather the last bits of evaporating tradition and knowledge of the spiritual and liturgical know-how. I saw the hasidic dynastic courts becoming extinct, the giants of Torah and *Musar* disappearing, and the liturgical palette becoming more and more limited as the specificity of the different forms of *nusach* got blended beyond recognition. It was a strategy of despair. Hoping that the dark times would pass and that someday—when we or those who would follow would rebuild and restore *Yiddishkeit*—they would have living carriers of these traditions and lineages.

I have moved from this position, the one we call "restoration," one seeking to restore Judaism to its pre-Holocaust status. I am no longer interested in the Noah's Ark. Instead, I have embraced and propagated a vision of Jewish Renewal, one in which we metamorphose in the paradigm shift to be transformed again now as we have been transformed in the past. In this way the reader can trace the development of this point of view through the book.

Therefore, I have not "updated" my previous essays to make them conform to where I am now. The various stations of my journey may still offer shelter to those who follow. So I have kept the different stances I held in relation to the vision and the tasks connected with them. Each "burden" of vision came with her "burden" of action directives. I invite you to read these reflections with me and allow yourself to enter the "mansions" through which I passed.

Jewish Renewal is based on the Kabbalah, Hasidism, and other forms of Jewish mysticism. These sources support a transformational and developmental reading of our current place in history. This is augmented by offering the reader a sense of my personal-philosophical and phase-developmental journey so I move to pieces — mostly interviews — dealing with the sliding scale and the psychohalakhic process. This takes us into a reconsideration of the theology of *goy* and leads us to writings that deal with ecumenical and dialogical issues relating to other religions caught up in the same dilemmas of renewal or restoration. Restoration is ultimately not a viable option because of the impact of the paradigm shift.

The new paradigm deals with what is coming down the revelation-redemption line. This expresses itself in the emergent voices of the emerging cosmology, in which old reality maps are scrapped and new ones emerge that are, if not identical, at least parallel to the intuitions and traditions of Jewish mysticism.

This voice is augmented and at times even reshaped by feminism. The other half of humanity, whose input is essential for our survival, finally is getting the beginnings of a hearing. This in turn leads to a kind of healthy planetary homemaking and is concerned about ecology. This also calls for an eco-kosher *halakhah* and ethic. In order to become the kinds of Jews/persons who can effect the needed changes, the intra- and interpersonal work related to meditation and liturgy that are the laboratory of the spirit need to be renewed, and this leads to making prayer and meditation into a science as well as an art. Hence the need for a davvenology that is (1) an art and a science, (2) based on the Kabbalah, and (3) a generic empiricism.

The language of these essays is not what I would choose today. I am in a different place concerning egalitarian, gender-equalized language, and my attitude, which is harmonious to feminism. I did not wish to change them for this book since that would have led to some ludicrous anomalies in which the thought of the past would transdress in the language of the present.

As I am now involved in the intensive work of "spiritual eldering" and life harvesting, I am not doing this only with and for others. I am making my own life review, and this collection gives me a few of the many threads in my life to follow and to review. In each section I have prepared a "vestibule" describing some of the aspects of time, place, and person.

There are some acknowledgments of persons due at this time. As my working title for this collection of essays, I used the label *Mar'eh Kohen*.

I am grateful to Rabbi Daniel Siegel, my first *Musmakh*, who urged me to collect the scattered texts and to bring them together. His was the first pass at editing and collecting these essays. The blessed conversations with Hillel directors, the Oconomowoc "Ben Hammonites," the colleagues at Manitoba and Temple University, the Reconstructionist Rabbinical College, with the enduring and cherished friendship with its president, Rabbi Dr. Arthur Green and his wife, Kathy. Yes, there was—still is— a *Havurat Shalom* and an *Itzik Lodzher* among the "New Jews."

The wonderful *Shabbatot* and holy days with the Aquarian Minyan of Berkeley—in parallel with my dear friend and colleague in the work of reenlivening *Yiddishkeit*, Rebbe Shlomo Carlebach's House of Love and Prayer, on the other side of the Bay, both hothouses for the growth of a New Age Hasidism, when we "hung out" in the "far out" and learned Torah in a new way, where we blessed one another, Bless you Barry Hakohen Barkan—those were the days with my friends.

On the east coast, first visits to the *Farbrengen* in D. C. then delights of building our own *P'nai Or* community and the Shalom Center with the Oceans, Dr. Arthur (Moreinu Avraham Yitzchak Yishmael) Waskow and his wife, Phyllis (Esperanza) Berman, the working, praying, and playing together, the planning of retreats and *kallot*, those are a highlight of my life.

Some of the most challenging and profound work was what my partner, Eve Penner-Ilsen, and I did together in the Wisdom School. It was Dr. Jean Houston, who conducts her own Mystery School, who challenged me to conduct a Jewish one, based on the traditions of Jewish mysticism. In the first year, when we still called it Mystery School, we reenacted the teachings of the Baal Shem Tov, the *Maggid* of Mezritch (Rabbi Jonathan Omer-Man served authentically as the *Maggid's* stand-in), Rabbi Shneur Zalman of Liady, Rabbi Nachman of Bratzlav, and Rabbi Mordechai Yossef of Izhbitza. Coming closer to our time, the rebbes of the Holocaust period, Rabbi Ahrele Roth and Rabbi Kalmish of Piasetzno. From there we came to the spiritual directors of the present, and we dreamed of the Hasidism of the future. It was an exhausting and glorious year.

The next year, when Eve and I called it the *Mashal Hakadmoni*— Primal Myth Wisdom School—we felt the call to deepen the connection with the Bible and the difficult issues we had to deal with in life. This difficult and ever-so-transformative work called for imaginal, medita-tive, introspective, interactive mimesis, journal keeping, and dream assemblies. We dealt with Genesis and expulsion from Eden, sibling rivalry, dreams, addictions and the Exodus, Leviticus and shamanic technology, Deuteronomy and Ecclesiastes, Esther, Ruth, Jonah, and Job. (What an awesome night vigil it was when we wrestled with Job, danced with the whirlwind, and prayed the reconciliation prayer at dawn.) Isaiah and Proverbs completed that year. The next year we dealt with beginnings — *Gaia* and the emerging cosmologies and end-time issues — Messiah and resurrection. We learned about what it takes to live with a GRATEFUL MENTALITY, with angels in CLOSE ENCOUNTERS OF A HIGHER KIND. My appreciation for my partner, Eve, for the support staff, for the participants, is immense. The echoes of these intensives will reverberate for a long time. Fortunately, we also have recordings of these sessions that deserve transcribing, editing, and publishing.

I want to acknowledge and honor Phillip Mandelkorn and Stephen Gerstman, Donald Gropman, Howard Schwartz, Rabbi Arnold J. Wolf, Ed Hoffman, David Meltzer, Diane Sharon, Michael and Sharon Strassfeld, Richard Siegel, and others who were my early editors and whose encouragement got me from the Torah of the spoken to that of the written word.

Esther and Harvey Ekus, Robert Friedman, Rabbis Phillip and Shonnie Labowitz, Rabbi Jeff Roth and Rabbi Joanna Katz, his partner, and Max Sampson helped in so many material and emotional ways, supporting my writing and the staff at *P'nai Or* that helped me. And may the people of all the *havurot* in which I was privileged to participate and my students all be blessed. They will all see themselves and identify with one or another phase.

From time to time I meet colleagues from my Lubavitch days; we wink at each other, I hope in some appreciation. Their efforts on behalf of restoration are enormous and heroic. Ultimately, we work for the same *takhlit*, they under halakhic rules and we under the dictates of the psychohalakhic process and for Jewish Renewal. After all, *Mashiach* comes as he promised the Baal Shem Tov, when the well springs have reached the "outside." This book is to serve this intent.

Besides the active work with the "outside," I want yet to write to that aim. Since the Lurianic recasting of the Zoharic materials, there has not yet been a restatement of the perennial truths of Kabbalah in post-Einsteinian terms, taking the findings of physicists, macrobiologists, and so forth, and harmonizing them with the intuition of the Kabbalah.

At the *P'nai Or kallah* of 1989 I gave a series of lectures on the *Kabbalah of Tikkun Olam*. In 1991 at that *kallah* I taught a course, "Renewal Is Not Heresy; Where We Differ from the *Sabbatians*." These are being transcribed and will, with God's help, be edited for publication.

I pray that I be granted the opportunity to complete and publish these writings. Waiting to be completed are also *Mayanot* (Sources), translations of hasidic texts that inspired me; *Beyn Hamtzarim*, Hasidism from between the two world wars; *Yavneh II*, a study of the impact of the paradigm shift, parts of which are included in this book; and *Yishmru Da'at*, a hasidic *sefer* in Hebrew in the classical style, still mostly in fragmentary notes.

The *P'nai Or siddur, Or Chadash*, is now available in an experimental version. It is the work of our *hevrah*. Egalitarian and theologically connected with the emerging cosmology, it is based on the *davvenology* of the four worlds. Some selections of my translations appearing in the *siddur* are included here.

A companion volume to the *siddur*, *Yedabber Pi*, dealing with *kavvanot* and other davvenological psychospiritual methods, is in notes. *Gate to the Heart,* an updated and enlarged version of the First Step of the *First Jewish Catalog*, that now includes materials my partner, Eve Penner-Ilsen, and I developed for our Wisdom School is now in the process of being prepared for publication.

I would like to thank Ellen Singer for her contribution to the completion of this project. She skillfully helped turn what began as disorganized cartons of my writings into a coherent outline for a book. She sorted through the pieces, read and reread them, and helped to make the sometimes difficult final decisions about what should be included and what should not. As our work progressed, my respect for and trust in her insights and input grew. She consistently worked to keep me and this project on track; and she did so with grace and a sense of humor.

Throughout the editing of this volume a sentence stood out for me: "Through countless visions they have tried to compare You. **Behold through all their visions Thou art One.**" That last bold sentence was my choice for a title. Arthur Kurzweil offered reasons that convinced me to call it *Paradigm Shift*. It is true that it chronicles my own shift from an anxious restoration of a vanishing Judaism to hopeful and optimistic expectation for Jewish Renewal that comes from a harmonization of the Jewish vision with the emerging new cosmology.

This book is largely longitudinal in its historic progression. Contemporaneous with the unfolding of this work, I wrote on the updating of Kabbalah and Hasidism, translated many texts from the core of these traditions, did liturgical-davvenological, psycho-halachic and psychospiritual work, training and ordaining of rabbis and ecumenical work. The texts of these activities still await editing and publishing.

This book would not have taken shape if not for the encouragement of Arthur Kurzweil. Blessed be those who, like midwives, assist and encourage birthing. So blessings on Arthur Kurzweil, who encouraged, challenged me, and set limits to size in the service of quality. To slightly paraphrase our sages: "He does constant *Gmillut Hassadim* — practical

generosity—who publishes books and makes them available to others."
His vision for content and quality has brought the best of Jewish
spirituality to readers at a very crucial time. How to bless you? May the
seeds you sow be as blessed in their fertility as what you have created and
may you receive the *s'khar*—reward—in the worlds to come and the
p'rass—the bonus—in this world.

While a few minor finishing touches had to be added later in the
process, I finished my work with the book on *Erev* Pesach 5753, and in
this way it was my *siyyum*. *Hadran alakh Paradigm Shift*, may God
grant that as this book was completed, that I merit yet to complete the
others. I conclude with the sentence that has lately become my guiding
motto in which Moses told the Pharaoh, "And we, we do not yet know
how we are to serve *Yah* until we get there" (Exodus 10:26).

EDITOR'S PREFACE

For years I have been reminding Arthur Kurzweil that someday there would be a Jason Aronson Inc. project for me to work on. But when he called and asked me if I wanted to help Reb Zalman Schachter-Shalomi put together a collection of his writings, I told him I would have to think about it.

My initial questions were about the specifics of my role in this project. I also hesitated to jump at this opportunity for other reasons. While Reb Zalman and I share many acquaintances through our connections with the *Havurah* world, we had never met. In addition, I was completely unfamiliar with his work. I wondered what it would be like to work with a man whose reputation cast him somewhere between genius and eccentric. Would I feel intimidated in his presence? Would it be possible to establish a good working relationship where my input would be respected? In search of answers to these questions, I set off for Philadelphia to meet with Reb Zalman.

Upon entering Zalman's home, I knew that I was in warm, inviting, and completely unintimidating surroundings. After a long day of work, we both agreed that this was indeed a good *shidakh*. From the beginning we worked together in an atmosphere of mutual respect and a sense of equality. I returned home and began the process of reading through, sorting, and organizing the vast collection of Zalman's writings. Slowly but surely the book began to take form. This item needed clarification.

That item should be omitted. Always there was *just one more* article for me to read and consider including. Often we were not able to move at a consistent pace because our project was just one item on a long list of commitments constantly being juggled by Zalman. Nonetheless, we did proceed.

I came to this project never having read anything written by Zalman. As a result I brought to it the eye of an "outsider." On numerous occasions I recommended that points be clarified and questioned assumptions about the background of the reading audience. I hope that my perspective contributed to this collection by making it more accessible and appealing to an audience that extends beyond those who already know Reb Zalman personally and/or know his writings.

There have been two unexpected personal benefits for me as a result of my involvement with this undertaking. I have been introduced to the writings of a tremendously creative, spiritually alive individual. So much of what I have read has challenged me to take a fresh and penetrating look at the world I live in. Finally, through working on this book I have been fortunate to gain both a valuable colleague and friend.

I

Between Faith and Faith

1

THE SINAI GATHERING

Prayers of Peace

This report to the P'nai Or *community appeared in the* B'nai Or
Newsletter, June 1984 issue. *The contents speak for only one part of me.
There were levels beyond description to others. What was happening in
me on deeper and higher levels is not accessible to verbal description, and
yet, as you follow in your imagination—had you been there—and even
better on the level where indeed you stood at Sinai—you can gain
something by this description.*

*While the impact of this gathering was far beyond what is described,
we could not then follow up with the kind of political and social action
that this meeting required. Our hands were tied by our agreement with
the Egyptian authorities not to publicize this meeting in the media for
fear of repercussions from religious and political hard-liners.*

*Many months of constant work on the part of many individuals, in
particular, Ms. Maurine Kushner, had made this meeting possible. To
this day I am warmed by the memories.*

Between March 5 and 9, 1984, I celebrated Shavuot as I never had
before. I will remain affected by this experience for the rest of my life.
Sinai will be a reality for me on all four levels any time I will flash on
desert, mountain, echo, *shofar*, and the divine imperative that issues at
times in a small still voice and at times in thunder.

To tell you about this is to include you in this. I was your representative there. The presence of souls current, past, and future was palpable.

Who were the participants? People who were attracted by the call of the voice of God today urging us peace. They were:

Japanese—Shinto priests and Buddhists of all varieties headed by a venerable 80-year-old abbot wise and childlike, camera and all of them gadget happy, robed in their vestments and impressive in their cohesion despite obvious religious differences. I have yet to see such real tolerance for each others' faith and practice forms among other religionists.

A Native American shaman and healer—so utterly serene and sane and absolutely fitting into the desert.

Moslems—men and women, professionals and village elders, who, on the horizontal level, were exemplars of "adaba," a gallantry of soul, and on the vertical did the prescribed prayers five times a day. People from Egypt, the United States, and Israel.

Sufis—Some close to the Moslem tradition, others more universalist, doing Zikr in the oasis and on the mountain and seeing some of their holy hopes on the verge of realization.

Christians—Byzantine Orthodox, Copts, Melkites, Baptists, Anglicans, Quakers, Roman, and other Catholics, a rainbow of Protestants, praying and speaking in many tongues and doing this together. Some from Israel, others from Egypt, some from the USA and Europe.

Jews—from both Americans and Europe, from Israel and the Diaspora, secular and religious, New Age and traditional and feminist. The age range spanned from 11 to 80.

Some of us met in Cairo, others in Israel. I had the good fortune to be among those who got to Sinai via Cairo.

Egyptian hospitality felt genuine and appropriate from the airport on. And what an airport! What contrasts, ranging from veiled women at Arabic/English computer terminals to people of all shades and features from Chinese and Japanese to all sorts of Africans with headdresses from turbans and tarbushes.

And the traffic! It takes a long time to get in and out of Cairo. I kept thinking of the miracle of getting us out of Egypt in the night of Pesach on roads less well built and with packs carried by humans and beasts and on vehicles drawn by oxen and asses. We, in our day, enjoyed all this in air-conditioned comfort.

And the sounds. Cairo is the honkingest place I ever visited. Yet for all the tumult and bustle, people were close to polite in traffic and accepting of the way things were. The Nile Hilton was where they put us up.

Rabbi Marshall Meyers from Buenos Aires was my roommate at the

Nile Hilton. He serves on the new Argentinian president's commission dealing with the thousands of victims of the past junta, and he shared with me tales of the horrors of that time. God give him *koach*, the one permeable Jew in South America who has to present the best values of our tradition to a world that needs to be told of them. Oy! Did I feel a strong connection with him. He created a conservative rabbinical seminary to serve Jews in Latin America, translated the *siddur* and the *machzor* into contemporary Spanish, and in all this has a huge feeling heart and a soaring soul.

Pyramid Power

The impact of the pyramids! Their massive immensity dwarfed me to insignificance. Today they are worn by time and the elements. Yet the Great Pyramid still has some of the ancient finish on it and points to a splendor beyond that of any skyscraper.

The Sphinx, on the other hand, was small in comparison and the mutilated once-noble face that may have belonged to Sekhmet, cat goddess, does not so much deal with riddles and mysteries as with wear. My own riddles and questions had to wait for Sinai.

On the way to Cairo from the airport we also passed the necropolis, a whole city of mosque-shaped graves and mausolea. Ancient Pharaonic Egypt and Moslem crypts, it matters little, the dwellings for the dead are magnificent.

I could really identify with Jacob, who said to Joseph, "Don't bury me in Egypt." The Makhpela and the Safed cemetery reveal a very different attitude when compared with the pyramids and the necropolis.

The next morning we started through the desert to Suez. There is a tunnel underneath the canal that we went through and then found ourselves on the other side going north after a while, along the coast toward the Sinai.

We passed through the Firaan Oasis at night, the biblical Paran, a lush jungle of green in the midst of the reddish-brown stone and sand. Against the fragility of our modern technology, the forty years in the desert began to make a different sense.

From time to time we passed small villages, and at last we came to the tent compound that was to be our camp for the next few days. Everything from the spade stuck in one's belt to cover one's excrement, from the preciousness of a drop of water, to the virtual absence of wood—brush and, yes, camel dung campfires to cook coffee over—the cold at night—the voices that called for predawn prayer . . . in the desert.

DESERT DAWN

The next morning I got up before dawn and went up the nearest hill to *davven*. The sun rose behind the mountain to the east of me. The blueness of the sky—the dry crispness of the air—the reddish-brown craggy terrain, the intense red on the top of the mountain to the west of me, reflecting the sun that set it ablaze. "The mountain was burning."

Sentences from Exodus, Numbers, and Deuteronomy rushed into my mind, Elijah's trek to the Sinai an immediate reality. The desert has a holiness diametrically polar to that of the ocean. In this so-different, stark earth-and-fire element setting I can see the God word in craggy, deeply carved in lapidary script and terse DOs and DONTs. Against such immutable and massive realities the story of my personal life is a tiny graffito on the mountain rock.

As I prayed, I faced north to Jerusalem, and the *siddur* words spoke with an eloquence that life in the city cannot evoke.

At breakfast the Cairo group and the Israel group first met. We let out cries of surprise as we saw who else, of whom we had not expected was there. *Sabbah al kheyr—Sabbah an nur, Ahalan wa sahalan*, we greeted one another. *Ohaio Gozaimas, Boker Tov* regards and news exchanged spanning from the Pacific coasts of America to Japan in the fashion of a tribal gathering, the Sinai Gathering as we came to name this meeting.

And we planned to do the first big event, a peace prayer offered by each group in a total liturgy on the plain facing the mountain. The difficult and tricky protocol issues that loomed in the background were there, and yet the unseen hand that guided our deliberations, translated into Arabic, Hebrew, Japanese, or English, could be felt on our shoulders with reassuring calm. We managed to come to agreement with more ease than when we first had met to sketch it all out at the Nile Hilton.

PRAYERS OF PEACE

I believe that if peace negotiators had to do their work in that setting, camping together, kept awake by large writ thoughts at night and snores and the wind's wail and dry throats, all feeling the lumpy and sagging mattresses beneath their backs and cheerfully sharing toilet paper and toothpaste—it would get sooner to consensus.

Sitting on stones, or the gravelly ground, after having done some plain chore (like picking up the garbage after a meal), our basic humanity, from the bottom to the soul-soaring vision of God's plan for us as one humankind, the real issues are clear and the pseudoarguments to protect our ego veneers get unmasked before they are uttered and discarded as essentially irrelevant.

When we got to the site at about 10:00 A.M. we were seated on the ground in a formation of a lotus, each petal open to the center and facing the mountain another religious community, distinct yet one with the plenum.

Moshe Dror (Davidovitch), dean of the Ramat Hanege College in Yeruham, had brought a stone engraved by a laser with the words "*Dona nobis pacem*" done at MIT, which was later on placed on the top of the mountain. This stone was passed from hand to hand, and each person put some energy and prayer into it.

By now the Japanese were in their magnificent white-and-red trimmed robes, hats in black laquer from medieval feudal Japan, ceremonial fans in their hands preceded by a Shinto group of three in front and three behind with the center priest in front holding a long white whisk with which he whipped an arc and in all directions to purify the air and remove the demonic forces that might block the prayers, and after chanting an invocation Sutra he read the scroll with the peace prayer brushed for this occasion.

The prerecorded cassettes being heard over the kinds of portable stereos we have at times suffered from at the hands of rock fans: this time with gongs and temple chants that the ever-practical Japanese found easier to transport than heavy temple bells. These gave a curious and ancient dignity to their bass chants and the reading of the peace scroll.

Each group did their thing with dignity and dispatch and in an incontrovertible order, the older religious forms going first and the modern Buddhists last.

The Christians were next. Dean Morton of the New York Cathedral of St. John the Divine, a good friend from days back when he in the '60s worked in Chicago and I in Manitoba and we met, presiding, towering, booming, building the order of the liturgy that moved to Coptic Bishop "*a geshmakker mensh*" I would sigh in Yiddish over him, Melkite-rite Christians moving from *Kyrie Eleison* in Greek to prayers offered in Hebrew, Arabic, English, readings from Psalms, Gospels, and Epistles amidst Halleluia chants and, of course, the Our Father, which each community in unison with the others said in their own tongue.

Our turn had come! My colleagues who had been given time for the other branches of Judaism decided for a unified liturgy. I felt really honored to be asked to serve as *shaliach zibbur*.

HOLY GROUND

In commemoration of the burning bush, I removed my shoes to the verse from Exodus and then turned to our group with *Borkhu et HaShem Hamevorakh*: they responded and after *Birkat HaTorah* I chanted the words from Exodus 19:1–6, and the echo came back from the mountain and we said the last blessing, then the *Kedushah* of *Musaf*, which also has the *Shema*, and then I urged all present to join in a chant, each one in their way petitioning for peace in the name of those who otherwise would become the victims and visualizing the region united in peaceful interaction. *Anna HaShem Hoshia* was joined by *Kyrie Eleison* and *Yah Rachman Ya rachim* and *HehVah! HehVah!* (peace in Japanese) while I recited the *Malkhiyot* prayer of the High Holy Days and we blew the *shofar*, Samuel Avital and I, and again that echo! *Aleinu* and *BaYom HaHu* with a *Kaddish* for the past victims of the Middle East wars was our contribution.

Phillip Deer, the shaman, introduced his prayer with some heart words for the Traditional Peoples' vision, and by that time it was noon and the Moslems prepared for the Salaat in rows to prostrate themselves to *ALLAHU AKBAR!*

The tension of the significance of the event gave way to a happy buzz with embraces, salaams, handshakes, the sharing of water, and our return to the tents for food and rest.

I skipped part of our process. It was important we were divided into groups in which we all had co-conveners and representation. The work in these remains our business. We also needed to rest because we were to climb the mountain at 2:00 A.M. to get to the top for sunrise.

We woke at 1:30 A.M., got into the vehicles and to the Santa Katerina Monastery to the wadi behind which the ascent paths had been carved by an unnamed monk who had spent 24 years of his life to make the way up the mountain safe for pilgrims. May his soul bask before the Glory and reflect that grace!

It was a hard climb.

There were those who were eager and strong ahead of the rest of us, impatient, and they, regardless of nationality and religion, were a tribe onto themselves. There were the older and heavier huffers and puffers who had to take sips of water and little rests and yours truly among them who came along in the rear and another tribe in the middle carrying jugs of water.

We needed to help one another. The guide was Danny Rabbinowitz from the Israel Nature Preservation Society: deft, caring, humorous, inspiring, and unsparing to the ego that looked for comfort and consolation.

Arab helped Jew and Jew helped Arab and both shared with Christian and Buddhist, at times with a hug, a boost, and shared a word of encouragement.

How steep that mountain is. We climbed more by starlight than with flashlight, which made for a retina burn. The dawning day gray-blueing-pinking at the east urged us to further spurts of energy. Limbs and lungs did not want to obey anymore. Rest even for ever as long as it brought rest was immensely inviting. And yet the spirit was willing where the flesh was not and the spirit won as we helped each other the last 500 meters up the rocks to the top where church and mosque share scant space perched on craggy rock.

PEAK EXPERIENCE

And then the top—and the eastern mountain far ahead. Phillip prepared a smoke offering of sage, sweet grass, and cedar and holding the incense bowl began his chant just as the sun's first pierce came to touch us. We felt presences of prophets and ancestors, chains of traditions from times more ancient than Jethro's forebears. (Jethro is *Shu'aib* in Arabic and mentioned in the Quran—we passed his tomb on the way.) As soon as the sun was half risen over the horizon, the Japanese banzaied it three times, we davvened *Zikkred*, blew the *shofar*, and chanted, then Pir Vilayat Khan led us in a pledge to serve the spiritual government of the world with our body, mind, and soul; we each in our way accepted the Kingdom of God and pledged to bring it down into our lives and into our world.

And all the bone-tired ague was forgotten for the moment. Soaring in songs celebrating the chains of transmissions that connected us with Sinai, we joined each others' refrains and hugged.

DANGEROUS DESCENT

Oy was it ever a peak experience! The climb down was not easy either. Here we had to help one another even more.

There were times when it was not clear how one could get down farther when the path ended seemingly at the precipice. And then out of need and fear we looked again and the boulders to the right or the left turned out to be the stepping-stones that would get us down.

The sheer drop ahead and the way the mind scrambled to find the possible foothold and then did see it made me think of how we in so many situations need the goad of danger and urgency to discover the

Gestalt of the possibilities that are ours and to our saving advantage. It was a penetrating lesson in stone on problem solving.

A feast awaited us at the Elijah plateau. "And they ate and they drank and they saw God" (Exodus 24:11). And also had rides on camels' backs.

We descended farther. To the left of us on one of these seemingly impossible turns we looked around a rock and there were huge slabs of rock shaping an A, forming an entrance to a spring welling up from the center of the floor. There was a small slab of rock forming a table before it. I was deeply impressed by the feminine mystery dwelling there and in my mind named that place Miriam's Well.

I could not imagine a better place to celebrate women's mysteries than at that well. How I wished that rabbinic ordinations could take place at the Sinai and after such a climb.

Exhausted, we came back to our tent camp and seeing that from a height below us brought to mind "How goodly are thy tents O Jacob." One could really see how impressive a peaceful tent encampment is and how Balaam was moved from cursing to blessing.

We had work to do while our bodies got a little rest and dealt with tacky issues and there was another even more integrated cooperative session. All of us had gained a perspective that went way beyond political considerations.

Rainbow of Truths

The next morning we went to visit the monastery. It is very ancient. It has a library with the oldest extant manuscripts from the time of the Desert Fathers, who followed in the wake of the Jewish hermits and healers of the Qumran and Therapeutae-Essene tradition.

We heard a story of how during one of the times when a Christian monarch from Byzantium wanted to build the monastery on the very top of the mountain, he sent an architect, who after visiting the site, concluded that it was not feasible to build on the mountaintop without cutting the top off and leveling some of the ground in order to build the huge monastery envisioned by the monarch. When he asked why he had not been obeyed, he got the answer. He ordered the architect to be beheaded. That person will in my mind forever be the patron saint of those who want to leave holy sites alone to be what they are in their stark reality.

We had gotten the word that some monks might want to have some words with us. It turned out that the abbot was the one with whom we the rabbis and Dean Morton had a great conversation.

As an Orthodox Christian, he said he was not interested in dialogue, believing that his church had the spiritual nourishment that Christians need and that was enough. I suggested the model of the rainbow of truths rather than a mere relativization, and we fenced for a while.

Then I said something warm to him acknowledging the conflict of becoming abbot because he is so contemplative and how he has to keep being a manager and the one who faces the world. He melted to this and we really got to talk about Soul and God and Breath and Prayer and the vocation to serve in the world and also in the hidden sanctuary.

We felt blessed when we walked away. I hope to get to go back again to *davven* with him.

COOPERATIVE CLIMB

So I learned so much and wanted to share some of it in this way with you.

Mordechai Kaplan o'h envisioned the reconstitution of the Jewish People. I can see how the Sinai would be an appropriate place for this, for us, and for all others whose living message is anchored there and that now includes Shinto and Buddhism.

God willing, the coming Shavuot retreats will reflect this in the future. For this year my *kavvanah* will be that the *mattan Torah*, the revelation we are to receive may take us to unprecedented places, to give us what we need for the well being of the whole planet and our families and selves. It is so clear to me that we cannot lean only on old theophanies, which were good for the times they were given.

We need to renew the old in the light of the radically different. We need to climb that mountain together. Never before have we teetered on so precipitous an edge, pushed by past mistakes and sins into the direction of global destruction.

As I typed this in Jerusalem, I feel that if the Torah is to come forth from Zion, Zion too needs a new Sinai. Otherwise the new elections will only shift the old Karma a bit this way and that.

2

THE DIALOGICAL MENTALITY

This piece was prepared for a meeting when we, a group of professors and graduate students from Temple University under the leadership of Professor Leonard Swidler, traveled to German universities to meet with our counterparts. It was first offered in German and then translated into English. One can discern a verbal gestalt patterned after the Sermon on the Mount and 1 Corinthians 13. The classical form is used here to wrap a radical content, in much the same manner as the original material, which departs from the established norms.

You have been told that the dialogical mentality consists of the ability to allow for another's point of view. *But I tell you* that unless you have the ability to see beyond the Pharisees Hillel and Shammai you have not entered into that Kingdom.

You know well the oft-quoted story of Hillel and Shammai. The Greek goes to Shammai and wants to learn the whole Torah while standing on only one foot. Shammai beats him with a builder's rod. The Greek leaves and goes to Hillel. He responds: "What you don't want to be done to you don't do it to someone else. All the rest is commentary; go and learn to the finish." And the Greek became a Jew.

You have been told that the dialogical mentality consists of the ability of Hillel to teach not only the point of view of its own school but also that of Shammai—and this, by the way, is why Hillel's opinion prevails, because in his school the words of both Hillel and Shammai were taught.

But I tell you that the dialogical mentality really consists in knowing that *"the words of these and of those are the words of the living God."* Beyond the tale of "you are right" and "you are right"—"how could they both be right?" "You, too, are right." Beyond this, to the point of knowing that if Shammai had not hit the Greek. Hillel's pointed "don't do something to someone else that you would not have done to you" would not have convinced him on one foot. Only because of the Greek's resentment of Shammai's builder's rod did Hillel's *verbum* touch him so deeply. The dialogical mentality knows somehow that the Greek's pain at Shammai's beating carved the space for Hillel's teachings to flow into his awareness.

You have been told that there are negative theology and positive theology. There is the negative theologian who would strip God of all the attributes and whose certainty grows as he strips them one by one, saying *neti neti.* Then there is the positive theologian whose certainty grows as she invests God with omni attributes. This and That and more. *But I tell you* that the dialogical theologian is the one who sees that what the negative theologian discards is what the positive theologian picks up for attribution. He then realizes how the process of divesting and investing is what gives the certitude and not the arriving at the goal that is inexhaustible and endless.

The *dialogical* mentality differs from the *disputational* mentality. The disputational mentality begins with premises that it is uncritical about. They precisely serve as premises because as PREMISES they have a regression stopper built into consciousness. You cannot and may not ask me how *I arrived* at the premises because they are not conclusions I arrive at. You assume the assumptions; they are given, not taken. Now when you have a given in the mind of one who disputes with another who has another given, then all you can do is convince the other to give up that given in favor of *your* given, but you cannot have a dialogue. Like in the "pick up" the question is, "Your place or mine?" The turf of the game decides the outcome. In the disputation I want to impose *my* turf, *my* given, *my* one and only true hermeneutic, once and for all abrogating all others, and I have a proven one, self-coherent and strong. The dialogical mentality *you have been told* is greater because it has made relative all turfs and rules and leaves them open for consensual negotiation.

But I tell you that unless even the assuming of the assumptions is open for inspection by awareness there has not been any dialogue—only a sporting event.

Dialogue does not happen where we are adversaries.

Dialogue is collaborative.

Dialogue sees that there is better sight in two eyes than in one.

Dialogue seeks to communicate.

For where there are turfs they will be laid waste.

And where there are rules they will paralyze themselves into constriction.

But where there is dialogue there is a process that even when it passes away continues in that passing.

In dialogue there is a sharing of reality maps in which two seekers share experience — both as *Erlebnis* and as *Erfahrung*, in an ever-clearer seeking of *under*standing one another rather than *over*standing one another.

Dialogical mentality is at home anywhere in the *Uni/Verse*.

When it moves *Toward the One* it seeks the polarity of the *Uni*.

When it moves *Toward the Many* it seeks the versatility of the *Verse*. Its Universe of discourse courses back and forth and is independent of either polarity.

You have been told that dialogue implies two dimensions. *But I tell you* that the dialogical mentality, being aware of them both, implies three dimensions and transcends them in the Self.

You have been told that it is the substance of dialogue that matters. *But I tell you* that it is also the form that needs minding.

Dialogue is aware of mutual form and loves each other's form because it gives depth to the cognitive dissonance and helps one to really get to see the *out*- and *in*-lines of one's own cogitations. So, as the structural strokes of this presentation are appreciative of the beatitude of *the peacemakers*, the substantive issue calls for a new beatitude: Blessed are dialoguers, for in their concerned sharing they fulfill what is written (Malachi 3:16): "Then did those who respect God [more than their own creeds] talk with one another and YHVH attended and listened in and wrote it in a book before Him titled: *THOSE WHO FEAR YHVH AND RECKON WITH HIS NAME.*"

Amen, Alhamdullillah, Shanti. Om

3

BASES AND BOUNDARIES OF JEWISH, CHRISTIAN, AND MOSLEM DIALOGUE

The two articles that follow appeared in the Journal of Ecumenical Studies. *The "Bases and Boundaries" articles were not given at a meeting. The symposium took place only in the pages of the journal. The participants were my colleagues at Temple University, and we had talked about these issues on more than one occasion.*

The article on Jesus was my review of Dermot Lane's book The Reality of Jesus *(Paulist Press, 1977). The issues dealing with Jesus are painful ones in the Christian-Jewish dialogue, and often the responses come from a panic reaction. We have it between the rock of wanting to maintain our belief in the* Mashiach *and the hard place of our history with those who wanted to force us to accept Jesus as our Messiah. The arguments tend to raise more heat than light. I attempted to show where there were possibilities for further dialogue that would allow some permeability to the person and the teaching of Yeshua ben Miriam of Nazareth that would not result in an automatic rejection response. Let the reader then follow my arguments and see for her/himself if these considerations helped. I believe that there still is some mileage left in the dialogue and/or disputation over these issues. Most of the time, they are addressed by Jews who come from legal-rational quarters. I sought to speak from a place that recognized the soterial-mediating function of the* tzaddik *in Hasidism and who access the inner realities of* Tiferet *she beTiferet of Yetzirah, the place of a sacred heart in the cosmos.*

*Still, I feel that the creedal issues we discussed here, while not having
been yet laid to rest, are not the ones burning with current relevance. And
so I brought the challenges of our own time to bear on our conservation
in print.*

PROLEGOMENA

I am deeply aware that the unprecedented dialogue a-trois in this
conference is fraught with new problems that increase the complexity of
our meeting. There are places where Christians and Jews will be able to
ally themselves against Moslems, and Moslems and Christians against
Jews. There are positions of three-way mutual agreement as well as
situations of mutual disagreement. I cannot take for granted that the
Moslem and I will share what the Christian and I do, and so on, round
and round. What is tacit in one relationship is necessarily explicit in
another. When I make explicit what is tacit, I may create problems.

Moreover, I am convinced of the need to conduct our dialogue with
other members also, not physically present, who are committed to other
ways, Bibles, and dogmas that express emphases concerning God and the
Cosmos that are different from ours. All of this makes our dialogue
exceedingly delicate. We cannot retreat from the challenge, though the
dynamics are very complex, and we will need to keep all of this in mind
while we are trying to evolve the right manners for this new phase of
dialogue. May God grant that we stay conscious of this.

OUR DIALOGUE TAKES PLACE IN EXILE

How does one live with exile? Exile is one of the ways in which
traditional Jews experience life differently from the way their Moslem
and Christian counterparts do. We are in *Galut*. We participate in
dialogue against the background of exile. With the exception of a few
exalted souls, Christians lost the sense of exile in the year 321 when
Emperor Constantine converted to Christianity. The religion of oppressed ghetto dwellers now sat in the driver's seat of the *saeculum* and
controlled political events. From that time on, salvation for Christians
became a private matter between the soul and its God. The messianism
of Christians no longer needed this world to come into its own.
Triumphalism claimed its fulfillment here on earth under the rule of the
triple-crowned vicar of Christ. All that now mattered was the spread of
the Holy Roman Empire. Only oppressed nations after the resurgence of

nationalisms had messianic dreams of temporal significance. If a Christian felt alienated and marginal, it was interpreted as his or her personal problem. Until Vatican II the church did not see itself as the *ecclesia* in waiting for the end of the exile, but as the church arrived.

In Islam, to my knowledge, although there too an expected Mahdi is part of the eschatology, there is no sense of exile. Once the Jahaliyin and idolators were removed from Mecca, a new world order began.

Except on the Sabbath when we Jews share a few moments of exilelessness, we stay aware of exile. I ask my partners in this dialogue to remain aware of exile, which I believe we all share, as the basic condition of an unredeemed world.

Dialogue Is Not Arbitration or Disputation

There is a myth, begotten by marketplace and parliament, that the individuals involved in dialogue will have power given to them to change the thinking of the faithful of their own community. The Jewish community has given me no such power. If I go too far out, I will be repudiated by my own community. The dialoguer who goes too far afield is discredited, and with this the effectiveness of dialogue as a changer of consciousness is undermined. Dialogue is not even part of seminary curricula. With the notable exception of the Hebrew Union College of Cincinnati, there are no chairs in Christianity and Islam in Jewish seminaries. I suspect that the same is true of Christian and Moslem seminaries vis-à-vis other religions. In the past we have studiously ignored one another, and still there is tension between us. But in conferences such as this one we become the instrument of the Power that wants us to connect, the Power that I believe is at the core of the urge for dialogue.

Thank God we are not in a disputation. We may look to a discussion in which all partners are equal, open to each other and caring for the truth, each responding from the position of a loyal adherent to his or her own religion, standing in the presence of the God who witnesses this sharing. As Malachi 3:16 has it, "Then did those who respect God speak, each to his fellow, and the Lord heard and listened and wrote it all into his book entitled 'The dialogues of those who fear the Lord and honor his Name.' "

Our Poor Acts of Faith

To us Jews, and in some measure to Christians and Moslems, the revelation at Sinai is crucial. But what if we could construct a working time machine that could take us to participate in the receiving of the Torah at Mt. Sinai? As we teach this event in the tradition of scripture and *Midrash*, there were present the souls of the born and yet unborn receiving the Law in seventy languages. All the earth trembled when the entire Torah, up to the last insight yet to occur to a diligent student, was given to Moses and the vast multitudes, of whom the 600,000 men from 50 to 60 years old were only the nucleus, surrounded by elders, women, children, slaves, and the mixed multitudes. Echoes of that event are still in the air and can be heard by those with holy ears.

Would this, in fact, be what we would find at the other end of a trip in time? When I am in a mood for historic facts, in touch with what I know of the nature of Hebrew — with the documents of covenants of the ancient Near East — I think there were fewer people there. All the isegetics of the *Midrash* that came in subsequent times managed to help people accept the momentousness of the revelation, but were they warranted by the factic reality, or were they a pious strategy intended to exhort the faithful?

The *Midrash*, even if unfactual, was not untrue. I am in need of the *Midrash* where I am a viscerotonic celebrator of the holy feasts and mysteries, a devotee. On that level and in only that universe of discourse do I accept the *Midrash* as reality. The *Midrash is* true in the same way that God *is* love, or Brahman *is* Atman, and the Lord *is* King. (The word *is* is a convenience for the English ear. In Hebrew it is lacking, as in *Adonai Melekh*.) Rabbi Yishmael stated that "the Torah speaks in the language of men." I understand this to mean that the symbolic language of the Torah motivates our hearts and behavior more powerfully than would a factual record of events.

I do not base my values and my life as much on facts as on faith. So, despite the facts, I make an act of faith that places me at the foot of Sinai, and I accept the Law and the revelation. If this is so with regard to the Sinai revelation, how much is it true of an event less public and in the view of only the one person who reports it? Were not all the revelations of the prophets like that reported in Daniel? "And I Daniel alone saw the vision and the people with me did not see, though a great quaking fell upon them and they fled" (Daniel 10:7). Had we been present, all that we could have reported would have been that this holy man claimed to have experienced a vision. But what about the truth in that vision? This I allege by an act of faith, distinguishing it from a common hallucination. I base my life on such acts of faith, and I will try to persuade my children to make similar acts of faith. I will do so in emulation of Father Abraham, of whom the Bible states, "For I know him that he will command his children and his household after him and they shall keep the way of the Lord" (Genesis 18:19), but this is an act of faith and love. I have been talking about my own faith and the problems associated with it. If my own faith is on such shaky ground, then what about the claims of other religions, especially the ones with which I am in dialogue today?

Granted even the most generous reading of their positions, what facts do I have? A carpenter's son from Galilee spouts holy sayings culled from the popular piety of his day, heals some folks in the same way as did Elijah and Elisha, makes grandiose claims, and dies without fulfilling them. Then I have the testimony of his bereaved disciples, which is about on the same level of credibility as that of the disciples of Rabbi Judah the prince who, it is claimed, came back after his demise to recite the sabbath sanctification and, when this became part of local gossip, ceased to come (*Ketubot* 103). I also have the testimony of a zealot persecutor of Jesus' followers, who on the road to Damascus fell victim to a seizure and reported afterward that he saw an apparition reproving him, "Why dost thou persecute me?"

What of the claim that an unlettered man rode a miracle horse to heaven to get the true and latest version of the revelation that any form critic can see as a bowdlerized version of Jewish *Midrash* served up in new ethnic clothes and at the service of the children of Ishmael instead of those of Isaac?

DEFLATING INFLATED FAITH CLAIMS

I am aware that I am treading on pious toes. But please watch; I also stepped on my own. What I am saying is *not* that the world faiths to which we belong have no factual basis at all. What I *am* saying is that we are *all* on shaky ground, and that we need to deal not so much with the external facts but with our own *acts of faith*. These we need to take seriously because we stake our lives on them and invest them with supreme value. These acts of faith are not the result of facts. On the contrary, facts in this world are more often the result of acts of faith on which we base our actions. Our acts of faith create realities for us and others. So that we do not become arrogant in the process of inflating our truth claims that are based on our own acts of faith and put down those of others, I must make these statements so that in a sober and humble fashion we may talk about our traditions without undue triumphalism.

The major impediment to communication among our three religions is the dogmatic stance that we assume for the sake of the propagation of faith. We quote authorities who knew no more truly than we know but whose energetic assertions "snow" us. Their energy is the result of worldviews so dominated by their inner scene that they did not permit any of the doubts that are brought on by reality maps that did not match their dogma. Against the refrain, "it ain't necessarily so," we bluff others who are not of our faith, and we bluff our own people—not deliberately as con artists, but out of desperation at the lack of hard evidence, and we bluff ourselves as a strategy against our own fickleness, our "crooked heart" as Jeremiah 5:23 calls it. Then again, acts of faith are not made on an empty heart. We have within it our soul, the most reliable teacher. As we watch the process in which the soul becomes thought or speech, we notice that many a time we ease ourselves into convenient clichés that have little of the new insight in them. Once more we are trapped by habits that are the dunghill upon which the creeds feed. It takes vigilance and humble courage to make acts of faith. After all, where faith is weak, there is an abundance of beliefs. With this in mind we may be more humble about our tradition and our sureness, yet also a bit more proud of the holy process in our inner being that keeps teaching and guiding us.

THE AQUARIAN CHALLENGE

Besides the challenge of past history we also face the challenge of the present New Age. The Aquarian Age is empirical, experiential, humanistic, multioptional, fluid, mystical; it is existential, integrative, ecumenical, aware of nonverbal dimensions, with a view of God that is radically immanent, while at the same time utterly transcendental, nonanthropomorphic, and apopathic. Instead of being particularistic in regard to salvation and the conditions that make for it, it is universalistic and noninstitutional, heuristic and empirical. This view takes most seriously "by their fruits ye shall know them," and the fruits are manifest in the realm of better human living and interaction. It demands to see the fruits in better and more harmonious relationships, and to see a consciousness that is higher, more integrated with the physical, multidimensional, centered, and ecologically aware. The new humanism wedded to transpersonal psychology has challenged all of us by presenting a viable and deeply religious option to the Bible religions.

Here, too, we make some acts of faith. I believe that there is something in Judaism that is in some sense closer to the divine intent than even the best that Aquarian psychology can produce. At the same time I maintain that Judaism without holistic Aquarian psychology will be farther from the divine intent than Aquarian psychology alone. We three can meet the challenge of Aquarian psychology most significantly in the field of spiritual direction, *Tarika*, *Musar*, and Kabbalah. About these things we must talk with one another from real live experience, not only from books.

THE DIALOGUE OF DEVOUTNESS

Once we realize the shakiness of the factual fundaments of our acts of faith and come to a tentative agreement that the biblical and Qur'anic notions of holiness are not too far apart, then we realize that the holier we become, the stronger the impression our acts of faith make on the universe. But where do we learn how to fulfill the command, "Holy ye shall be for holy am I the Lord your God"? We search the sources of our traditions and find an entire literature devoted to spiritual direction. We read about holy souls and the paths they took on their way to holiness, the anecdotes in which their lives and conversations taught more than what one can learn in the academy, the counsels they gave to seekers, and their day-to-day, breath-by-breath witness.

There are few conversations in this universe as deeply satisfying to the heart as the dialogue of the devout. Unfortunately, such dialogue took place mostly among the people of each religion separately. If this profound sharing were to take place between *tzaddik*, saint, and dervish, monk, murid, and *hasid*, we would have a model of what one of the highest forms of conversation could be. One of the prime topics of that discourse would be counsel that would help the spirit gain the service of the flesh for the sake of the divine. This dialogue is a sharing of how best to surrender and conform to the divine will, how to receive divine wisdom for our guidance, how to read scripture for the sake of the spirit, how to emulate—imitate—divine attributes. The counsel gained in such dialogue helps the worshiper to worship, the meditator to meditate, the adorer to adore, and the virtuous one who wished to become a devotee to become a virtuoso of devoutness, a saint.

NEIGHBORS ON THE SHELF OF THE HEAD BOOKSHOP

In the past such exchanges were rare occurrences. Most of the instances found in the literature were motivated by a competitive spirit that might be expressed as follows: "If this goy—kaffir—pagan serves God with such zeal and devotion, how much more need I who have the true religion serve God with zeal and devotion?" Nowadays these exchanges are becoming the more common. The conversation is motivated by the consideration that one's own tradition may lack a certain way, approach, attitude, or advice that another tradition has deeply fostered. The popularity of bookshops specializing in how-to-become-enlightened literature is an index of New Age spirituality. Their shelves are packed with Yoga, Vedanta, Zen, Tibetan and Teravada Buddhism, Tantra, Sufism, Kabbalah, Hasidism, Tarot, I-Ching, and Christianity in its mystical form.

In the literature, in retreats and workshops, and by attendance at workshop with others, Christians and Jews can learn about Zikr; Moslems and Jews can learn from the stately rising and abating rhythm of the Mass; and both Christians and Moslems can learn much from *shabbat* and *davvenen* for their own holy resting and praying.

Shankara, Ibn Ulu 'Arabi, Luria, and Eckhart meet in the mind and discuss how the infinite becomes finite. Reb Nachman, Ramakrishna, Shams al Tabriz, and St. Francis prod one to adoration among the trees. Reb Moshe Kobriner, St. Jean-Vianney, Junaid, and Hakuin keep urging us to the simple, humble essentials of steady, everyday holiness. This dialogue of devoutness produces such hybrids as Christian Yoga and Catholic Zen, and it once produced a Raimond Lully, a Kabir, a Bahya ibn Paquda, and an Abraham, the son of Maimonides.

The dialogue of devoutness is the dialogue of devotional empiricism. It does not seek to improve on what is divine in the spiritual life, but on what our human response is to the divine challenge. What used to be secret teaching from master to initiate has now come out of the closet.

The Eso/Exo-Teric Switch

Andre Guenon and Friedtjoff Schuon found in Houston Smith their American spokesperson. His point is that the greatest sharing between religious takes place in the realm of the esoteric, not the exoteric. Behind all religions there stands the philosophia perrennis. This view accounts for the differences between religions as mere accidents of time and clime, space and race. Though I find this view not quite convincing, for reasons I hope to detail elsewhere, it is nevertheless pervasive in our culture. There is much agreement today that what all religions share is more important than are their differences.

The hallmark of the Aquarian Age is that the esoteric has taken the place of the exoteric, and there is more agreement concerning the esoteric teachings and their empirical value than concerning the exoteric aspects. Many of the exoteric observances are being discarded, often out of ignorance and carelessness, or lack of proper instruction in doing them so that they work in one's life. Pragmatic rationalists among members of the hierarchies give their consent to this because the practices seem to divert a person from the essentials toward minutiae that in superstitious minds have taken on a magic heaven-coercing quality. Thus the Catholic Church is discarding Latin, novenas, holy water, incense, and the concern for extreme unction; "tantric" means formerly at the disposal of the faithful. This is on the official level, while such practices as exorcism, use of incense, and anointing have moved to the counterculture.

Among Jews there is less observance of the midnight lament, the ablutions of the *mikveh*, the *kapparot* with live rooster or hen, and the holy days of Succoth and the New Moon. As I hear it from Moslems, Ramadan has for some become less a period for fasting during the day than for feasting at night. This switch is akin to the one that occurred in the use of our sacred and vernacular languages. Hebrew, once referred to as the holy tongue and reserved for prayer and sabbath conversation, has become the language of the marketplace and the election campaign, while Yiddish, the once secular, vernacular, is now used for the study of Torah and colloquy with God.

The esoteric aspect has become the public face of religions. As mentioned before, head bookshops are stocked well with St. John of the Cross and St. Theresa of Avila, but one will be hard pressed to find a catechism or a Kyriale. The Kabbalah is much better represented than volumes dealing with home life and daily prayer. On the Moslem side, one will find only rarely a book of Hadiths or Salaat, but Sufism is overflowing the shelves.

All this causes the guardians of religion great anxiety and concern. Does it mean that what once was considered essential is no longer valid? Was the synagogue/church/mosque wrong in maintaining our differences all along? Is the effort to get us to dialogue together nothing but another ploy to homogenize all religion into some syncretistic melange in which each one can find some way to cop out from real commitment? These anxieties cannot be averted by reverting to a strict fundamentalist position. Whenever tradition is challenged to renew itself, it must meet these crises. Whenever a religion refuses to renew itself, it finds itself without adherents. How do we steer the course between removing all the surface tensions between religions, thus losing what is special in each, and the building of concrete walls between us? Perhaps we need to explore this again and, after exploring, reformulate our teachings on the differences of our religions. Let us each look at the teachings concerning the status of the adherents of our sister faiths.

The Theology of *Goy*

In the age preceding this Aquarian era, known as the Piscean Age, we worked with words rather than with functions. Words were very powerful. "Abra Kadabra" (Aramaic for "it is created as it is spoken") and "Hocus Pocus" (a vulgarization for "*Hoc est enim Corpus meum*") were words for religious magic. The proper formulae for prayer were vital requirements for receiving an answer. Theology had to be in precise legalese, and a clause such as *filioque* could split a church. The difference between one synagogue and another was in the use of *w'yatzmah purqaney*, and Sunna and Shia split similarly over such either/ors.

It is easier to teach in flat blacks and whites than in shades of gray. The higher the contrast between right and wrong, saved and damned, the easier it is to run the magisterium and the institutions. For us Jews it was simply the choice between Jew and *goy*. Even Jews who were not well educated or did not abide by the expected norms were called *goy*. Originally the word did not have pejorative connotations. We are called *goy* too. "*Amkha Yisrael Goy Echad Baaretz*" ("Thy people Israel one nation on Earth"; from the Sabbath afternoon liturgy). I am sure the word became laden with pejorative meaning by all the pain inflicted upon us by Centurion, Crusader, and Cossack, to the point that when one referred to a Nazi by that word it had lost all human connotation and become synonymous with inhuman villain.

Today I am in dialogue with *goyim*. Who are you to me in that category? Jews are agitated by the question *Mihu Yehudi?* (Who is a Jew?), and the agitation extends to *Mihu goy?* which is the other end of this polarity.

In many aspects of Jewish thought and Law I have discovered, instead of a binary yes-versus-no relationship, one that is graduated in the middle range and this is what I wish to share at this time. In *halakhah* there is a descending order of persons. The highest rank is occupied by the High Priest. He is the only one to enter the most holy sanctuary, and this only on Yom Kippur. Below him is the average priest. Below the *Kohen Hediot* stands the Levite, and below him the first born in the family. All other Israelites came next, and they are followed by the *gerei tzedek*, the righteous proselytes who have embraced Judaism as their own religion. Below them stand the ones forbidden to marry Israelites, the *mamzer*, child of adultery and incest, and *goyim*. But even among *goyim* there is a scale in which the *hasidei umot haolam* (the devout of all nations) rate highest; they are followed by the *ger toshav*, the sojourner (to whom we will return), and any other son of Noah (that is to say, any non-Jew of general ancestry). Below him is one who worships stars and constellations (idolators); below these are the seven nations of Canaan, and below them the Amalekites.

There are occasional aggaddic statements to the effect that a learned *mamzer* is higher than an unlettered High Priest or that regardless of one's status each person is rewarded according to one's deeds. There are also distinctions regarding freemen, bondsmen, and slaves.

We are concerned here with the categories of Son of Noah and *ger toshav*. According to rabbinic tradition, based on the covenant made with Noah and his children, God prohibited to them idolatry, bloodshed, sexual depravity, theft, and the living limb (to eat part of an animal that is still alive), and ordained that they establish courts of Law. Anyone who accepts these commandments and lives by them is to be accorded all the courtesy with which the Torah charges us concerning the stranger in our midst. Such a person is to have the same rights before the Law and is invited to worship with Jews, though still forbidden to intermarry with them.

Whenever I have talked with Christians about this I found that the category of *ger toshav*, although satisfying to some,[1] is not satisfying to others, and it does not satisfy me. Under this category an *advaitin vedantist*, a *jnani yogin*, and a Zen Buddhist would enjoy the same status as a Christian and a Moslem. Somehow I feel that the Islamic model of the "peoples of the book" challenges our present thought on this matter. We must clearly separate two issues here. What happens if a Jew becomes a Christian or a Moslem? The Law holds that even if Jews renounce their religion, they still remain Jews; nevertheless, they incur severe ostracism in the community for embracing Christianity or Islam. The other issue deals with non-Jews who by their act of choice become Christians and Moslems. They are better than Henotheists (an option open for the children of Noah). They hold beliefs that Albo in his *Ikkarim* claims are essential; i.e., there is a supreme God whose will is revealed to humankind, and who rewards those who keep to this revealed

---

[1] During the last century, Aime Palliere became a *ger toshav*. He sought to become a Roman Catholic priest. During his seminary years he became a member of the Salvation Army. His search led him to Judaism, to which he sought to convert. He corresponded with Rabbi Elia Benamozegh of Livorno, went to visit him, and later continued his correspondence with him. Instead of leading him to full conversion as a *ger tzedek*, an option that would have required that Palliere renounce his allegiance to Christianity, Benamozegh suggested the category of *ger toshav*, an option that had fallen into disuse since the destruction of the Second Temple. By assuming the status of *ger toshav*, Palliere could participate in Jewish worship, though he could not lead as officiant, nor did this entitle him to marry a Jew. Palliere accepted this suggestion, and there grew around him a circle of *gerei toshav* in Paris.

way and punishes transgressors. Here Christians and Moslems definitely are closer to us than are Zen Buddhists.

Alas, we Jews do not have a forum such as a Sanhedrin in session these days, and opinions are private until someone publishes a responsum and this responsum is accepted by the majority. I know of no such work concerning the status of Christians and Moslems today. It is clear that the *ger toshav* category is inadequate to deal with members of the other Bible religions, who in my opinion deserve a special status ranking above *ger toshav* and below *ger tzedek*. This category will allow us hopefully not only to tolerate one another but also to learn from one another.

THE DIALOGUE OF GOOD NEWS

I am deeply intrigued to hear the good news others proclaim. It is in the nature of each religion to emphasize one or another aspect. Our daily prayer in the grace after meals asks God to send to us soon Elijah-Al Khidr with the good news of redemption and consolation. Elijah wears many garbs and disguises. When a Christian proclaims what he or she knows as good news, I want to hear it. I cannot hear it though if it addresses itself only to those who belong to the visible church. None of us here reject the truth stubbornly out of truculent recalcitrance to God; hence we can in some sense connect with salvation in what is called the invisible church. We Jews dealt with the category of the children of Noah. The Moslems accept non-Moslems who believe in One God as Muumin. So what is our message? All three of us share the good news of turning to God, *Teshuvah*, *Metanoia*, *Tawba*. All three of us share the good news of the ultimate kingdom of God right here on this planet. Can we not share in the dissemination of that message? We all believe in the consequentiality of human life. We all share the sense of *in illo tempore* time that allows us to keep in touch with the seasons of hope and revelation and the advent of redemption. We all share in the belief that some of God's blessed will and wisdom are manifested to humankind. We all share in the belief and hope in the ultimate transcendance of the limitations of the flesh and society.

In the areas where we do not share, we still need to be able to hear what good news the other proclaims, without getting "uptight." Each one of us has some aspects that are well developed in the faith and others that are either overdeveloped so that they have become top heavy or underdeveloped because we have heard only through a wall and seen through a veil. We need each other as mirrors. How do I look to you? I must tell you how you look to me so that we have accurate reflections of whether we manifest what we proclaim.

The Dialogue of Indebtedness

James Parkes once gave a sermon that has often been reprinted under the title "Christianity's Debt to Judaism." I think that there are some issues on which we all need to declare our debt to each other. Islam has given us the first thrust in the direction of scholasticism. Maimonides and Aquinas came on the heels of Ibn Sina and Ibn Rushd. It was Islamic thought and scholarship that made us enter into dialogue with philosophy. It was so fruitful in its own day that I cannot believe that there is presently hardly any of this dialogue going on.

It is clear to me that Mohammed, in his *hadiths* and in the formulations of the Koran that depended on his vocabulary and the state of his awareness, did what he conceived as bringing the *shariya* of Judaism and Christianity into line with the condition of his day and age. Even during Mohammed's life, Islamic law changed to fit the changing conditions. There must have been developments in the *shariya* to deal with the industrial revolution. I would like to learn more about this. I would like us to be able to enter into a dialogue on ecology, holy places, medical ethics, food technology, etc. We all owe Islam a debt for keeping an untarnished *Tawhid* — unity of God — before our eyes in the past. We now need to dialogue on *Tawhid* in cosmic terms.

The issue of abrogation also needs detailed and caring exposition so that we know clearly what Islam teaches on the abrogation of the other Bible faiths and prophecies. It will be delicate and difficult, but necessary to do, since there were many developments in Judaism and Christianity after the Koran. It is a situation similar to that of Vatican II when it dealt with rabbinic Judaism after Christianity.

Judaism, in its concern for the practical and the mystical, owes much to Christianity for systematic theology. The current rabbinate as a clerical and pastoral, instead of a judicial, vocation came to us as a result of the influence of Christianity. One cannot listen to synagogue music without sensing the influence of sacred music from the church. Modern seminary education is clearly modeled after the Christian paradigm.

At times I wish that the dialogue had developed before we copied from Christians and Christians from us. We might have voiced our caveats to the total vernacularization of the Christian liturgy. Our experience with Reform Judaism might have helped the church. Conversely, we needed to learn some of the caveats for candidacy to seminaries without a sense of vocation. Heinrich Heine said, "*Wie es Christelt sich, so Juedelts sich,*" "As Jews jewel, so do Christians crystal." I only wish that had been the result of critical scrutiny, not merely external emulation.

THE DIALOGUE OF HERMENEUTICS

In this dialogue we need to share information. How does a Jew read the Bible? What are the canons of legitimate interpretation? How does the Christian come to an interpretation of the same text? In recent years teams of scholars have worked together in new and very helpful translations of the Hebrew Bible. Some Jews have made fine contributions to the understanding of the New Testament, bringing to bear parallel sources from the Talmud and the *Midrashim*. Other Jews have worked on the Koran and made worthy contributions quoted by Moslem scholars.

For all that books can offer us, the vital contact comes from studying texts together and getting to see with the eyes of the other. In this way I have come to a fair understanding of Roman Catholic and Neo-Orthodox Protestant hermeneutics. I have met a number of Christian Old Testament scholars who knew our hermeneutic of *Tanakh*, though I have yet to meet a Christian scholar of Talmud rabbinics.

Unfortunately I have no sense of Moslem hermeneutics of the *Kitab al Muqadas*, the Bible. It seems to me that the way in which the Koran views the Bible is more a reworking of oral midrashic material than of the texts themselves. I am not even aware of an Arabic translation of the Bible that is authorized for Moslems. I do know that Sufis have a four-level hermeneutic close to that of our Kabbalists, but I have as yet no sense of hermeneutical dialogue with Islam.

WE AGREE TO DISAGREE

What is it that we will not be able to agree on? What is it that we will have to learn to live with in each other?

It seems to me that a Jew will have to learn to live with the following aspects of Christianity: the person of Jesus of Nazareth is bound to stay central and in the position of the Christ, the Messiah of the first coming. Both Jew and Christian will have to wait for the Shalom order to be instituted by the one who will complete history and fulfill the messianic expectations dealing with turning swords into plowshares and having lions living with lambs. The teachings of Paul concerning the Law will remain a *shibboleth* between us until the day comes when we all no longer see by looking through the glass darkly, and the Tree of Knowledge will have been supplanted by the Tree of Life.

With Moslems we will have to negotiate matters of the *shariya* and the issue of abrogation. On the matter of the Razulship of Mohammed, we may find accommodation. I pray that we learn to agree first on matters dealing with more practical issues and find a way for the children of Isaac and Ishmael to live in peace.

I am convinced that learning Torah together is an important prelude to the kind of dialogue we will hold with each other when our eschatological expectations will have been fulfilled. I trust we each will find that we were right, though not quite in the way we thought we would be. Only by holding on to our shape and color do we form the mosaic in which we are God's tiles.

4

JESUS IN JEWISH-CHRISTIAN-MOSLEM
DIALOGUE

Treat this discussion as an exercise in hope. I would for this moment only suspend past pains and disappointments and suspend also my conviction that where we are now as Jews and Christians is better than any other place—better because it is our reality. Further, I also believe that the separate voices of our official religions will ultimately contribute more in the unanimous peace in praise of God than a plain chant in which all blend. . . .

There is little that a Jew can say upon reading Lane. This book puzzles me. Here is a man who documents how all of present-day Christology hangs on a hair. The further he returns to the past the more traces of the unique, special, the second person of the Trinity vanish, and what remains is a teacher of aggadic Pharisaism who differed from the other teachers of halakhic Pharisaism.

Lane's method is a sort of last-ditch stand when a person encounters the conflicting claims of historic material and of creedal dogma. The two are not compatible, and the means of the low-ascending theology are just not able to sway the historian while the believer is threatened by the historic stuff that makes his or her lush creedal affirmation look inflated and exaggerated. But if the believer cannot assign the special unique creedal significance to his or her Christ who pales into one of the many teachers in the *Sitz im Leben* that the historian gives, then why bother believing? I cannot believe that just another rabbi teaching *aggadah* to fisherfolk would excite the regular Christian to participate in a Mass done in Jesus' memory. So who is Christ?

Call him by his Hebrew term, the *Mashiach*, annointed one, and claim his descent from David in order that there will be fulfilled that "a sprout come forth from Jesse . . ." and you run into the trouble of (a) the job description given to that messiah has not been fulfilled by him. The irenic order of universal *Shalom* has not yet arrived. As we are told of R. Menachem Mendel of Vitebsk who, when he lived in Jerusalem, once heard a madman blow the ram's horn on the holy Temple mount. When people came to him and said, "The Messiah has arrived; he blew the ram's horn," R. Mendel opened the window, looked out, and said, "No. He has not come. Everything is still as it was before." The state of exile continues unrelieved and for us Jews aggravated by inquisitions, expulsions, pogroms, and extermination camps. One might cry out: "If it is as you say that *you* are saved—how come you make *us* suffer so much?" No, the seat of the Davidic Messiah has not yet been occupied by his rightful descendant, and that is that. And (b) what sense is there in the genealogy that traces Joseph's descent from David if Joseph had nothing to do with the biological event of Jesus' birth? So, even if the *Shalom* order had arrived, Jesus could not be billed as the Davidic Prince of Peace. Both on the fact of exile and on the theory of Davidic descent, we have no Messiah as yet. To some extent I feel ashamed to raise those old disputed issues, but somehow the Christologist is not ashamed to lay the heavy claims on Jesus, and there is after all this tradition that we Jews experience in countless ways as leaning on us and urging us to accept this Christ as the Messiah we expect, and we can only push back by retorting: We will accept a biological descendant of David as the Messiah when through him the *Shalom* order is established.

But wait, is there only one Messiah spot for Jesus to occupy? Ever since the break between Judah and Joseph, the Kingdom of Israel from the Kingdom of Judah, there has been a claim for the coming of a Messiah, son of Joseph. This Messiah comes not to redeem sinners—this belongs to the Davidic Messiah—but to redeem the righteous and to teach them that they too need to come to *Teshuvah* (turning—*metanoia*). Being a descendant of Joseph the *tzaddik* he, as the *Midrash* (*Vayosha* 24) has it, will, after having served as a leader of the Jewish troops, be killed by a warrior from the West named Armilus (Romulus). He is, as the Jewish tradition places him, the righteous suffering servant of Isaiah 53 who is to be martyred. Let's put this together. An Ephraimite, a descendant of *Joseph* who comes from Galilee (no need for the census story at all), who lives an exemplary holy life (perhaps there is an underplaying of other companions he may have had in favor of fisherfolk, publicans, and sinners, which may have helped in making converts among

the Gentiles of the Roman Empire, but not in Jerusalem, where Nico-
demus and Joseph of Arimathea become more important), and is
martyred by "Romulus" could very well have become the *Mashiach ben
Joseph* for Jews. If Christians had spoken of Jesus then the chances are
that Jews would have been able to join Christians in the Good Friday
lament and count Jesus as one of the ten Martyrs of the State and included
his death with that of Rabbi Aqiba in the dirges of the Yom Kippur
martyrology. Jews could have even added the extra bite of bread at the
conclusion of the meal as a memorial and have had a cup of thanksgiving — Eucharist — for the same intention and prayed in the daily liturgy for
the resurrection of the Josephite Messiah that he might lead us to meet
the Messiah ben David. But . . . the Gospel writers were prisoners of
hope. Too impatient to postpone their hopes for the salvation of this
world, they pushed it up to heaven, and as soon as the temporal order was
in their hands Christians became triumphalists in an unredeemed world.
Not content to assign the dignity of Messiah Ben Joseph to Jesus, claims
were made for the New Adam that the world's condition refused to
substantiate and all the transubstantiations subsequently did not change
the accidents of wine, bread, death, and martyrdom.

But why identify the second person of the trinity with the messiah and
come with inflated claims when we can, instead of turning to the syn-
optics, turn to John? His formulation of Jesus as the *Memra*, the *Logos*,
the Word that was God, was with God, was made flesh, creates the more
significant Christology. Of the three tasks so well described by Rosenzweig in his *Star of Redemption* — Creation, Revelation, and Redemption — the real claim was made that Jesus is the *revelation*. That equates
Jesus with Torah, not with *Mashiach*. If there be a being who so lives as
the Creator in Heaven wishes the being to live that he or she becomes a
living Torah, at least Jews of a mystical, aggadic, kabbalistic-hasidic
persuasion seem to have a stronger theological warrant for dialogue. The
tzaddik is God's possibility for humanity in a physical body. The *tzaddik*
is Torah, who decrees and God agrees; for the *tzaddik's* sake the all was
created. "God does not need a world," the *Magid* of Mezeritch teaches,
but since *tzaddikim* like to lead worlds, he creates worlds for them.
Tzaddikim can heal and help, but most of all those who see them utter
the blessing: "Blessed art Thou Lord our God King of the Universe who
hast apportioned of thy wisdom to them who fear thee." The *tzaddik*, at
once an archetypal model for behavior, is also an accessible model and
anyone who will follow the *tzaddik* — in the older sense of *imitatio* — can
also become a *tzaddik*. There are tractates of all other commandments in
the Talmud, but for Love, Faith, Awe, and Devotion only a living *tzaddik*
can serve a generation as the tractate of the duties of the heart.

The *tzaddik* is the Sinai event for all those who stand in a positive relationship to the *tzaddik*. The *tzaddik* serves the souls of the disciples and devotees as a general soul that is for the disciple the interface to God's grace, light, and love on this plane. Now all those teachings are more compatible to the soteric claim of Christianity. The Paraclete, the mediator, the WAY to the Creator, all these are what the *tzaddik* is for mystical Jews and the Torah is for all Jews in general. The Christian can say that, fulfilling the Torah, Jesus became the Torah now immament in his heart and soul without making at the same time the extravagant claim for Jesus to be the fulfillment of the redemption. For, although the Torah was given at Sinai, no Jew expected that this would so transform the whole world that it would usher in the irenic realm of God's Kingdom. It is on the contrary a revelation—a survival guide and handbook of how to manage in a world that is not yet redeemed.

Having stated the foregoing from a Jewish position, is this not also close to the Christian one? The final redemption still awaits another COMING. In the meantime, there is the word made flesh, the paradigm of the fullest God in the fullest human, the *soter*, reconciler, connector to the Creator. On the Jewish side such an open and clear statement gives possibility to the notion that Jesus is for Christians who follow in his footsteps, pray in his name to the Creator, love one another as he had loved his disciples, and await the redemption with the light of the world having poured itself—*kenosis*—into the souls of his followers. He is the word that the Christian hears spoken of the Creator in the tongue of the man, the *rebbe* from Nazareth. His followers once named Nazarenes can now be seen by Jews as Nazarener *hasidim* in the same way as Jews who follow the Satmarer Rebbe are Satmarer *hasidim*, and those who follow the Belzer are Belzer *hasidim*.

There is yet a deeper aspect of Christology worth considering from the principle of dialogue. There is the experience of the Christ (I do not mean the Messiah aspect, but the Son of God aspect) that is the confidant, the compassionate, the Holy, the one who is all sacred heart, who is the love of God that is also the God is love and he who abides in love abides in God and God in him. True, this aspect is far from the ken of the exoteric Jew but close to the esoteric one who is a *hasid* or who follows the Kabbalah. I remember a conversation I once had visiting the late Thomas Merton at Gethsemani. Merton responded to my question what the Trinity meant to him by quoting the Greek Fathers who said that God in awesome might and creative power is the Father. God as loving and compassionate and working to bring all souls to their reconciliation and salvation is the Son. God as this love is revealed to the human mind and gives human being the revelation of God's will and wisdom is the Holy Spirit. I responded to this that I believe that God creates, and, if this dimension of an infinite number of dimensions is talked about under the name "Father," this has not only enough biblical and theological warrant for Jews but is no point of quarrel. That God loves and in this capacity is called the Son also makes a certain amount of sense to a Kabbalist. For in the Zohar the Tetragrammaton is interpreted to mean YHVH as follows: Y is the Father — *Hokhmah*, wisdom. H is the Mother — *Binah*, understanding. V is the Son — *Z'eyr Anpin*, the heart and the compassion, the one really pointed to in the word YHVH; and H at the end is the Daughter — the *Shekhinah*, the sabbath, the Divine Presence and, yes, the *Ruach HaKodesh* — the Holy Spirit. As long as we do not exclude the other manifestations by declaring that there are only three, we have further room for dialogue and understanding. Now it is also true that the Kingdom of the YHVH has not yet begun on this earth and, as Zechariah foretold, that will happen on "THAT DAY on which YHVH will be one and His name ONE."

What this calls for is a willingness to admit that all our formulations about God are nothing but tentative stammerings of blind and exiled children of Eve responding to the light deeply hidden in the recesses of their nostalgic longing for the untainted origin in which one needed not to look through the glass darkly but could see. This can even make us proud of our traditions and heritage as the storehouse of those stammerings of the souls that were filled by God with the grace of that holy moment that defied definition and that was forced by ecclesiastical lawyers to be encapsulated in a stateable wording. The mistake that was made was to take the ecstatic exclamations of the overwhelmed souls and to make them numbered articles of creeds instead of acts of faith made in fear and trembling.

It is this move that, for all the balance in Lane's book, he did not make. It is indeed difficult to say that the magisterium of the church — that the Torah and all its commentaries — are *deo gratias* what we do have and treasure, but only as the human snapshots of moments of God's nearness; that, although we cannot improve on the divine that flows into our vessels, we can and must take responsibility for keeping these vessels clean and transparent and not at all as essential as the light they contain. Perhaps we are as dogmatists small souls of small faith who do not dare trust that God will be with us as God was with our forebears and that God will not abandon us nor forsake us.

It then behoves the poor of the spirit of all creeds and denominations to support each other in the desperate acts of faith that we make in the face of the exile and the holocausts and enter into a dialogue among fellow servants and children of *one* Creator.

5

For They Bow Down to Emptiness

and the Void

Dear Harold,

You write that you read the exchange between me and an Orthodox colleague in *Sh'Ma*, April 1974. We discussed what ought to be our attitude vis-à-vis the spiritual teachings that come from non-Jewish Eastern religions. You state that you are now disquieted since you have been doing Zen sitting for the last year and a half and have gained much benefit from it.

You point out further that in the past, if someone had said to you, "*Zazen* is against *halakhah*," you would not have cared. As you have from time to time told me you saw in *halakhah* the skeleton of an outworn parental tradition that, so you experienced it, betrayed you at your *bar mitzvah*. When we talked about this we decided not to look upon whom to lay the blame. The parents and teachers were no less misguided than you. But we left this and spoke of your soul's awakening, first through chemical aid, then through communal experience, encounter, and sensitivity training, and finally through the aid of many variants of Far Eastern religions and some profound love relationships; ultimately with meeting your beloved Roshi, Ananda upon his atman (How else can I say *alav hashalom*?).

You told me of your becoming a lay devotee who "sits" every day, practices "Beginner's Mind" during your daily pursuit, and seeks your

39

Roshi's (your late Roshi's successor's mondo) counsel from time to time. And yes, I need to add that our friendship began at a weekend at . . . when out of curiosity you wanted to see what an Aquarian hasidic *Shabbat* was all about. You began to read Jewish books, *The Jewish Catalog,* Jewish periodicals, and *Sh'ma* among them, when this exchange occurred. You made, I recall, a great effort to attend the Torah Dharma Day at Berkeley.

You told me that you were glad to hear a Zen prior, Sufi Shaikh, and 3H Sadhu, all of Jewish birth, discuss their journey. Especially when it was (in a somewhat pained and humorous way) admitted that almost all the seekers of Jewish extraction had experienced the intrusion of *schmaltz*, warm Jewish devotional, images in either their own *Bhakti*, or making talmudic insight connections in Jnana, intellectual contemplation or other Jewish intrusions into their emptying.

They concurred that repressing the Jewish stuff brought about an inner drying up, and so they reopened themselves to the Jewish stuff, to varying levels of Jewish involvement. Now you wonder, is Rav Hollander right? Then what are you to do? You trust me enough to be able to help you, and I intend not to betray that trust.

As Rav, I have to agree with Hollander in his general view, though not in his extremist formulation. As spiritual guide (let us grant that I write now from that place), I disagree with the most basic of his premises.

I trust that the movement of a soul toward God, enlightenment, and self-realization is not under the category of routine service for a Jew, but under the category of *teshuvah*, turning toward God. *Halakhah* is not the body of law that knows about this. Spiritual direction by living persons is. This is what Hasidism has taught me.

In the movement of *teshuvah*, we are told of two things: one is the *teshuvah* done out of fear, the other is the *teshuvah* done out of love; his intentional sins are reckoned as merit.

By no stretch of the imagination can I think of the Jews I have met at encounter groups in ashrams, zendos, etc., as people driven to return to God out of fear. A deep love and longing motivates them and nothing could be further from their minds than either the hope for monetary gain, social prominence, or the fear of punishment, human or divine.

The one important category under which I can think of them from the Torah perspective is that of *baalei teshuvah* — out of love. The process of their movement toward God is not ours or Hollander's or anyone else's to predict. The process I am talking about is God and the soul finding their most fruitful interaction for the growth of the soul, and for that soul's participation in the building of the divine Kingdom here on earth.

I must tell you of an occurrence that touched me profoundly: I was at

Naropa Institute (Boulder, Colorado). While I taught a course in Jewish mysticism there, my father, of blessed memory, passed on. I did the *shivah* in Boulder. Reb Allen Ginsberg participated in the *minyan*. He read Psalm 49, the one to be recited in the house of the mourner, as if he had written it. I led the *Aleinu*, and as I came to the words, "for they bow down to Emptiness and the Void," the teachings in Chogyam Trungpa's *yeshivah* in Boulder and the words emptiness and void (*hevel varik*) made an altogether different sense to me than they have ever before.

You call it *kensho*, don't you? That is, when the inner and outer, the upper and lower, the momentary and the eternal all coalesce together, and regular reality comes back just so. Once emptiness and void had been freed from a bad value judgment on my part and seen in the same perspective as King of Kings, the Holy One, blessed be He whose highest attribute is NO-THING, I was once again in touch with the one aim of all religions.

I wished I had an eternity to reflect on this, but Kaddish came up, and I had to put my super-WOW into the words of *bechayeykhon uveyomekhon* and was once more connected with the here and now and with my Jewish expression of it. With it came the rhythm of *Kaddish* in the morning, *Kaddish* in the evening, the seven days, the thirty days of mourning, the High Holy Days, and the most delightful time punctuator: the *Shabbat*.

Suddenly, I am aware that the discussion of this matter has translated itself to another plane, one in which the categories of the *Shema* exchange are insignificant. What is significant is that there is a mountain, and we are all climbing it, and we all want to get to the top, and we all call that mountain and the path leading to it by different names, and when we get to the top we get to see what we are, always were and will be. Then we get our orders to go down and fix this place, our mother earth, to establish the Kingdom of Him, whom we call the Almighty, and get to live the heavenly days right here on this planet.

To get this to happen we have to be spiritual empiricists. So what works is what's true. Behind the discussions such as Rav Hollander's and mine, the following slip stands back of the argument. It concerns the nature of the man whom God had created in his image. The means we use to create such a perfect man is the path. The view of God one holds, and hence the view of the perfect man made in his image who is led on path, that path being *Halakhah*, the Tao, the Dharma, etc.

But is this *etc.* not *Avodah Zarah*? An alien form of worship? No halakhic objection could be raised even from the Hollander camp to the worship of an anikonic infinite God. To call the encounter with the Void the worship of a heathen god is absurd. First there is a mountain. Then there is not the mountain. Then there is. This is not religion. And even if it were religion, how could anybody forbid this, least of all, God? So there is in that Zen part a portion that is a religion; that has customs, ritual, images and forms, a hierarchy, a liturgy, etc., and as much as you can participate in it, it is universal. And as much as you cannot participate in it, because it is Japanese, ethnic, located in a different kind of space, and appearing under archaic forms, it is *Avodah Zarah.*

If *Avodah Zarah* is not the category under which you can be supposed to sin, sitting for endless hours in the presence of a void, not doing anything, there remains only the category of having wasted time from the study of Torah.

However, I do not think that you would have difficulty convincing the heavenly tribunal at the final judgment that you were *not* wasting time, investing, perhaps, in no-thing. If you ask whether it is okay for you to adorn Buddhas, light incense sticks, chant mantras, etc., from what I know of Zen and its aims, yes. But from what I know of the Hare Krishnites and their aim, no. What I'm saying is, that from what I know of the attitude that Zen has to the function of the sacramental acts and their meaning, I know of nothing objectionable, given a lucid under-standing of Zen aims by the strictest Halakhist. On the other hand, Iskon (Hare Krishna), besides participating in every single aspect of what the Pentateuch considers idolatry, it also demands the total abnegation of any other religion and demands that you give up Judaism. That is the basis for my decision that it is *Avodah Zarah,* idolatory.

In all this I am saying that some people have not made it to God, to realization, to Judaism, to *halakhah,* to *teshuvah,* through that way. So please God, we will yet talk about this and meditate and *davven* together for more and clearer light. May you have luminous years ahead of you.

6

THE TRANSCENDENTAL EXPERIENCE:
AN EVENING'S MUSE-IC

There is daytime talk and there is nighttime talk. Nighttime talk is much better suited to this subject than daytime talk could ever be. Indians know that you don't make day music during the night. The mood of a morning Raga is different from that of an evening Raga. When we wake up in the morning in a wise way we can enjoy the day. Very few of us wake up in a wise way because we have an alarm clock, and to wake up to an alarm clock is to wake up all wired—and then comes coffee!

Vinoba Bhave, who is Gandhi's disciple, was jailed by the British. After a while they understood that here was a man who deserved to be Hindu chaplain of the prison. Every morning they had an awful way of arousing the prisoners: clanging, shouting, ringing bells. Then they complained they had so much trouble and riots, so Vinoba said to them, "If you don't mind, don't make that noise in the morning. I promise to awaken the prisoners on time." And he went from cot to cot and took hold of the hands of the sleeping prisoners, until the person opened his eyes and said "Good morning" to him. "Namaste," and he went on to the next cot. Now that's the way to wake up. You then have a sense of "It's a nice world." You can wake up as our liturgy prompts us, with a prayer: "Thank you, living and existing God, for having given back my soul to me. Great is Thy trust!" You trust me with my soul for another day. What an amazing thing.

Now if we were to wake up like this and move through dawn into the

morning, the morning liturgy would make sense to us too, in its own
contemplative way. We would understand again the phrase: "At the
dawn I seek Thee, Refuge, Rock sublime." Or, as I once wrote,

Dawn

Each day another version of the dawn.
  Gentle pink blushes
  color the blanching horizon
  and billow-pillows softly promise
  to receive the rising sun.

Lo this quiet hour when the day begins to break forth
  from the fetters of the night
  and stretches arms across the sky
  and with pink floods yawns aloud.

And in the hearts of those whose eyes
  have witnessed miracle
  so common yet so new
  a joyous hope makes its debut
  each day again as ne'er before.

Now if you pray my friend do join
  the ranks of yogis in surya namaskar
  and betallissed Jew
  or celebrant who greets the sun
  with dominus vobiscum.

And then at last the sun appears
  and over silhouetted horizon peers
  with golden blinding ray
  does kiss your soul and
  melts the last hard lump not
    solved by night and rest.

Yes bring on Oh day what bring you must
How can I this day forsake this trust
Which dawn again has kindled in this breast
HOLY LORD, AMONG YOUR ANGELS
I LIKE DAWN THE BEST.

But we have an alarm clock, and before we are awake our blood-stream is full of adrenaline. We get into fight and flight before we even wake up. No wonder then that we are irascible for the rest of the day.

Evening again has a different quality to it; while in the morning we would like to be able to learn how to concentrate on our tasks, in the evening we want to be able to get rid of concentration. Concentration is sort of a pinpoint kind of awareness. Many people feel that this is what sobriety is all about: that kind of highly focused pinpoint awareness with which one repairs an intricate mechanism. But there is a kind of diffused, panoramic, multilevel, soft focus awareness people have and that's the awareness of before falling asleep. When busy movement quiets down, when our stomach does its quiet digesting, when our blood pressure drops to another level, then we could, if we wanted to, let our mind float free and roam. But most of us don't know how to let our consciousness journey; we fall asleep. Tonight we'll have to go there in that state of mind. We can't stay in the daytime state of mind and talk with any sense of empathy about transcendental experience.

There are internal physiological tides in which time is coupled to a person's diurnal rhythm, and in this sense there are the early risers and the late risers. When you look at your chart—horoscope—you may find the time on which most of your houses are filled as the sign of this internal tide system. Those who do not understand this ridicule people who flow to different tides.

There was a *rebbe* named Bunam of Pshysskha, and people accused him of saying his morning prayers too late each day. He answered: "It is written: 'All my bones shall praise You, O Lord.' Now there are some little bones in me that don't wake up until 10:00 A.M. so I must wait for them to wake up too before I pray."

Each person needs to find the time in which his soul rises with greater ease because of the help that his physiology gives him. And so there are morning Yoga people and evening ones.

Besides this tide pattern, which is personal and individual, there is also a texture to time that is more part of the fabric of the global space time continuum. Mircea Eliade has pointed to two kinds of time, linear and cyclic. Linear time is the duration against the background of which events take place in history. Cyclical time—which he also calls "in illo tempore" time—deals with the tides of our myths, the cycles of nature and experience that flow with them that the seasons and holy days bring along with them. In curves that are smaller than the year there is the texture of the moon phases and of the Sabbath and the various days of the week that we, not by mere happenstance, name by deities or heavenly bodies, Sun-days and Woden's days. So time has texture and Mondays and Fridays differ more than Mondays and Thursdays for instance.

> Palaces in Time
> Evenings, palaces in Time:
>
> You, my rich God dwell in them.
> Please let my longing here remain
> To glean the wonders of each nook
> And serve your treasures to a
>   world in need.
>
> Evenings, palaces in Time.[1]

And so evenings have their texture. Anyone who needs to do something that runs contrary to the texture of time has felt that he was going upstream. The effort to achieve the same ends is much greater than when one floats downstream. So we will try to stay in the flow of evening time and in this way launch into our connection with the transcendental moment.

We Anticipate Fascinating Marvels

If you want to find out about transcendental experience, you have to posit that "there is such a thing," because if you believe there ain't no such thing you're going to be a drag, not only on yourself but on the rest of us.

There is anticipation. Most of the time, when you go to a religious service, you don't anticipate "I'm going to meet God." Instead, the inner climate of your anticipation is, most of the time, "It's going to be another service." Maybe there will be a collection. You have such and such things

---

[1] 4th c. A. J. Heschel, *Des Shem Ham'forsch Mensch* (Warsaw, 1934). My translation from the Yiddish.

to do after the service. With such anticipation what are you going to do? Transcend? You are going to find exactly what you came to find. Anticipations are gates. So if your anticipation makes space for it at least there is the chance, if there is such a thing, that you might get there.

You have been to places of ecstasy. You were born. You saw a sunrise or a sunset. You most likely had what Maslow called "a peak experience." And what's so exciting about being at such places is that there is always the feeling that if you were to be able to go one more step, you would go to that special, light-filled place. How come we didn't take the other step when we almost knew where the gate was? Because we were frightened that if we would take one more step, we might not be able to come back.

We lean back and it looks as though the wall is dissolving a little bit; it's beginning to shimmer and we have the feeling that it is moving farther away, it's coming closer; distances begin to shift. We hold on to the chair, grit our teeth, shift around, look for something to eat to bring ourselves down to earth. We disturb enough of the gently balanced mind-expanding equilibrium because we fear that if we were to go there, we might not be able to make it back. So we postpone heaven by another few years or lifetimes. At such moments we are afraid we are losing our minds, or rather the ego becomes anxious that we are going to lose control of our minds. We are afraid that we will be only an *I* and not a *Me*.

AND DREAD THEM TREMENDOUSLY

I have an *I* (subject), *I am*, and then I have a *me* (object) and that me is what feeds me, what does things for me. I'm afraid to leave the *me* behind, that it would be irretrievable. I would no longer be anchored in a body, in time and space, the recognizable features of the here and now of a threatened reality. But that's where transcending takes one. So if we are to talk about the transcendental experience with empathy we must be able to follow into chaos at least in our imagination. You object: "You are going to take us to lose our minds; we won't be able to return to our *us*ness. We'll be forever in hell. We have commitments for tomorrow, we can't come with you, you are poisoning our mind's ecology!" Now it's true that this might happen. I don't want to take your anxiety away; it has kept you safe and protected in the past, but I want to give you testimonials from people who have gone there and come back. The journey worked for them very well to enhance their life in everything that they subsequently did.

Four Who Entered

We are told in the Talmud *Haggigah* about four people who entered PaRaDiSe. Three of them didn't have such good results. One of them went and he died. The second one went and lost his mind. The third one went and lost his faith and the fourth one entered in peace and came out in peace. The statistics seem not so good for transcendental experiences.

Rebbe Chayim Tchernovitzer, one of the hasidic masters, says in his *B'eer Mayim Chayim*, "Why is it that Rabbi Akiba went in peace, and came out in peace, and the others didn't?" He answered: One person was Ben Azzai, a Rabbi, who didn't want to get married. He said, "My soul desires Torah. All I want to do is study," and he had no hold in this world. He took one look and died. Why? It was too good there to come back; death was no tragedy for him. We consider it a tragedy.

The next one was Ben Zoma, who describes himself as being "like a man of 70 years"; he was a widower, and was much younger than that. He went and lost his mind. On the other side of life he must have seen someone for whom he cared very much, so he left his mind there and sent his body back.

The third one, Elijah ben Abuya, lost his way. And he saw, he saw through it all, but along with seeing, he didn't find peace. Because as Kazantzakis describes this in the book *Report to Greco*, "Not only have I seen the face of God, I have also seen the chaos behind the face of God." And that is also part of the transcendental experience, to go there, to see the face of God and beyond it. When we speak of God we are not talking about the Godhead. Meister Eckhart makes it very clear. "As far as Heaven is from Earth, so far is God from the Godhead." The Godhead transcends God, as Heaven transcends Earth. That order which we human beings called God, which we might approach, still has another face behind it, the face of the Godhead, in which there is chaos.

Elisha ben Abuya, the third rabbi, a divorced man, came and saw an order in which God the Creator runs the human race like a puppet play in which all human freedom was illusory. Behind this he saw the force that melts the created order again into the uncreated state is that prior to the state which we know God as "God of the World." Ribbono Shel Olam, the King of the Universe. Then he felt that there was no purpose to the order ruling this world, and "there was no judge and no justice in this world!" He returned and opting for a freewheeling, sensate esthetic, lived no longer in a world of moral and ethical order.

The other one was Rabbi Akiba. Do you remember the story of the holy Rabbi Akiba, who was martyred by the Romans when he was 120 years old? As a young man he was unlettered. He was 40 years old when he first decided to study Torah. His wife, Rachel, waited patiently and lovingly while he studied. He really dug love, as can be seen in his legal decisions and *Midrashim*. He went in peace and came down in peace because before he entered the transcendental experience his Rachel, the wife whom he loved so much, sent him off and greeted him on his return with carnal love and spiritual blessings. "Go in peace, come in peace," and so he went and came in peace. He had gotten his earthplane scene together harmoniously before he entered the garden.

Somebody who hasn't got his scene together ought to be anxious about transcendental experiences. He might, like our other three rabbis, not land safely.

So, we have now described some of the gates of that experience. What was the experience like? If it's truly a transcendental experience, there isn't anything like it in the world.

In Search of a Language

Our big problem in theology is that our language has referents only for our everyday life. What can you say about God? Well, you can say nothing, but if you say nothing, you can't witness Him. So you say, "God is like this or that, only more so." "Like what?" "Like a Father." We use root metaphors in order to be able to apprehend that reality which is behind it, but we also realize that this root metaphor is not more than a gate. Besides, is God only a Father? What about the problem we have with the word *Father*? After Freud we can't use it without washing our mouth out. So it is with king, so it is with almost every model that we have had for apprehending that reality which is God. So, what can we do?

As long as we speak of God's immanence, we can do lots of things. We can say God is like a tree, the Arbor Vitae, the Tree of Life, and we can say, "God is like a tree, and the roots are up and the branches are down and we are the fruits." You know, you really can talk like this. God talk about God immanent is no problem. The sages talked about it: "As man's body is filled by his soul so the world is filled by God." In all the circles where God talk is talked about and being analyzed, we know that we now can talk about God within but we can't talk about *God Transcendent* "up there" and "out there" anymore. We have reached the limit of God talk. In talking about the transcendental experience, we have to agree that we have no analogues or metaphors, we have no definitions that will be able to contain that experience. So why bother to continue talking?

Eloquent Shrugs and Stammers

Remember when we talked before about how you get almost close but
don't quite take the other step. What is it that makes us want to come
close? Rudolph Otto talks about it as the *mysterium fascinans.* . . .
"Come!" It beckons while we may not see his face, but we might see his
finger. So, we come closer, closer, and as we are about to lift our face
and look up, bah! The *mysterium tremendum* says, "Get out of here, if
you want not to be burned up in the great fire! It is a terrible thing to fall
into the hands of the Living God." It is "fire, fire, fire," as Pascal wrote
in his memorial amulet; "for three hours I felt nothing else but fire; it is
not the God of the philosophers, it's the God of Abraham, Isaac, and
Jacob!" That's what happens to people. Some run. Others, like St. John
of the Cross, stay and later write:

> I entered in, *I know not where*,
> And I remained, *though knowing naught*,
> *Transcending knowledge* with my thought.
>
> Of when I entered I know naught,
> But when I saw that I was *there*
> (Though where it was I did not care)
> Strange things I learned, with greatness fraught.
> Yet what I heard I'll not declare.
> But *there I stayed, though knowing naught*,
> Transcending knowledge with my thought.
>
> Of peace and piety interwound
> This perfect science had been wrought
> *Within the solitude profound*
> A straight and narrow path it taught,
> Such secret wisdom there I found
> That there *I stammered*, saying naught,
> But *topped all knowledge* with my thought.
> (Emphasis added)

He walked first through the attraction of the *fascinans.* But then he knew
he couldn't walk any further until he was able to shed all his senses and
walk through a dark night of the senses. What do we call it today?
Isolation experiments! What St.John of the Cross describes to us as the
dark night of the senses is exactly what some psychologists are doing.
Bringing about a withdrawal of every kind of stimulation to all our five
or six senses. And then, illumination! A hasidic rabbi once said, "Don't

trust it. You know what illumination is? God gives you a candy. If you want to take the candy, you'll stay with the candy; if you are wise, don't eat that candy; go past it." Ramakrishna would talk about the same thing when he said, "When you get an illumination, you need to use the sword of discrimination and chop the illumination to pieces, because there is more to do." So then, when all kinds of insights into scripture, into liturgy, and into wisdom are offered to the mystic, he must reject them as final goals and say like R. Shneur Zalman,"Master of the Universe, I don't want Paradise, I don't want the world to come, I only want You." To leave the illumination, we move on and where do we come to then? To the dark night of the soul.

THE SILENT LONELY VOID

Let's talk about the dark night of the soul in terms that are familiar to us. Everybody has a lonely place, "within the solitary profound." The lonely place is when you're deeply wounded and not necessarily by physical wounds, where you crawl into that lonely place in order to just let your wounds be alone. You also know that you might die in that lonely place and nobody would know. So why do you bother to go to that lonely place? Because you just can't stand to be around and be vulnerable. But being invulnerable also means not to be in contact. Can you imagine how we go to that lonely place? It feels like dying. You know that just before you die you will have to go to that lonely place one last time. That's only an analogy of what St. John the Cross talked about when he talks about the dark night of the soul. Is God to be found in that place? R. Nachman talks about that place as The Void. He has a great teaching in which he says,

> God,
> for Mercy's sake,
> created the world
> to reveal Mercy.
> If there were no world
> on whom would Mercy take pity?
>
> So—to show His Mercy
> He created the worlds
> from Aziluth's peak
> to this Earth's center.
>
> But as He wished to create
> there was not a where?
> All was Infinitely He,
> Be He Blessed!

The light He condensed
sideways
thus was space made
an empty void.

In space days and measures
came into being.
So the world was created.

This void was needed
for the world's sake,
so that it may be
put into place.

Don't strain to understand
this void!
It is a mystery—not to be realized
until the future
is the now.

Now
speaking of the void
we must say two things
—opposites—
is-ness and is-not-ness.

Void means absence of God
for world space's sake.
But in truth's deepest truth
God is still there.
Without His giving life
Nothing is is-ing.

Thus we speak of the void.
There is no way to realize
the void before the future
is come to be now. . . .

And the void?

It is nothing but
the no-thing which takes up
no space at all.
All it does is separate
between the Divine which fills
and the Divine which surrounds
the world.

Without the void
all would have been One.
But then
there would not have been
any creature — any world.
So the void is a kind of
Divine Wisdom of not being
so there can be division
between one kind of being
and another.

This wisdom of not being,
the wisdom of the void —
cannot be realized!
It is not a something,
but it makes all somethings
possible.
Each something is infused with
God
and surrounded by God:
There is in between
a void that is not.

This cannot be known
by knowing
but it can be faithed
by faithing past and through it.

The wisdom of the void
is dangerous,
because where it is strong
there is no sense and no knowing.
So, be guarded,
and seek to escape the void trap:
"Those who come there do not
return."

The void has no limits,
no echo.
Burning questions
are not answered there.
Martyrs who want to know Why?
are told "Silence."
Thus is the decree of the Thought!
Such thought is not given
to words.

What makes the difference between God immanent and God transcendent? A very thin line, which is composed only of surface tension between the two aspects of God. There the void is. Now Reb Nachman discussed the void not like someone who has understood this only conceptually but like someone who has been there. He says, "There is a place where some souls fall." And that to me describes the lonely place very well. There is no way to get out. And if a soul falls into that place, it just can't make it. All the places where a person gets lost, another one can find him unless he is lost in the void; no song can penetrate that region.

Every country has a song, and if you know the song of that country, you can help the people who are lost in that country. And it shall be on that day and the great *shofar*, the ram's horn, shall be sounded. And those who are lost in the land of Ashur, and those who have been pushed to the land of Egypt, they will all be gathered together because of that great *shofar*, the sound will be able to reach into that country. And they will all be brought together from there. What happens in a void? No *shofar* sound can reach there!

Is there any way in which anyone can save any other person being in the void? Rebbe Nachman said there is only one way to do that. If one knows how to sing the song of silence in the void, in the dark night of the soul, he can be heard by the souls lost in the void and can show that soul the way out. "Who knows the song of silence?" said Rebbe Nachman. "Moses knows the song of silence!" "How come he knows that song of silence?" "Because he's tongue-tied." This is the penalty he had to pay for entering the song of silence.

> But "Moses,"
> the tongue-tied one,
> is used to thought
> that cannot be worded,
> and he must give thought
> to the void
> to save the lost souls.
> (Moses, the humblest of men,
> knew his full greatness
> as well as his lowest
> vilest self.
> Others would lose
> their mind
> would they know the full
> debasement
> and the full glory of being

a Man of God.
One who hides the full truth
of yes and no,
of is and not-is
cannot be in the void
without bursting to pieces.
In speaking,
only one side can be worded
and then there is the other side
clamoring.
Moses can contain yes and no,
noble and save, in one wordless
thought.)

THE FULLNESS AND THE UNITIVE

One can become tongue-tied also by the fullness. The mouth—the tongue and lips—are at the service of the word and the words come out only one at a time. Man can hear and speak only one word at a time. Thus staying with the word he stays with one side only of the paradox of the whole truth.

Imagine a judge swears me in and says, "Do you promise to tell the Truth, the whole Truth, and nothing but the Truth." I can reply that I am only prepared to swear to tell the truth and nothing but the truth, but the *whole truth* I cannot swear to tell. Who as a human being knows the whole 360-degree truth? Enlightened beings manage to get 120 degrees of the full circle of truth; really enlightened saviors make it to 180 degrees. To tell the whole truth makes one tongue-tied. Which word first, which side first. And so the psalmist puts it, "God spoke ONE and we heard TWO." And the sages of the Talmud, "I AM and HAVE NO OTHER GODS, were just one word when spoken by God. They became two when Moses repeated them."

FAR OUT, TOO MUCH were phrases from the input overloaded 1960s, and the 1970s have chosen Incredible, Unbelievable.

Now in the transcendental experience the empty and the full are one. Jung, in his "Seven Sermons to the Dead," recorded how he heard Basilides of Alexandria speak:

Here Ye: I begin with nothing. Nothing is the same as fullness. In the endless state fullness is the same as emptiness. The Nothing is both empty and full. One may just as well state some other thing about the Nothing, namely, that it is black or that it is white or that it exists or that it exists not. That which is endless and eternal has no qualities, because it has all qualities.

The Nothing, or Fullness, is called by us the PLEROMA. In it thinking and being cease, because the eternal is without qualities. In it there is no one, for if anyone were, he then would be differentiated from the Pleroma and would possess qualities which would distinguish him from the Pleroma.

In the Pleroma there is nothing and everything: it is not profitable for one to think about the Pleroma, for to do that would mean one's dissolution.

The CREATED WORLD is not in the Pleroma, but in itself. The Pleroma is the beginning and end of the created world. The Pleroma penetrates the created world as the sunlight penetrates the air everywhere. Although the Pleroma penetrates it completely, the created world has no part of it, just as an utterly transparent body does not become either dark or light in color as the result of the passage of the light through it.

We ourselves, however, are the Pleroma, because we are a portion of the eternal and the endless. Still, we do not possess it, but are exceedingly removed from the Pleroma; not in space or time, but in being, inasmuch as our being is different from the Pleroma, inasmuch as we are created beings, and thus limited by time and space.

Transcending and Returning

And then there is just the back and forth, flipping between fullness and emptiness, faster and faster, until they have become one. And so have Yes and No and Life and Death and Creator dies into His creation that lives into its death back into the Creator. I am living God and I am dying mortal and I am everything and I am nothing. All opposites tear at my center and I must bear them all. I am all fire, all ocean, all space, all stone and rock. Every being in every galaxy is in one continuum with my day-to-day being. The infinite revolves majestically around its own axis, which is the heart, *THE HEART*, the most sacred sanctuary, the heart of the holy of holies. It bears the weight of all life and death. It is all ecstasy and all agony. It is the I AM THAT I AM—I AUM THAT I AUM—the Void, there is no one there anywhere, My God why hast THOU forsaken me. Hoc est enim corpus meum, ABRACADABRACADABRA. In the Beginning, Blessed be he who spoke the WORD and the WORLD came into being. THERE IS NO GOD BUT ALLAH. *Adon olam asher malakh beterem kol yetzir nivra!* The body is aflame with ice, the cells light up in electric Glorias. All nerves become a Tree of Life. Each breath breathes the universe in and out and costs every ounce of will and at the same time happens without volition and effort. All the feelings are arrayed around Awe and Love and each is MOMENTOUS on the one hand and so much madness on the other. All Ideas are TRUE and cancel each other against the rock of ESSENCE and it is now that I must die and Now I am born. In the telling it is never as simultaneous and NOW RIGHT NOW as in the actuality. In all this I long to be at home just one more minute with my loved ones, loving, making love, coming forever, LET THERE BE LIGHT! More light! I rebel and I surrender to the Self of the Self. . . . And I want to escape into other lifetimes which I see and in which I lose myself only to die again and to sink into a milky ocean of light, light, light and freedom and bliss and sure, pure being from which there is no escape because it is everywhere and always and I am that I am again here and again, now. . . .

And somehow I have had a reprieve from this burden of eternity of being, of BEING, of BEING THE ALL, and I cuddle with my little *me* intact, being creature again. I want to feel and sense with new eyes and heart and body, with a mind that is clear in all its all connected indiscriminate intuiting and associating, and there is so much to think about, so much life to be lived, and so much to forgive and be forgiven for, the kingdom did come and the will was done in earth as it is in heaven and I got my daily breath—careful now, no more evil, no temptation just to live for the kingdom and the power and the glory. AMEN.

Well, that was a flood of words and still nothing but a suggestion of the total simultaneity that allows itself to be put into words. But alas, it left out dimensions upon dimensions for which there is no analogue in experience and language. So if this is the case, why bother with this inadequate description? Because for a small moment in all this we were together at the Gate of Transcendence and we both, you and I, remembered, became members again of that mystical body of one-ness and shared in the experience of transcendence.

Though the questions will come and the doubts return and the ego will in its anxiety at getting unseated from the manager's position want to deny that all this ever happened even for a small moment. The fair witness within our awareness will testify that it was present and this is at times all one can expect to remain in the memory of the one who transcended.

II

SHOAH

INTRODUCTION

The following two articles form a Gestalt. Each one is another facet of the same topic. When read as a unit, they provide an overview of my thoughts on the *Shoah*, the State of Israel, and what I propose we might say and do about them.

7

SOME DAWN THOUGHTS ON

THE *SHOAH*

When Michael Lerner of Tikkun *magazine invited me to write on the*
Shoah, *I was able to bring the thoughts expressed in the earlier article to*
further development. This version differs somewhat from that printed in
Tikkun *2:1. Some notes and paragraphs that were omitted in the* Tikkun
printed version are restored in the present version.

In these meditations, I want to first point to the need for transdialectical
thinking about the Shoah *and to make a liturgical suggestion; second,*
look for the implications of the Shoah *for the planet; third, consider the*
possibility of making Auschwitz a place for the work of t'shuvah, *for*
one's final witnessing and for the work of psychic rescue; and finally I
want to deal with the psychic issue of "recycled souls."

For forty years have I contended with the generation.

(Psalm 95)

It has now been some 40 eventful years since the *Shoah*. Elie Wiesel
has been awarded the Nobel Peace Prize. His witnessing message has
reached many and they have affirmed it. By and large, however, we Jews
have yet to reach a consensus of understanding about the Holocaust at a
level responsive to Wiesel's message.

I, who am also a survivor, do not write these lines lightly. I write from

my own firsthand experience. Thank God, I was not interned in one of
the Nazi camps. Instead, I was a refugee internee in two Vichy camps
before coming to the United States in 1941. Our suffering in France at
that time was due to a series of events that to us then seemed simply
unfortunate. Had we had our way, my parents, siblings, and I might
have joined our family in Oswieczim (Auschwitz). They were *shochetim*,
a position they had inherited from my grandfather, a fervent Belzer
hasid. They were also among the first to be forcibly inducted into the
ghastly task of building the KZ.

I hesitate to make my statement here, knowing that even I, one
haunted by The Great *Shoah* Question, have difficulty maintaining an
awareness of it. The inner work that allows one to do creative thinking
instead of falling into reactive defense is hard. The blind spots are many.
The mind circuits have a way of overheating and underlighting on this
issue. Affirming the popular "explanations" set forth by our tradition
would not be of much help here. None of the theology derived from
Deuteronomy ("Blessing if you harken . . . Curse if you don't") helps us
to understand our fate and destiny in the world. And to view the
Holocaust from the dialectical viewpoint would lead only to the wish for
getting even.

There are those who claim there are no lessons to be derived from the
Holocaust. Its evil is too unique, the concatenation of circumstances too
weird to help us transfer meaning to other situations. They maintain that
we cannot persist with the theology of self-blame. The murder of
children as punishment for the transgressions of *Shabbat* and *kashrut*
does not make sense to our souls. The enormity of the massive Nazi evil
will never make sense. Still, I disagree with the notion that one cannot
derive any lessons from the Holocaust. As I previously wrote:[1]

> What Jewish guilt is there in Auschwitz? No single-valued reductive statement
> can serve to answer the question in a sociological frame. But, ethically and
> morally, our weakness was not enough righteousness toward the *goyim*
> [non-Jews].
> "What?" I hear exclamations all around me. "*We* should have been more
> righteous? Why don't you preach to the Germans, why to us?" And here is the
> answer. Why did we not preach to the Germans (as some of us are preaching
> to the Johnsons about Vietnam and as many non-Jews are preaching to the
> South Africans)? Why did we not preach to the Arabs? *This is the point.*
> Thinking that we, as victims of the Nazi Germans' oppression, somehow had
> no right to preach in order to save our own necks, we kept an anguished

[1]In Zalman Schachter-Shalomi, "Homeland and Holocaust," in *The Religious Situation*
(Boston: Beacon Press, 1968).

silence. In response to Nazi hostilities, we judged *all* Germans to be inhuman, predatory beasts, and the Germans returned the compliment. They were stronger, and we, by definition, the vermin to be exterminated. In short, *the Holocaust was partially caused by Jews who did not think it worthwhile, or even possible, to reprove the Germans.*

This brings us to our next point. *Jews are responsible not only for themselves but also for* goyim. *Their responsibility as the chosen people (chosen to be responsible and to be a kingdom of priests) must work paradoxically to eliminate their own chosenness by delegation of the responsibility to others who will also become God's people — Germans Arabs, and Russians included.* And here *halakhah* [Jewish law] enters the picture.

There has been much refinement in Jewish Law. Prior to the Holocaust, the Torah of the Jew had proliferated into the most minute levels of life. But the Jewish Torah of *goy*, by and large, did not have any specific action directives. Those that it did have were ambiguous and self-contradictory. We, who were charged with the responsibility of reproving our neighbor when we saw him involved in a sinful act, had excluded the *goy* from our reproach. The *goy* was given the same consideration as a compulsive beast: no amount of rational reeducation could possibly help him. At best, we sought only the application of subtle pressure: "You are such a nice Minister of the Interior; please stop the pogrom." The *goy* who could be bought and cajoled was not good enough to hear with us the word of the Lord. Our theology will continue to fail us as long as our *halakhah* — that which provides us with our action directives — has not yet come to grips with our relations with *goyim*. *Jewish halakhists must provide us with an application of God's law, which will be more in the service of the total redemption. They cannot do this by recourse to old patterns, because these will bring only the old results.*

So I say they are a people of confused heart.

(Psalm 95)

Our[2] vision has indeed been narrowed by reinforced old suspicions and new-found vigilance. We are frustrated that we could not find all the Nazis who went underground and punish them for their crimes. More-

---

[2]When I think *we, our, us*, it is a con-*fused* identity. Fused of many differing "I"s, it is at times the I of a traumatized, brutalized individual who has not yet healed from the *Shoah*. At other times it is the I of one who is planning *aliyah* and already identifying with Israelis. Most of the time when I think of myself in terms of my political *hashkafah* I see myself in the same camp with the New Jewish Agenda people. Religiously, I am at home with the post-denominational Jewish renewal folks, and spiritually I am committed to generic spirituality deriving deeply from the hasidic tradition. At other times I am just *amkha*, a Jew like all the other Jews, who feels that some things are fitting for us and others are, while not *treif*, nevertheless *s'passt nit* for Jews. I am happy if good things happen to Jews and I wince when a Jewish name is connected with crime. So the *we, us*, and *our* are fluid and depend on the context.

over, how can we leave bygones when we are still confronted by the threat of genocide, this time at the hands of the PLO and its allies? Did not the special vigilance of the El Al security people save that plane in London? How are we then to let go of our preoccupation with self-defense? In such a climate it has once again become *them against us* while "the world" shows more concern for the price of oil than for our lives. In turn, we feel justified in holding on to our defensiveness in the absence of any willingness on "their" part to enter into any accommodation with us. This deepens our entrenchment in our difficulties, because without giving up the wish to better ourselves at the expense of others, we cannot figure our way out of the automatic response pattern that has us lost in a maze of retaliatory moves. We are locked into a system that compels us to repeat the plea of being blameless victims—or, in desperation, to take on the tactics of those who threaten us—while trying to get even.

So I say to you in the pool of blood "Live!"

(Ezekiel 16:6)

At times, in deep meditation, it seems to me that I hear a horrifying scream from a catastrophic future alarming us to wake up and correct our course. It seems almost too late because there is so much sophistication in the technology of destruction and so little in the technology of making peace. The distance between what *is* and what *needs to be avoided* is too vast. Who can live daily life and remain conscious and aware in the presence of such stress?

We are numbed by the anguish of our impotence in the face of such overwhelming evil. We are even blocked from turning to God for solace and help. We are still angry with the God of our ancestors of whom we learned in Hebrew school. When we turn to those who claim to know God and God's will, we realize that they, too, are paralyzed. The *gedolei yisrael* (halakhic authorities) have not even once met in council to tell us of their consensus on the meaning of the Holocaust.

We are on our own now. We must open our minds to important questions. Are *we* not—even as victims—playing supporting roles in the evil system? This until now unvoiced question comes with a "yes" for its answer. We cannot just hide in our victim status.

We, who want the world to learn something from the Holocaust, what have *we* learned? How do we deal with our *own* people and our cousins in Israel? Are we not aware of how victims can internalize their oppressors and emulate them? Are we not steadily and forcibly being pulled into the place of the oppressor? How can we, as conscientious supporters of Israel, allow our high-tech weaponry to be exported to those who openly are bent on Israel's destruction? Why do we, in our search for hard currency, abandon all principles and sell arms to repressive, totalitarian governments—into whose hands we press our Uzzis?

These questions make us very anxious. How can we remain so complacent and ignore the reality that Israel may cave in, not due to external pressure, but from inner and moral collapse?

At one time the reluctance to change gave us the advantage of cultural and traditional stability. Now we cannot any longer afford this. The victim scripts have to be abandoned if we are to survive. Our traditions do not have to be discarded. By transforming the cultural treasures of the past to help us in the present-future we can maintain many of the major values in the deep structure. By adapting the surface structures to new scripts we can enhance our lives. However, for many of us, letting go of the martyr script would create an identity crisis.

Survival as an integral part of life on this planet is worth it. The tides of constant arming amidst conspicuous and wasteful consumption, our excessive use of energy and goods, cannot be stemmed by morals-as-usual. We will have to create an ethic and a morality more effective than the present dialectical ones.

We want to maintain our identity. However, we are confused as to how to play Jew in the present world. Looking into some mirror of truth, how do we seem to ourselves? From Woody Allen to the IDF para-trooper, from Communist to *neturei karta*, we caricature conflicting postures, none of which makes us into winners in the game of life. Without a clear archetypal model "JEW" we know not whom to emulate. Have we yet envisioned the process—Lammedvovnik AM 5786–5800? We have to design such a type today if we are to survive that era as Jews. We have to package the information, directives, tropisms into accessible models for the future righteous men and women and inject these resources into the educational system in order to produce them.[3]

---

[3]Children learn some things that adults are not able to learn so easily. For example, the Rubic's cube has stymied and frustrated me. I have seen children master it in a short time, but I have only seen a small number of adults who could do it.

This much I do know: the place where I get stuck with the Rubic's cube is that I am in such a hurry to get it done that I do not explore the ways that seem to lead away from getting all the same colors on the same side. It has taught me to be more humble in relation to those who, in order to reach their ultimate goals, will be willing to go temporarily in an opposite direction that seems only to divert them.

In solving the Rubic's cube, it looks at times that in making the right and appropriate moves, you destroy the gains you have already made, creating more chaos than order.

We may have to scrap some of our old scripts. They have the cultural inertia of tradition on their side—it has to be this way in order to give each paradigm the needed stability. The paradigm has now shifted as our technology shifted. The benefit of global communication is part of the same system as the threat of global destruction. Alas, we may not have the moral power to change the karmic path we are on.

For all our vaunted Jewish intellect, we have not yet demonstrated that we have what it takes to reassess the dynamics of our Holocaust involvement. We are still caught in the reactive strategies of victims who have not seen the full and dynamic drama of their intimate reciprocities with their oppressors. Hypnotized by the constant need to make countermoves, to defend and retaliate, we have not yet had the safe space, time, and energy to develop the vision and the metastrategies needed to get out of the victim-oppressor cycle.[4]

The *Shoah* warns us that no ethnic victory over others and at their expense can serve as justification for destroying the planet. Yet we still have not learned to think in transdialectical global terms.

Where a pervasive process is concerned, the answers cannot be gained from any single individual. The only way to get it together is TOGETHER, and that includes those with whom we'd rather not talk.

God! I remember and am dazed.

(Selichah for Neilah)

We have yet to attend to the Holocaust liturgically. With only a few notable exceptions *(The Authorized Kinot for the Ninth of Av* by Rev. Abraham Rosenfeld: London, 1965 [p. 173] and the Yizkor sections of the RA Machzor written by Rabbi Jules Harlow), we have still not incorporated the Holocaust into our liturgical repertoire. Somehow, this

---

[4]This too was written in an article from 1968, way before there was an oil crisis. The Middle East crisis excited us because we were threatened once more. Unconsciously, we were predisposed to new action directives. The grief and guilt over our silence in the thirties and forties have done their unconscious work. The next step can be taken only consciously and deliberately. . . . Arab refugee relief is our problem too, and it is our obligation as Jews not only to contribute money, but also to organize the Arab world to help their own and others. (Perhaps a penny per gallon on Arab oil to help the refugees resettle and start life in the places vacated by Jews who emigrated from Iraq, North Africa, Russia, etc., is worthy of consideration by the Joint Distribution Committee.) We cannot forget that the State of Israel is God's grace to Israel (the people) and affords us the opportunity to apply the lessons of Auschwitz in terms of action directives. In order for these action directives to have reality, they must stand in a dialogical relationship with those who are part of the total redemption. They must be located, not on the continuum of a righteousness that has a precedent, but on an unprecedented *teshuvah*-center *Aggadah*.

demonstrates more clearly than anything else that even the *religious* people have not found a way to include *a kinah* (lamentation prayer) on Auschwitz.

I have written a Hebrew version in the style of the medieval *kinot*, with an English rendition. Both can be chanted to the melody of *Eli Zion V'areha*.

Dirge For Auschwitz

Alas, how poor are words to state our pain
In remembering the millions slain
While yet upon our souls the stain
Of standing by while brothers called in vain.

Unshriven here we are depressed
As long as somewhere someone is oppressed
As long as the murderers the meek suppressed
And grieving mothers wail distressed.

Shalt Thou, O God, not bear Thy guilt this day
For standing by while multitudes in blood did lay,
And silent Thou unmoved didst stay,
Thy covenant to help us didst betray.

While millions' lives to ash were turned,
To their last breath Thine intervention yearned,
Still hoping day and night, while all the ovens burned.
Why were our prayers of desperation spurned?

If Thine own we are, O Lord, and Thou art King
If only by Thy leave occurs each thing,
Then butcher Thou, and we the offering.
Yet who, but Thou, can heal our suffering?

The help Thou sendest must renew
All of mankind, not just the Jew
The Arabs and the Russians too
Must be freed, ere peace is true.

Send Thine anointed Saviour, Lord,
To turn to plowshare atom's sword.
May each in Him see One adored
And prophesied by prophet's word.

I have been to Germany since and taught there. I must say that I enjoyed the experience of teaching at Tuebingen. I found that both students and colleagues sought to know, and wished to set right, what a generation before them had wronged.

I met Germans in Israel who are motivated to work for *tikkun*. I met German converts to Judaism there and in Germany who live noble Jewish lives. I met Christians in East Germany whose sympathy for our people and heritage causes them to live close to the edges of danger. I salute them.

I cannot say that the warm and touching experience at the university healed me completely of my traumas. On a train from Heidelberg to Tuebingen, I became terrified when the train filled with soccer fans returning from a game, and a rowdy cadre of youths were making their way through the aisle. Suddenly, one of them noticed me and shouted: *Da sitzt ein Jude*! I, then sixty years old, felt the fear of a preadolescent again. I felt as if some time trap had plunged me back to the late fall of 1938. I calmed down when I spotted a train policeman patrolling the car, but the incident put me in touch with some unconscious fears still active in my guts.

Your brother's voice cries out to me from the earth.

(Genesis 4:10)

My wife and I visited Auschwitz, a painful pilgrimage, to see if we wanted to bring more children into such a terrible world. The most terrifying impact the place had on me was a psychic one. There are souls there that still haunt the site. "The voice of your brother's blood cries out to me" was no longer a mere metaphor for me. According to Rabbi Gedaliah ben Yossef ibn Yachyah (sixteenth century), souls cut off tragically and suddenly "hover about the area where they have lost their bodies" (*Shalshelet Hakabbalah*, Treatise on the Soul and its Nature).

I felt then that it was imperative for some of us to go and live at the scene of the horror for at least a year to raise those *neshomes* chained to their hells. I envisioned a *Bet HaMidrash* in which psalms would be said, the *Mishnah* (*Neshamah*) be studied, and *Kaddish* recited, a place where those of us who wish to work for peace could meditate and think, mourn and grieve, and do that work to which we would be drawn by the souls who need our work and help.

I gave up on this "dream" because of the unfriendly government and because of the sad fact that it would be most difficult to find the right people to do this work. By "the right people" I mean those who know the meaning of psychic rescue and release work and who believe in it. While there are some who are capable of doing this, they are, understandably, too preoccupied with the enormous spiritual needs of the living.

I spoke with some people about this. When I raised the possibility that some souls may still be chained to their suffering and to their wish for revenge, I was attacked with such vehemence that I dropped it. My conviction still holds.

> I forgive whoever has hurt me . . . in this *gilgul* or any other.
>
> (From the bedtime *Shema*)

One does not need to visit the death camps to come across their impact. Even if I had not believed in reincarnation as a result of my study of Kabbalah I would have begun to believe in its reality for reasons of fact. My reputation as one interested in spiritual phenomena has attracted people who have confided in me about memories of having lived during the Holocaust years in their past life cycle. Some of them have vivid memories of having been victims. A few have memories as oppressors. Some have come back in Jewish births, others in non- Jewish ones. Some of the Jewish ones have chosen blue-eyed, blond-haired bodies that would make them pass as Aryans. Others, born to non-Jewish parents, have felt an overwhelming attraction to Jews and Judaism and feel themselves haunted by that pull.

Recycled souls are still around us. Here are only two of such phenomena as I have witnessed them.

Mark (not his real name), who had never spoken Yiddish before, attended a *Havurah Shabbat* session during which a visitor had introduced a breathing exercise calling on the participants to breathe deeply and rapidly, alternating the breathing in and out more and more rapidly. Mark entered into a state of panic, beginning to cry in Yiddish for *Mashiach* to come. He banged on the door, could not open it, and collapsed, whimpering. Fortunately, he recovered in the warmth of the gentle ministrations of his friends. His story, when he could be coherent, was that during the exercise he had lost touch with the reality of the present and had fallen into a state in which he re-remembered his dying in the gas chamber.

A woman from upstate New York was referred to me by her psychiatrist because of the strange anxiety attacks she experienced each time she tried to *davven* in a traditional *shul*. She belonged to a progressive congregation. Though she preferred the traditional *davvening*, she felt terrified when she would attempt to *davven* in a more fervent *minyan*. I instructed her to shut her eyes and imagine the *davvening* going on, and as she did so she began to weep. She re-remembered *davvening* in the traditional fashion in another lifetime. When the fervor rose, it triggered in her memories the outcry of the last *Shema* in the gas chamber. Working together with her therapist, I was able to help her to remain present to both the horror memory *and* that this was not in the present lifetime.

Sitting in the secret of the Highest — in the shadow of Shaddai

Each technology has its shadow cost. Each mile of highway has a statistic of lives lost. Each advance of science brings some chaos with it. NASA's achievements are limited by the Challenger. Three Mile Island and Chernobyl are the shadow costs of nuclear energy. In common cost accounting the shadow costs are usually not included. We do not wish to be made aware of them. Still, as we look to the insurance companies to cover us, they charge us the actuarial rates that the shadow thrusts on them.

If we could become aware of the costs and of the dynamics of the shadow energies, then we might be able to reduce them. Here, too, we are just at the beginnings of glimmers on our awareness. Kabbalists called these energies *Klippot*. Some have voiced that the *Shoah* was the shadow cost of the State of Israel. Our tradition has taught us of the *Hevlei Mashiach* as the shadow cost of the planet's redemption. How tragic it would be if we did not derive from the *Shoah* what we must learn to be able to say "Dayenu."

המקום ינחם את העולם כולו
אושביציון

אֵיכָה יֶשְׁמְשׁוּ מִלִים לְהַבִּיעַ כְּאֵבֵנוּ
בְּזָכְרֵנוּ אָבְדַן מִלְיוֹנֵינוּ
בְּעוֹד עַל שָׁכְמֵנוּ אַשְׁמָתֵינוּ
עַל עָזָר אַחִים שֶׁבֻּקַּשׁ וְלֹא עָלָה בְּיָדֵנוּ.

וִידֵי תְּחוּשׁוֹת אוֹתָנוּ לֹא יְנַקֶּה
בְּעוֹד מִי שֶׁהוּא עָשׁוּק וּלְעֶזְרָה מְחַכֶּה
עוֹד הוֹרֵג נָפְשׁוֹת עֲנָיִים יְדַכֶּה
וְאִם שְׁכוּלָה בָּנֶיהָ תְּבַכֶּה.

שְׁמַע יְיָ כִּי גַם אַתָּה אִתָּנוּ
אָשָׁם, כִּי מִתְבּוֹסְסִים בְּדָם רְאִיתָנוּ
וְעַל שְׁתִיקָתְךָ לֹא נָבַרְתָ לְהַצִּיל אוֹתָנוּ
מִי הֵפֵר בְּרִית? לָמָה רְמִיתָנוּ?!

בְּמַחֲנוֹת הַהֶסְגֵּר מִלְיוֹנִים עֵינוּ
וְתִקְוַת אֲנִי מַאֲמִין לֹא סָרָה מִפִּינוּ
כָּל הַיּוֹם, כָּל הַלַּיְלָה לִישׁוּעָה קִוִּינוּ
וְלַמְרוֹת אַכְזָבוֹת מִמְּךָ לֹא סַטִינוּ.

יָ-הּ! אִם אָנוּ עַמְּךָ וְאַתָּה מַלְכֵּנוּ
אִם אָנוּ חֶלְקְךָ וְאַתָּה חֶלְקֵנוּ
אִם אָנוּ צֹאנְךָ אָז אַתָּ זוּבְחֵנוּ
אִם אָנוּ שׁוֹבְךָ אָז עָלֶיךָ לִפְדוֹתֵנוּ!

צַנֵּה יְשׁוּעַת יַעֲקֹב חִישׁ נָא מְהֵרָה
הַ"בְּעִתּוֹ" כְּבָר עָבַר וְעוֹד יַד רָשָׁע גוֹבְרָה
יְהוּדֵי רוּסִיָא נֶאֱנָחִים מֵאִין בְּרֵירָה
וּסְבִיבוֹת יִשְׂרָאֵל עוֹמְמָה הַתַּבְעֵרָה

גְאָלָנוּ הַגּוֹאֵל לֹא אוֹתָנוּ לְבַדֵנוּ
כִּי יִגְאַל אַךְ יַעֲקֹב וְלֹא בְּנֵי עֵשָׂיו אַחֵינוּ
אָז הַגָּאֵל עוֹד מוּכֶה, עוֹד עוֹרְכִים טִבְחֵנוּ
אִם לֹא יִגְאַל הָרָשָׁע עוֹד חַי רוֹצְחֵנוּ.

וְאִם עוֹד מִי סוֹבֵל הַגְּאֻלָה פְּגוּמָה.
בֶּן חָם אוֹ בֶן יֶפֶת אוֹ אָדָם אוֹ בְהֵמָה,
אִם עוֹד בַּעַל חַיִּים סוֹבֵל צַעַר וּמְהוּמָה
אֵין שָׁלוֹם וְשַׁלְוָה לְיָחִיד אוֹ אוּמָה.

נָא-רַחֵם, הַנֶּאֱרָץ מֵרַבִּים
הַמְכַוְּנִים לְךָ וְלֹא לָעֲצַבִּים!
גְאוֹל-נָא כָּל אֶחָד בִּלְבוּשֶׁיךָ הָרַבִּים
בָּהֶם תִּוָּאַרְתָ מִפִּי שְׁלִיחִים אֲשֶׁר בְּשִׁמְךָ מְנַבְּאִים.

8

JERUSALEM AND THE COMPLETE REDEMPTION

This article, not accepted by several Jewish journals in May 1967, was written in response to the gathering clouds of the 1967 war. It was written about the same time as my response to Richard Rubenstein's "Homeland and Holocaust" that appeared in The Religious Situation 1968. *There I wrote, among other things, a proposal that we set aside one penny per gallon of gas to contribute to the United Jewish Appeal to be earmarked for the resettlement of Palestinian refugees.*

The United Nations is today not the instrument it could have become then. Perhaps in the current conflicts about the territories, we are approaching another nexus for rethinking these issues.

Jerusalem must be internationalized. This is the burden of these lines. The purpose of an internationalized Jerusalem is to make it possible for the Jews to keep Jerusalem, while at the same time opening the way for the complete redemption.

There are many intoxicants in humanity's blood. Some of them are the result of the inhalation or ingestion of foreign substances; others are the result of experiences lived through. Pride, victory, and success create such intoxicants, and the voice that tries to speak a sobering word is shouted down.

This is an attempt to say a sobering word in the service of the same objectives that most Jews hold. Perhaps all we wish to do is to extend the aims and to make more feasible a long-range view of peace in the Middle East, along with the redemption of Israel and all nations.

A Jewish Jerusalem would be good, but it would postpone the complete redemption and recycle the possibility of a Jewish defeat. We want the world to recognize our claim to Jerusalem. On no other basis can we negotiate with the world. One can negotiate only that which exists as a claim. Even a de facto recognition of the claim makes negotiations possible. This we want.

Those who want to raze the Moslem and Christian holy places and rid Israel of "abominations" invite dangerous "liberations," "holy wars," and "crusades." This we don't want. A Jewish Jerusalem in which the right of access to the holy places will be given as a matter of natural right to Christians and Moslems is what Israel is offering. An internationalized Jerusalem that will be under territorial autonomy of the United Nations is what "world opinion" is demanding. We wish to state why we think that this is even better for Jews and for the "complete redemption" than a territorially Jewish Jerusalem.

A complete redemption is one in which all parties are redeemed, judged, and justified before God. There are still some Jews who believe in and hope and pray for the complete redemption. Some think this is a dream that cannot be realized. Some think that for the sake of the complete redemption, only Jews need to be redeemed. We think that a complete redemption must not enslave another or cause him loss of property or face. The Hebrew words *G'ullah Sh'lemah*, total redemption, imply no halfway measures. Because of this, we hold that a redemption that causes distress, upset, loss of face, honor, or any other form of enslavement must include in itself the seeds of the same for the "redeemer." In this way, Versailles included Auschwitz. What is gained by might is lost by greater might. A Jewish Jerusalem will suffer the Christians and the Moslems but will not greet them as its own. When the Ukrainian peasant had to get the keys of his Provoslavna (Russian Orthodox) Church from the Jew because this was the way the Roman Catholic landowner had arranged matters, we suffered under Chmielnitzky. The salvational value of a pilgrimage to a holy place is undermined when a pilgrim has to pour out his heart to his God that he may free the place from the hands of infidels. We wish no Moslem or Christian to pray for another redemption. Their holy places must be their own. It is in our interest to keep the messianic spark contained in Christianity and Islam alive in order to motivate Moslem and Christianity to the age of the plowshare.

The messianic element demands that the Moslem, Christian, and Jew need the messianic era as Moslem, Christian, and Jew. Just as we cannot be asked to enter a redemption that excludes the very basis of our wish to be redeemed — Judaism — so cannot others be asked to give up their basis for redemption. Just as our own messianic hope cannot be fulfilled by means of the Christian or Moslem channels, so cannot we demand that others relinquish their hold on the source of their values.

The messianic new "Torah which will come forth from Me" (Isaiah 51:4) must be more redeeming than any previous one *(Jeremiah 31:33)*. It will have to transcend the best that we know of God's will at the present. The Holocaust and the atom bomb point to the fact that previous truths have not been good enough. This is why we are in various stages of exile. Exile of the soul, the mind, and the emotions. Exile from plenty and the good life, and exile from God and from our best selves.

A United Nations capital in Jerusalem instead of New York would be a move in the direction of the complete redemption. At present the United Nations is weaker than ever before. Humanity cannot afford this. When Castro and the People's Republic of China are out of place in New York, peace is impossible. The United Nations needs sovereign territory of its own. If Jerusalem is to be what the New Jerusalem ought to be, it must not miss the opportunity to be the host of the United Nations. To be the house of prayer of all nations, Jerusalem must belong to all nations. When Jerusalem belongs to all the nations, then she is safe. Perhaps this is what is meant by "Jerusalem is destined to be spread among all the lands." Israel ought, therefore, to demand of the United Nations that it move to Jerusalem, and, only on that condition, internationalize it. The sentiment of many UN member nations will move in this direction and we have a right to exact this price. Whatever financial expense this will entail, it could not exceed the cost of Arab-Jewish blood spilled for it. And not only the blood of Arab and Jew, but also of Jebusite, Assyrian, Roman, Saracen, and Christian. There is hardly any nation that did not contribute with blood to its soil. The Israeli armed forces have shown that they have what it takes to be the core of a United Nations peacekeeping force. The discipline that sought to prevent overkill and civilian hurt and pillage is one that ought to become worldwide.

Any person serving in the United Nations peacekeeping force should have to relinquish his or her nationality and become a world citizen. With the Israeli draft in force for the United Nations, Israel will become the first "no nation" under United Nations auspices. There is no worthier vocation of the kingdom of servitors and the holy folk than to serve peace. *"Sim Shalom Tovah Uverakhah,"* we pray thrice daily. Other people could, upon serving the United Nations in any capacity, become world citizens.

Jerusalem would be surrounded by Israeli territory. The currency of Israel would be hardened, employment increased, and security guaranteed. In dealing with Jerusalem and the holy places, one of the most benign myths in the world — that of the city of peace and goodwill — is placed in the service of these objectives. Just as the Vatican brings commerce, money, and pilgrims to Rome, which is only part of the world, how much more would Jerusalem enjoy these when it belongs to practically the whole world.

When, with the United Nations, mankind's resources became located in Jerusalem — computerized libraries and communications making them available instantaneously and globally — a United Nations University would grow out of the Hebrew University, as well as colleges of various nations and cultures and seminaries of various religions. All this would be a step in the direction of the complete redemption: "and out of Zion shall come forth Torah." It could take us as far as humanity can reach toward peace. What would God say when all of God's children ask for God's blessing and to dwell in Jerusalem?

III

THINKING ABOUT GOD, REALITY, AND LIFE

9

PATTERNS OF GOOD AND EVIL

"Behold I set before thee today"

In the early sixties a number of colleagues met every year at the Union Institute at Oconomowoc, Wisconsin. We would spend a few days sharing our insights and finding delight in one another's company and pooling our travel and other expenses. We met without publicity or fanfare, and most important, we shared our struggles with faith. Since the academic meeting served as our model for sharing papers with one another, Arnold Jacob Wolf suggested that we put some of these into a book. He called it Rediscovering Judaism. *We also studied texts, davvened, and meditated together, enjoying our differences as well as our shared concerns. Many a seed concerning spirituality in Judaism took root in those meetings and are felt in all wings of Judaism.*

Existentialism and psychoanalysis were in the air, and we reexamined doctrines many moderns had discarded. A. J. Heschel's style had impressed me as a way to say what linear logical rationalism could not say. This long meditation on the theodicy—why bad things happen to good people—was based on ideas I had found in Chabad *and in* Personalism. *A. J. Wolf edited and shaped this, and my thanks are here again expressed.*

BEHOLD

Of course, one can close one's eyes, stop up one's ears, and just live.
No! It would not be quite correct for any of us to say, "I live," and

81

make it stick in the active grammatical form. In order to be able to speak in the active form, one must be capable of deliberate action. Most of us are passively *lived*, driven, and determined by our environment, by our heredity, and by the people around us. Nevertheless, one can close one's eyes, stop up one's ears, and just be lived. This would be far more comfortable than to engage in attempts to live deliberately that at the outset seem doomed to futility.

But there are some of us who cannot close our eyes.

We are aware that we are being called. We are not yet certain whether the voice calling imperatively, "Behold!" issues from within or from a nebulous without. Still, the imperative causes us to pay attention, for this voice commands the ear to hear, to heed, to pay attention ("*Shema!*"), or forces a choice inescapably upon us here ("*Hineh*"), or gives us the grace to see a little ahead toward the fork in the road and tells us to look ("*R'eh!*").

Set Before Thee

Life inexorably moves on. It is impossible not to choose in the face of the challenge. If life were to stand still, we could postpone choosing, but with our own life at stake we cannot afford to be objective, to wait for all the evidence to come in. Choosing not to take up the challenge is still a choice as deliberate as the choice to say yes. In either case one has to take the responsibility, that is to say, be answerable to someone for the choice made.

The variegated pressures that we face are always before us. Each field of tension in the pattern of challenges is loaded with potentials to which we attach values out of our inner hierarchy.

To choose would be a simple task if only the hierarchy of our values were clearly defined, if the values that are the ultimates of our life did not change their shape and color in the many and terrible contingencies of life. Try as we might to put our values to work within the subjective life space of the I, they evade our will. As into Zeno's river, we can never step into the same I-stream twice. The coordinates shift and are so fluid that "the world is a spinning die, and everything turns and changes; man is turned into an angel, and angel to man; and the head to the foot, and the foot to the head. Thus all things turn and spin and change, this into that and that into this, the topmost to the undermost and the nethermost to the topmost." We are not yet ready to say with Reb Nachman, the author of this quotation, "For at the root all is one, and salvation inheres in the change and return of things." Our consciousness is fluid, our I-stream flows on. If only we could have *one* fixed coordinate, according to which we could bring order into our chaotic interior, we might be able to attach values to the gaping potentiality of the fields and the patterns that are before us and of which we are a part.

I SET BEFORE THEE

God is the Name that man attaches to the Origin of the Voice. Man must do so, because somehow, despite all the confusion between the within and without, the Origin of the Voice is "realer than real." Despite the bump of the world's "reality" on our senses, we know that our senses are easily deluded. But this Voice does not speak to the senses and because it does not share the bump of reality as we know it, we feel it to be the more real.

Even without God, man's predicament is hard enough. Uncommitted man is constantly forced to choose among the clamoring stridencies of loyalty and attachments, which are frequently mutually antagonistic. In the very instant of anticipating one fulfillment, he faces the pain of separation from another loyalty, which he cannot but betray. The stress is too much to bear. The pagan cuts up his life, allotting Sundays to the worship of the sun, Mondays to the worship of the moon, etc. Sunday and Monday are irreconcilably antagonistic to each other. Yet even the pagan lives hermetically sealed in the loyalty of the day, because if man were to pass Sunday by only "sunning" and Monday by only "mooning," he would feel the inherent hostility of both sun and moon as they rip at the wholeness of his being and fragment it. In order to survive, he must, after a quick propitiation of the ruler of the day, set about ignoring him. Once the quick compromise has been made, the pagan has either to tranquilize or to overstimulate himself into oblivion, in order to maintain some vestige of wholeness.

A JEALOUS GOD

And at the same time, the Voice from that certain uncertain region constantly insists that man consolidate all his holdings, that he be made whole and that he be set free. But if he rebels successfully against the sun and the moon, he is still not free. A person's family, his people, his country, his livelihood, his friends, will still continue the tug of war for supremacy, none of them to emerge a final victor. The easiest way, so it seems, would be to give up the gods and to enter into the Kingdom of

God. However, this cannot be done with one's outer will, one's instrumental will. If one were to attempt to enthrone God merely with his outer will, he would find that he has jumped from the frying pan into the fire. At least at one's entrance into the Kingdom, the Voice is antagonistic to all other values within man. A jealous God demands that man "forsake his country, his birthplace and his father's house."

Today Must Ye Do It

God increases the terror of man's predicament, whose dread is compounded by anxiety over God's unknowableness. Pagan deities are predictable; they live in their assigned roles, they are conditioned to specific functions by their mythic necessities. Not so God; He obliterates all security that comes from being able to predict anything about Him. Truly He is jealous of all the little supports, of the coordinates of comfort into which we would sink for a little bit of rest; if at this stage we wish to sink into Him, the dread of vertigo paralyzes us. We dare not yield to a free fall because we are not really sure that "underneath are the everlasting arms." The inner will has not yet entered the Kingdom. Since the outer will is impotent, the temptation for man to plead, "the heaven is for God and the earth is for men" is immense. Terrified by the immediacies of today, we would like to do tomorrow, *mañana*, that which we are challenged to do today. If one is to take God as the prime coordinate for ordering his inner self, if one is to yield to Him one's inner will, there is no living "as usual." But neither can living as usual be sustained if one does not yield his inner will to God.

Before Thy Many *Panim*

We have already noted that there are many choices "before thee." The "before thee" of this morning is wholly other than the "before thee" of noon. There are times when it seems that one's identity is nothing but a skeleton on which hang a number of ever-changing presents.

"Before thee" also means "before thy many faces." How exact Hebrew is in its vagueness: The word *panim*—face or faces—is not singular. Many faces, many facets make up the outer self, the *persona*, and the inner self, the *Penim*. The facets of an individual person, of a corporate person—a community—constantly dance in tune and rhythm with the cacophonous calls that challenge it. It would seem that we confront them all at once, though this is not so. Our predicament is worsened by the fact that "face" nevertheless indicates direction, for our *panim* point to one direction and our back to another.

Our first choice would be to define ourselves, our face, in terms of essence, but our existence precedes our essence, and in our existence there already exists a direction into which our face points. Those slices of life that we already confront are an existent fact. And yet, if one is aware of having a *panim*, then at least there is a possibility of pointing the face into the direction of the Voice and replying to its "*Hineh*—Behold" with "*Hineni*—Here I am." To use this possibility is by no means a solution, but it often is the only possible turning toward a solution, for it allows us to turn, to return, to do *t'eshuvah*.

Today Is the First Day of the Week

The temptation to escape from history, not to pay for the consumption of yesterday, and not to prepare for tomorrow, is great. If only the statute of limitations were not to exceed 24 hours; if only we were not responsible for yesterday and tomorrow; then at least we would have today as a wonderful day to get lost in. On the other hand, the temptation is often very great to pay for all the yesterdays and all the tomorrows today, so that not a minute of today remains, and then today is overwhelmed and crushed by all the yesterdays and the tomorrows. *Today* is a great challenge, for it is the only one and thus unique today, while there are many tomorrows and many that will soon be adding themselves to even more yesterdays.

The yesterdays are determined, the tomorrows will turn into yesterdays and also become determined, but today is brand new and free. It never happened before and may be altogether different from all other todays we have ever experienced. Today need be determined not by yesterday but instead by the self, which is addressed by the Voice and turns not into a new direction but toward itself. It can be free and can redeem all the yesterdays and shape all the tomorrows. But, if one free *today* from determination, if one lives in an ahistoric today, one unconnected with yesterday that plans not for tomorrow, or if one pays all yesterday's debts today and is overwhelmed by anxieties for tomorrow, one finds no escape. The debt of an irresponsible today as it turns into yesterday will ultimately have to be paid, crushing all future todays.

Today the Messiah Comes—If Ye Hearken to My Voice

Curiously enough, at the beginning of each day we may tend to say that today can be free, that it can be made manageable, that one can live deliberately in it. At the beginning of each day when the sun is shining one may say, Yes, and at the end of each day say, No, because clouds or no clouds, the sun has set. Unhappy creatures we are, wishing to escape into a wholly spontaneous world, to flee back into the world of child's play. But this is a wish that we cannot fulfill anymore, for if we are given a day free from routine, we embrace a routine diversion in order to escape the responsibility of freedom. An adult deliberateness, the spontaneity to be deliberate, is responsibility.

But to evaluate all todays as tomorrow-determined yesterdays in a cynical manner also will not do. We all remember momentary snatches of todays; we change direction deliberately yet spontaneously. Even if 99 percent of our experience tended to justify a cynical evaluation, the real experience of the one case out of a hundred in which we lived and achieved freedom is a serious ally to the Voice that speaks to us in unceasing challenge. We claim that we cannot do this every day, that we cannot afford the tremendous inner expense of living deliberately each day. We claim that we do not have enough strength.

How much strength do we have and how much strength do we need? Surely today we do not possess enough strength *forever*, not even enough strength for a year, for a month, or a week, but today we do have enough for a today, and if we only dare to expend all today's energy today, we may rescue this day from a misdetermined in-place-ness with dead yesterdays.

Looking back on such days when we did manage moments spontaneously deliberate, we also know—and this is so humiliating—that our deliberation was not completely our own doing, either that we had "luck" or that we were "blessed." Which word, *luck* or *blessing*, do we use? The way in which we shape our inner chaos determines the word.

THE BLESSING OF FAILURE

Maurice Samuel has given the word *blessing* a new yet old meaning. It is not success. Failure can often be a blessing. Did not Jacob, the one who bought, stole, was given (what difference does it make?), finally get the blessing? Was he not the supreme example of a persistent failure? As we follow his life we see that there appears one success, in itself also a failure, when we see him limping away from the one encounter at which he did prevail. The blessing is that out of the successful failure he received the name Israel.

As infants we are such blessed failures that we can under no circumstances shift for ourselves. The blessing is inherent in our failure, for in the measure in which we are not successful in dealing with our environment, in that measure the blessing of parents becomes apparent.

Blessing—*b'erakhah*—is a pouring down, a channeling down of energies, standing pooled above a field in need of irrigation. In order that the *b'erakhah* channel may exert its blessed work, the field in need must be below the source. Obviously, success cannot command the flow from the pool. If the successful field is too high, it remains dry. The water does not flow upward.

In the choice of today we face both the blessing that failure and humiliation bring and the curse that success brings when it blocks the flow of blessing. In our parable of a field in need of irrigation, the fluid is one that we know—it is water. But in the analogue, what kind of fluid are we talking about? "Water" means the flow of that positive polarized energy that we call holiness, an energy that is very much like the energy of the Voice, an energy that polarizes the things it saturates in the direction of that Voice. Truly, in this sense, one can say that blessing is the substance of the power that makes for salvation.

What moves a human father to bestow his blessing? He has *nachat*. *Nachat* refers to an exhalation, a sigh, a centering down and skin-tingling energizing of fingertips, a transfer of that which is in the father's hands onto the child's head, a transfer of power that makes for a certain committed deliberateness as a young *panim* faces an experienced-furrowed *panim*. The blessing saturates its recipient, a few of the many lines of the bestower transfer themselves to the recipient—at least this is what a child confronts in facing his father's voice. As he humbles himself, he receives the inflow of blessing.

If the positive flow of energy is a blessing, then a negative flow of energy would seem to be a curse, but it isn't.

GOOD AND EVIL—HAM AND EGGS

Matter is recalcitrant. It does not conform easily to the polarization of the good. Matter is far more at ease when it can avoid polarization, when it can remain "*and*-evil." In the world's prize boner, Adam and Eve, we, are turned into hopeless suckers. The hawker's promise then was that we (like God) would be knowers of good and evil. At least, this is what we thought. We would know good clearly and absolutely, and we would know evil clearly and absolutely, and we would be able to embrace the good and avoid the evil.

We, however, want to experience life. So we continue to think that the wider our exposure to loyalties of all sorts, the more godlike our knowledge will be. But exposure tends to contaminate us with polarizations of attachments to things that we face and to energies that possess them. As a result, we do not know good and evil but, in all things, only *good-and-evil*. We are affected and infected and cannot escape innocently from any exposure to good-and-evil. Whereas, before our exposure, before the primal sin we, mankind, Adam and Eve, needed no *persona*, no mask to hide behind, we now feel naked without one. Having exposed ourselves to so many things makes us anxious about our exposure. The very fact that we have to assume roles vis-á-vis given immediacies (or else shrink into bottomless anxiety unmasked), means that we are now incapable of immediate relationship. Our mask interferes with our immediacies, so that it is almost impossible to relate spontaneously in an unqualified manner.

Even in this sense, the manner in which we must turn our skin into "leather garments" has our sin become the dividing wall between us and the other. We cannot face God as we are. We can only face Him in one of His roles into which we construe Him, and in one of our roles into which we construe ourselves vis-à-vis Him. In this good-and-evil fiasco, not only have we become contaminated but so has every bit of the matter that surrounds us, and it too faces us not as it is in itself but as a "something." This "something" we define in terms of usefulness, pleasure, or libido object. Even the world plays the roles assigned to it by our conceptualization as if it were an end in itself. Would that Berkeley were right! How easy it would be then to live and to choose!

The Eminence of Gray

We seldom face either of the two ends of the continuum of good and evil; most of our choice challenges fall somewhere in between. Pure blacks and whites would have made choice a mere automatic act. However, the many shades of gray place us in an insoluble predicament. In the gray we discern a little bit of white, and our pity for the little bit of white causes us to accept much of the black in the good-and-evil mixture. Our predicament stems from the fact that we are not too sure whether it is the white in the gray that attracts us or whether we are genuinely attracted by the black in the gray and are offering the white as a mere rationalization for choosing the gray.

No, that is not quite true: our attraction for the little bit of white is not merely a rationalization. We do not have any real inclination to choose the black; the white really gives the black its only appeal for us.

However, we ourselves are not objective, for we discern with eyes that are also gray and with a mind that interprets what our eyes discern, a mind that does not escape its own lack of polarity. Thus, we have no criteria that can come to our aid; we cannot quite gauge the scales of gray by matching them to an inner hierarchy. Due to the grayness of our own mind, to the good-and-evil restlessness of black and white in our own being, the standard for a hierarchy is constantly shifting. Hence good and evil are patterns that we cannot assess even momentarily. Good and evil are shifting shadows generated by a highlighting equipment over which we have no control and whose location we do not know.

THE JEOPARDY OF CAPRICE

Order is holiness and purpose. Order is plan and system. Order stands for harmony. Disorder is impurity and discord. Even a totally evil tyranny is an order and partakes of some of the virtue of order. However, it is not a total order, for it is not harmonious with all that is. Its good is not coherent, for it does not allow every other good to stand next to it. Yet tyranny, a man-made evil system, is at least an attempt at ordering chaos. A carcinoma, very much like tyranny and fanaticism, is the result of miniature order-making. Despite the evil of tyranny, the stark evil that appears in dictatorship is nearer to the good than existent blind, orderless caprice, which is a curse. Tyranny and dictatorship are evil because they are a mockery of freedom, and the dictator is a mockery of God. Orderless caprice, the curse, is anti-God. Orderless caprice — *tohu* — is a world that has turned into a ghost town its master has forsaken, abandoning it to chance.

He who approaches evil deliberately deserves the directed curse of *arur*. In this sense, the participle of the past, *arur* denotes not retaliation by God but the inevitable result of man's deliberate choice to derive his energies from chaos. In this sense must Deuteronomy 27:15-26 be understood.

The worst punishment that the author of Leviticus could conjure up was not *arur* but "If you will go with me *Keri* I will go with you in the anger of *Keri*." Hasidic masters interpret this to mean a *mikreh*, an accident, chance, mere probability. Hence, they read it: "If you are related to me in a capricious, accidental, and haphazard manner, so will I in turn relate to you." *Keri* is thus the disease of the grays, the evil that disguises mere means as divine ends. *Keri* is the taking lightly of life that leaves every *datum* to a *fatum*.

Pain is not a curse as long as it is inflicted by a rod held in a father's hand. Thus, "Thy *rod* as well as thy staff — they comfort me."

Pain is often purposive and good; it is the warning signal system of an organism. One cannot equate pain with evil unless one has yielded to catch-as-catch-can sensate hedonism. No *hasid* ought to say, "It is bad — '*shlekht*.'" Instead, the Baal Shem Tov said he ought to say, "*Ez iz bitter*." For the good Father never gives evil but often must administer a bitter medicine.

THE PACT AGAINST THE COVENANT

Random energies attaching themselves to such as attract them by using them are evil. At first, these energies come as diverting guests and playmates. They stay on, however, as tyrannical obsessions. Folklore always saw demons in this manner. At first they are useful and worthy of exploitation, like a fire in a stove, but as soon as fire changes from a way of cooking or warming to an all-consuming end, it acts out of a *hubris* of Promethean self-expansion and it becomes a *Molokh*.

Almost always, the price for excesses and the exploitation of random energies is the loss of soul. He who turns to these random energies, even if he arranges with himself the possibility of repentance after exploiting them, will find that he can no longer turn away. To allow himself to be fooled by the promise that the eternally Feminine would ultimately redeem Faust, is the price that Goethe paid to Mephistopheles for having helped him to write the play. Both Faust and Job (as popularly understood) are fictions that tranquilize the average reader to identify with the hero out of a self-deceiving consolation that "peace will be mine, for in the dominion of my heart I will proceed" (Deuteronomy 29:18).

DOES THE KING SEND HIS SON TO WAR WITHOUT ARMS?

Assessing our predicament: the fact that we must choose; that even God Himself is a dimension of our predicament; that we have so many choices before and in us; that we must choose today; that blessing is difficult to find uncontaminated; that means at first exploited turn into idolatrous ends; we are ready to yield to despair. All our experience has taught us that it is impossible to do anything about our predicament. We cannot trust any person's best intentions, nor can we trust our own. We do not think anyone capable of really choosing.

However, on the level where we hear the challenge, we are also given an assurance that not only must we choose, ought we choose, but we can choose and make the choice stick. The challenge is harmonious with the statement of our sages, "God does not tyrannically abuse men." Our very predicament carries within itself enough life space to make choice possible and worthwhile. The Voice trusts us more than we trust ourselves. Perhaps we are not able to find an answer to the question *Why does it trust us? or How can it trust us?* Nevertheless, the nature of the challenge and of our predicament make it very clear that it *does* trust us, with an intense loyalty that amazes us and embarrasses us and obligates us as a result of its costliness. We would be encouraged by the Voice if some of the coordinates of our predicament: God, the hierarchy of our values, our role constructs, the flickering highlights would hold still long enough. But if they held still, they would all be static and arrested, and this would mean our death. To be alive one must live in the shifting highlights and trust the cosmos for its trust in man. As long as one is alive one can make a fresh start, paradoxically learning from experience that one must forget all that has happened before, because this time it can really work. (See Milton Steinberg's "Our Persistent Failures" in *A Believing Jew*.)

A Program for Heavenly Days upon Earth

Like *panim*, the word *hayim*, life, does not occur in the singular. We do not live one homogeneous life. Our life is a number of flowing streams, some that are above the ground and others underground. Often those above the ground submerge and those below emerge, as in *emergencies*. Life is keying up and tuning down. Life for us is made up of "sitting in thy house, going on the way, rising up and lying down." In all of these we are bidden to make sure "that these words which I command thee today be upon thy heart; and thou shalt teach them diligently to thy children." While there is a promise attached to the challenge that we may someday live "heavenly days upon earth," there is no way in which we can make life stand still long enough for us to shape it to that heavenly form.

The Jewish tradition into which we were catapulted by the fact of our birth as Jews offers us a vital and viable way of living, polarizing energies positively rather than offering us an atavistic glorification of a salvation achieved only in death.

Death solves many logical problems. To write one's philosophy is to write one's last will and testament. The static conclusiveness of thought partakes of the anatomy of a corpse. Whatever lives organically must face dangerous complexities. We cannot help choosing life.

So we do not wish to commit ourselves to a static philosophy. We wish to be able to live and grow, we wish to be able to reply to the challenge as living beings, but we must turn our face in one direction, and we must be able to understand the direction in which we are turning. We cannot dismiss philosophy altogether; neither can we make our philosophy static.

HOME IS WHERE THE DEEP WILL RESIDES

Minds have a primary set. It is the set of a deep decision. The set of the mind is occasioned by the deep-seated will. In no way can the surface will to descend to that level, nor can a surface assertion or affirmation change the set of one's mind. This primary set stems out of a primary decision. It is an *eruv*, an anchoring to one's deepest personal domicile. One establishes one's domicile halakhically for the Sabbath by an *eruv*. Once one has by an *eruv* anchored his domicile to a particular locale, his permissible Sabbath orbit is established. An *eruv* is a guarantee that the person who established it is to be found around there at least on the Sabbath.

Thus a hasidic interpretation of Psalm 119:122 reads as follows: "Anchor Thy servant in goodness, then wickedness will not abuse me."

The problem is how one moves oneself from one anchoring place to another, a process often called conversion, which has preoccupied many mystical and ethical writers. The inner psychology of the spiritual life is built around this principle. For what one needs in order to effect conversion is no less difficult to achieve than fixing Archimedes' world-wrenching lever.

THE *BAAL TESHUVAH* — AN OUTSIDER

There is a set of the esoteric mind that is opposed to the exoteric mind. The person with an exoteric mind does not see himself in need of an overwhelming and general desire for *Teshuvah*. He may recognize that there are many times in which *Teshuvah* is required of him, but generally he is at home with God. We may classify such a person as having the *hakham* type of mind (very much like the "wise son" of the Passover "four questions"). His rightness is measured in terms of Torah behavior and the mutual approval of the pious. The *hakham* approach in Jewish theological problems is detached, as if merely reexamining already-concluded philosophical business. He advocates the study of *Maimonides' Guide to the Perplexed*, if at all, in terms of studying the answers before the questions — and then only in order to know how to answer the heretic. The *hakham* tends to be quantitative, form following, seeking the obvious. He is content to function with a dormant motivation that derives from a past decision. It is not that he is unconcerned about God but that he is too busy doing God's will. The *hakham* is basically democratic. According to the Torah dictum he seeks the majority opinion. He defines his thought in terms of quality and essence. The *hakham* looks to the past for justification. He is more a student than a disciple. He wishes to walk through the world with a cool head rather than with a heart afire. He is content to align his conceptual thought with a great authority and leave it at that.

The other type of mind is not "at home," is uncomfortable. If his is not yet the heart afire, it aspires to become fervent. It is more concerned to increase its present holdings than to maintain them. The *baal teshuvah* is intoxicated with his yearning and feels depressed unless he can maintain his intoxication. To live in the stress of the *baal teshuvah's* psychology is emotionally expensive. Not many souls can bear this expense, and sooner or later they align themselves with one or another form of being, having arrested the process of becoming. From that moment on they are not in a *baal teshuvah* relationship to Judaism; they have become *Hakhamim*. The *baal teshuvah* must tap very deep resources in his own soul in order to be able to maintain himself in this emotionally expensive atmosphere. He truly is a heart afire in a thornbush that is never consumed.

The *baal teshuvah* lives in an atmosphere of crisis. He sees the world as in balance, and by his act of Torah observance, he wants to weigh the scales of the world on the merit side. His own sin is not just deviation from Torah-true behavior; it is a cosmic cataclysm. Merely to square himself with halakhic criteria is not enough for the *baal teshuvah*. He is not satisfied with mere halakhic justification. Like the Seer of Lublin he asks himself: Will God take delight in my action? He places himself before the visage of God. This does not mean the *baal teshuvah* has reached such high levels of contemplative vision that he is sure of God's qualities or attributes. He is sure only of his yearning for them. He has no criteria other than "not yet, not yet." The *baal teshuvah* is not concerned with any rational proof of God's existence. God exists for him in his dissatisfaction with his present, somewhere at the end of his strivings. He seeks not so much to know God as to find Him, and he finds Him in seeking. It is often difficult to communicate with the *baal teshuvah*. He is impenetrably esoteric, highly symbolic. The *hakham* often accuses him of double-talk. But the repentant communicates his concern and his striving.

The *baal teshuvah* is not satisfied with dormant motivation. He strives always to bring it to full awareness. He lives in a state of tension. The consent of the majority is far less significant to him than the discipleship he seeks in one who has already trodden his path. He is concerned not so much with the *what* of Judaism as in the *how* of becoming a good Jew. No goal in the present can satisfy the *baal teshuvah*; he always looks toward the future. He speaks from want of reconciliation, always considering himself in debt. He makes demands upon himself and upon others which seem unreasonable.

These two types of mind stand opposed in this primary set. The esoteric mind wishes to anchor the deep will only in God. The exoteric mind tends to deny the deep will and concerns itself only with the surface ought.

MY SON, THE CATALYZING FOSSIL

If we permit ourselves another dichotomy, the poles of the continuum named after two abnormal psychological types, we could speak of the *paranoid* set versus the *schizoid*. We do not intend to say that either of these attitudes is abnormal. In fact these two attitudes make up the normal state of thinking of our time. We will use them only for the insight they give to us in the primary set that we are discussing.

The schizoid personality finds it difficult to see relationship and purpose, design, and the origin of design in a number of data. The schizoid mind does not get excited; it shrugs its shoulder and prefers to live in an atmosphere of Apollonian detachment and grandeur. It insists that real history does not exist. It is always unsure of its parentage and origin. It permits polytheistic appeasement. It capitulates before stress, and so it is totally un-Jewish. Toynbee *sees* in this mind the *acme* of the higher religions. Obviously, Hinduism and Buddhism, seeing in *samsara* an endless cycle of Karmic changes, can find only one way out, and that is to seek Samadhi or *Nirvana*. The Japanese variant does not so readily capitulate before stress. It seeks to increase this stress and to reorganize its primary set as a result of the prolongation of the stress. One of the translations for Zen is "distraction," for it drives itself to distraction until it can become converted in a moment of *satori*. In the Zen *Koan*, the moment of stress is prolonged until the mind bursts into *satori*, enlightenment, that makes peace with *suchness* as it is and allows one to move with creative caprice in the midst of chaos.

Not so the Jewish mind. It is "paranoid" in that it goes to great lengths to seek to see design and purpose. It claims a father and its own sonship to him, though it also is terrified by the father's hiding. This is why even the "rod" is a real comfort, for it points to the father. One of its higher hopes is, "Only goodness and mercy shall *pursue* me all the days of my life." Rain, flood, and drought are not results of atmospheric conditions, but of being judged in the eyes of God. "If you walk in my statutes . . . I will give you rain in due season."

How a yellowed leaf on a tree is to be plucked from its branch and wafted by the wind, and where it is to be set down, is part of divine design. The half-life of a decaying electron is determined by Him in the same manner as "He causes their hosts to go out in their number calling each one by name." Conditions, therefore, cannot be changed by manipulation of symptoms alone. One has to "rise to the source and root of the decrees in order to sweeten them."

A child sits in the rear seat of a car, looks out at the moon, and shouts to his father who is driving, "Dad, the man in the moon is following us." This is the phenomenal reality of the child's experience. Analytical thought would divest phenomena of personal meaning.

The tone of almost all the books of the Bible, of almost all the statements of the sages, of almost all the moral lessons of the pulpit, has been "paranoid."

This does not mean value judgment but rather a functional assessment of a psychological set. Freud has already shown us that on the deepest levels of our being, we share much with the insane. We may legitimately if analogically speak of the "paranoid" versus the "schizoid" set.

The secular mind, that of the modern pagan, is "schizoid." In order to maintain a semblance of sanity it must be pragmatically oriented. It sees life as a game, a sport, and its innermost criterion is pleasure. The Hindu, too, sees life and history as the sporting of God. The price for not being a "fossil" is to become a toy, a marionette for the cynical amusement of the capricious "fates."

THE BANKRUPTCY OF "ETHICS"

The only way one can exist in such a universe is to operate in terms of enlightened self-interest! If, from time to time, the secular mind experiences anxiety, it drowns terror in sensuousness. How else can it help to conquer anxiety if from infancy it has learned to still it by "hitting the bottle"? How can it do otherwise, if it was not reared by a father who is a repository of values, a father who becomes introjected into the child as the holder of values systematically demanding and exacting discipline by reward and punishment? The secular mind suckles at a breast that is too sweet or too sour because mother never acts but just *reacts* to the environment in disoriented caprice, the stony breast of an unresponsive mother or the impersonal consolation of a rubber nipple. Without the father, the child must learn to deal with mother's caprice on the basis of momentary and hazardous ingratiation.

The hedonistic mind then is embraced by a process of education that is empirically pragmatic and analytic, that never learns to think integrally or to refer to values. As a result it fails to develop any deep emotional responses. It is never "sent"; it is "cool" and schizophrenically detached; or, and this is perhaps worse, it develops deep emotional responses that remain capricious, chaotic, and manic-depressive. Either the anxiety of the existential questions is repressed, or it is drowned in self-pitying sensuous consolations. The secular mind cannot relate to the word *holy*. This word is not found in the dictionary of the pleasure-driven. In living with society on the basis of enlightened self-interest, the only coherent construct the secular mind can find is an "ethic."

This mind is far too pragmatic to be able to create. It may claim to create, but this is merely a rationalization, an *a posteriori* adoption of an action that was in fact motivated by enlightened self-interest. It is not concerned with letting others live except as part of the formula of "live and let live," with an emphasis that loads the word *live* with more energy than the words *let live*. The *let live* is merely a necessary compromise. A working hypothesis of "I will scratch your back today so that you may scratch mine tomorrow" does not deserve the word *ethic*. Neither does *égotisme à deux* deserve the dignity of the word *love*—nor does the occasional placation of a tribal totem deserve the dignity of the word *religion*. If the secular mind preens itself on a philosophy, its life is not bound to its philosophy.

I Plight My Troth to Thee in Righteousness and Justice

The religious mind is a bound mind (*religare*—to bind). It is bound to a coordinate and from this binding up, from its anchoring, it derives principles. It cannot "travel now and pay later." It is not free, because it is maintained in covenantal relationship. The religious mind realizes that the archetypal relationship of the soul with God was misplaced when it was projected on a father of flesh and blood; when an all-too-human father cannot quite manage to personify the values he demands, the religious mind displaces this projection and manages to focus it on Him, the Father who first fashioned the need for this projection.

The religious mind has opted for seeing all anxiety as the "echo that daily radiates from Mount Horeb calling 'Return, ye wayward children.' " It is impossible to still this anxiety, which is the carrier wave of His Voice, with sensuous consolation. The religious mind is not responsible to a pleasure principle. It is responsible to God. Thus it must seek its solution within the matrix of Torah. Often the religious mind is misunderstood by the secular. The secular mind cannot see in the word *Torah* — direction — a prime coordinate for shaping the chaos, but only a legislation that compounds man's chaos by piling a huge amount of new debris in his path.

THE TORAH IS NOT A TRANQUILIZER

"Straight are the ways of the Lord." *Yesharim*, the religious-minded, walk on it. *Posh'im*, the secular-minded Promethean rebels, stumble on it. The religious-minded see in a step the possibility of going higher. The secular see in a step nothing but an obstacle.

To one who is not involved in Torah, it is impossible to expound by the mere use of the printed word the process of studying it. He who has not recited a blessing that involves the Giver of the Torah in the teaching process sees only a legislation like all other legislations, which represents the social compromise, "as long as one does not get caught . . ."

As a social compromise the Torah is a failure. The Torah is not designed to ease the pursuit of pleasure and to make this pursuit more effective in terms of sensuous consolations. It does not intend to adjust man to the lowest possible tension among his various drives, in the face of other men seeking to fulfill the same aim. It is not concerned with "living and letting live" but with being holy, for "holy am I the Lord your God." The word *holy* is to the religious person the branch that connects the fruit to the tree, the fetus to the womb, the soul to God. And that is all the steadiness that the religious mind seeks, for it relies on the teleology inherent in the life that streams into his being, and the religious man allows it to form him into a shape that he by his own outer will cannot achieve.

Thus the religious mind, after announcing that "the world is a spinning die and everything turns and changes; man is turned to an angel and an angel to man; the head to the foot and the foot to the head. Thus all things turn and spin and change, this into that and that into this, the topmost to the undermost, and the undermost to the topmost," can also say that "at the root all is one and salvation inheres in the change and return of things." Thus, where the schizoid mind cannot discern a pattern, the paranoid mind manages to see a pattern, a *gestalt*, in the most chaotic mess. For the religious mind even the good is not absolute in itself. Surely "good" is not a euphemism for the pleasurable or for that which produces a game of life, but rather is that which is good-in-the-eyes-of-God.

Evil Is a Husky Husk

And evil is that which the religious mind, as it faces God, must learn to disown. All good is related to the process of thou-ing—facing God without a mask as a Thou. The Non-Thou, the absence of personal relationship, is for the religious mind the source of all evil. Evil then is found where, instead of a person, one is a mere shell, a mask, a *ke'lippah*. And so too does evil get its energy from a nonpersonal, nonthou, assignment, which is also nothing but a shell, of the energy that comes from God.

It may seem that good and evil are not ontological realities but verbal polarities of direction. One could say that good is what *goods*, and evil is what *evils*. But this is not quite so. The religious mind sees in these words *good* and *evil* a problem. It is "paranoid," and it sees in everything the image of God. Being at home with the statement, "Know you therefore today and set it to your heart that the Lord is God *and there is nothing else*," it is at once obliged to blame Him for evil. The religious mind goes so far as to say, "Former of life, Creator of darkness, Maker of peace and *Creator* of *evil*." He is All, and evil is part of the All, therefore that part of the All which is evil is also He. This relentless logic is a problem that only the most bound mind can face without breaking the bond and receding into the schizoid set.

The religious mind does not move from its premises. It remains anchored to its set, and shouts "In spite of it all and in the very face of it," and proceeds to ask God in prayer, "What is it you would have me do? What is it that you would have me not do?" The religious mind has experienced discovery by a Voice that speaks, saying, "Thy intentions are desirable but thine acts are not." The religious mind therefore does not want to decree its own acts.

If Y're So Committed, How Come Y'ain't God?

The problem of good intention that, in spite of itself, brings evil results preoccupies the ethical thinker but not the religious mind. The religious person "daily at all times and at each hour" commits himself to the covenant and its principles. The problem of the religious person is the problem of the act. He is only too painfully aware of the results of his acts and thoughts. He knows that despite the best intentions he is not God but a finite person and that many good actions bring results that are not good. The intentions of a given act may be pure and good; the results as they show up in interaction with the social world are not always good; and since the religious person cannot continue to exist in a world where any act, even with the best intention, is bound to have evil repercussions, he must consolidate his responsibility and be answerable only to One and not to many. William James calls this attitude the attitude of one who takes a "moral holiday." Stefan Zweig in his masterpiece, *The Eyes of the Undying Brother*, explores an ethic that seeks unfailingly good results. Like the hero of his story, any such person could not help but, in frustration, renounce the world and become a keeper of dogs. If one does not wish to take the moral holiday, what is the alternative? He must be God and take all responsibility to himself. Jean-Paul Sartre, who cannot take a moral holiday because his God is dead — and he wishes it were not so — must take all responsibility himself and do so in the face of the utter fear of nonbeing.

The religious mind does not stand beneath the sword of Damocles but beneath a poised Mt. Sinai that threatens to crush him unless he accepts the Torah. The Torah-bound religious mind cuts the Gordian knot of good result-ethics. It gathers all a person's investments (cathexes) and bets them on Pascal's wager. It trusts the "straight laws" that issue from God, but prayerfully, begging God for help.

TO PRAY IS TO BE DESTITUTE

Our society does not tolerate beggars. How paradoxical is its moral tone! While Protestant, and thus centered not in the deserving of grace gained by good works but in the free grace of God, it abhors the flesh-and-blood beggar. The *shnorrer* becomes an institutional fund-raiser. He never knocks on our door hoping to satisfy his hunger. He feeds on our own hunger for belongingness.

We may spend a great deal of our budget on "entertaining friends," but we do not invite the hungry for a meal. The real beggar is not fed but referred to a social agency.

At a time when we turn from the poor, it is terribly difficult for us to pray.

How often rabbis in pulpits insist that the Jewish meaning of prayer derives from self-judgment — *hitpalel* — and not from the Latin *precare*, precarious, beggarlike existence. Nevertheless, the praying person, while making any request to God, begs. Even if he builds God a magnificent temple it does not entitle him to negotiate a "deal," for "from Thine hand have we given to Thee." It does not matter whether he begs for material or spiritual benefits. In praying for either he says, "The needs of Thy people are all so many and their minds are all too small."

In the realm of the holy, the dichotomy between matter as evil and spirit as good does not exist. From a Jewish point of view it takes very little audacity to insist that matter is more holy than spirit. Physical "*mitzvah*" substances (leather *tefillin*, woolen *tzitzit*), when utilized by a commanded person in the covenant relationship, are almost more holy than the spiritual substance of angels. And it does not matter whether one fulfills the duties of the body or the duties of the heart.

We cannot glibly divide matter and spirit, nor can we glibly insist that in prayer we judge ourselves but do not beg.

At this moment both writer and reader are utterly frustrated by the merely descriptive material available on prayer. The Voice bursts out with threatening impatience, demanding that talk *about* prayer be stopped and that prayer begin. One is frustrated by hearing what the message of the prayer ought to be without being initiated into the process of speaking it. We cannot hesitate and defend ourselves against this urgency by ordering and polishing the verbal niceties of our intended prayers and thus escape from uttering them.

At moments when we face God, words fail us. The body does not know which attitude to take. A Jew casts a sidelong glance at an imagined Catholic kneeling before a crucifix and wishes that he, too, could kneel. At the same time, he knows that it would be all wrong and that kneeling would amount to anatomical apostasy. But then to sit in one's chair and to imagine that one is in the synagogue or to settle for formalized responsive reading is equally unsatisfactory.

Somewhere in the back of our mind we remember an ancestor wrapped in a *tallit*, his eyes closed, his body swaying, his hands raised in a heaven-storming gesture. But we are blocked in our self-consciousness and are ashamed before our own persona since we who see God outside of ourselves think Him to be so far away. One does have to descend into that desolation in which the modern Jew, who completely lacks a repertoire of prayer, finds his soul. Reading further will not help him. Meditation, at this point, is also an escape. Writer and reader have to become beggars and stop before God.

You God have . . .

I need . . .

Give . . . !

FROM THE SANCTUARY TO THE STUDY HALL

If writer and reader have prayed, they have come away with the conviction that "the righteous will live by his faith" or "He had told you, O man, what is good and what does the Lord require of you but to do justice, to like loving action and to walk hidden with your God."

Receding more from the prayer experience, the generalization gives way to particulars. Because one acts for Him, by Him, and with His help, one does not construct general principles but executes particular *mitzvot*.

The responsibility ends as far as we are concerned when we complete the commanded act. Only those who are demonically beset by scruples will not be able to relent and relax. Only wise and loving souls can exorcise the demons of scrupulosity in themselves and in others. Part of the comfort is contained in that man who knows that it is not only he who bears the yoke of the commandment, but that the Divine Commander also bears the yoke of the command and, especially, the responsibility for the results. Thus the *mitzvah* is not a means to an extrinsic end but the fulfilment of His will, and it is from the fabric of *mitzvot* that the pattern of good is woven.

THE REWARD OF A *MITZVAH* IS MAN'S GIFT TO GOD

Here is another logical paradox that nevertheless is a functional reality; on the one hand, God does not become real for any man except in the modification of that man's behavior and in the culmination of that behavior in *mitzvot*. On the other hand, man cannot begin to do a *mitzvah* in effectuality unless God is real to him; that is to say, unless he relates to God as a Thou facing him in a relationship that we call "holy." Then God is commanding at the moment of the act and observing the fulfilment of the commandment in the moment of the act and rewarding with his relationship the person fulfilling the act. To the secular mind objectively essaying the situation, this is a hopeless chicken-and-egg cycle.

To the religious mind which makes that leap of action, which is also a leap of faith, which is also an entering into the covenant, which is also a receiving of the law, which is also becoming disciple to a Teacher, an apprentice to a Master, the contradiction yields to committed beginning.

For inasmuch as man is absolved of the responsibility for his *mitzvah* acts he is not promised the result of his acts, nor is he given the fruits of his action. In fulfilling a *mitzvah*, the fruit of that *mitzvah*, the reward as it were, is presented to God as a votive offering. Every once in a while a religious person must defy the temptation to look back for results, a temptation to slide back into the pragmatic trap of demanding a messianic consolation.

One can respond only by fulfilling the command, and this one can do only deliberately. Being commanded, one can now live because being commanded is altogether different from being coerced. In the divine motivation for the creation of man there is no coercing. God does not wish to *live* man but to live *with* him. Such a relationship is possible only in reciprocal deliberateness. Why this should prove to be so delightful to God we may never know. What we may be given to know is that it is delightful to man.

To Do a *Mitzvah* Is to Admit God into One's Life

The Kotzker once embarrassed his *hasidim* by posing the question, "Where is God?" and to a shrug on the part of his *hasidim* and to their reply, "Where is He not?" he replied, "God is wherever He is let in."

Values reside in man only inasmuch as he has given life space within himself to significant persons to whom such values are important. To be holy means that one has given the power of attorney to God over one's entire life space. Our sages call the life space that each person occupies "the four ells." Furthermore, the sages say, since the Temple was destroyed, the Holy One, Blessed be He, has no more space in this world than the four ells of *halakhah*. These are the four ells that God and man occupy when man lives under the compunction of divine commandments. In occupying man's life space, God is not a nasty boarder. He not only pays "rent," He becomes a member of the family, indeed the *paterfamilias*. The rent that God, as it were, pays to the householder is the consolidation of all his values and holdings, the cessation of tensions and strife, for it is He who has now assumed the burden of the responsibility for the ultimate rightness of our acts. No more need we please either our environment or the society we live in, for even these relationships are part of His command. Whatever "sunning" or "mooning" is to be done, is done as a result of His commandment, for it is He who rules each day.

A Wise Son Says What?

Part of being in the disciple-apprentice position is to ask questions. The raising of objections is inappropriate to disciple-apprentice relationships. The question seeks to elicit information in order to complete the conceptual system, but an objection seeks to destroy the very skeleton on which the information is hung. He who seeks information has emptied himself of his own opinions, he is aware of their inadequacy, and he thus becomes a receptacle capable of containing the information; whereas the objector is full of his own opinions that are to him the only criteria of acceptance and rejection of information. The newly committed disciple-apprentice is a catechumen, and the answers to his questions may be called catechism. A catechism is the kind of teaching that is given by "those who know" to those who have to be initiated. It is not that the catechumen must receive information. If it were merely this, we could use modern educational methods that would begin with the motivation inherent in the pupil. But because the motivation of the pupil is bipolar and his cognitive apparatus is bipolar, he must be taught in an organic way. The catechumen literally has to swallow what he is fed by his master and teacher.

To the opinionated objector, the catechetic way of teaching is wholly unacceptable, no matter what one's religious situation is. Prometheus never asks how man is to merit fire, he never begs and prays for it; he begins with his objection to a situation in which man does not have fire. Prometheus cannot be a catechumen.

Tell Him Even about the Laws of the *Afikomen*

Every new item of information into which the Jewish catechumen is initiated makes terrible demands on him in terms of behavior change. The Jewish seeker is therefore less free to be convinced by the truth of a doctrine because, convinced, he becomes convicted of actual misdemeanors. The objections that a Jew is bound to raise to his instructor are therefore more often of a pragmatic nature than of an intrinsically aesthetic or logical one. No wonder, then, that the truths that are most readily confirmed by one's inner criteria are those that vote in favor of "the fatherhood of God and the brotherhood of Man" and "democracy." It is very easy nowadays for Jews to become convinced of neoorthodox liberal Protestant Christianity, whose value structure he has imbibed with his ABC's. He can even become "committed" to it, for it will not demand a radical change in his style of life. But what if the disciple-apprentice is exposed to Jewish indoctrination? It is not logic that will object but the introjected image of parents, spouse, and children, business associates, and others. Introjected as they are, they own a considerable emotive investment. Therefore these introjected factors are far more difficult to deal with than are logical objections.

The reality of the introjected significant persons is more profound than the reality of the values of neoorthodox liberal Protestant Christianity, because they are not merely conceptual and because they are in powerful control of one's persona. But the apprentice-disciple must be capable of jettisoning past roles if he is to be instructed further. For most people this is too harsh a demand, unless they receive not the catechetical instruction of tradition and its accumulated know-how, but a sugar-coated reasonable Judaism. Alas, there simply is no way of acquiring the information that those who have transformed their own lives from the dualistic to the monistic position can share with us, except by changing one's behavior. Otherwise, even to acquire information from *tzaddikim* who have realized God in their life here is an impossible task. One cannot listen to them long enough without losing patience, not because of what they say, but because of what they do not say, because of what their information demands in terms of behavioral change. Thus we are prone to raise objections before we have fully given *tzaddikim* a hearing. And yet what they say bears the authentic seal of that Voice that challenged us in the first place.

CONCEPTS ARE THOUGHT HANDLES

Neat theories are based on neat conceptual systems. There is one neat theory that holds that evil is an illusion. All is good because God is good. Man in his error invents evil. This theory begs the question how it came about that man fell into this error, because the creation of the very possibility of man falling into such error is evil.

Another theory holds that evil is as much a reality as is good. A good god opposes an evil god, and man is a poor creature caught in between a dual reality. But how could the good god be God if there is room for an evil one to oppose him?

In between these two theories there are a number of others. Some of them are closer to the first, such as theories that hold that yesterday's good is today's evil in the upward rising movement of man. In this gnostic view, the closer one is to earthy things the more embedded in evil one is. But somewhere, way on top, there is no evil at all.

Who made the "below"? Not a good God, of course, but an evil demiurge who wishes to play god and who has trapped us on a Ferris wheel in which evil keeps forever bobbing up and down and from which we must escape to the good God. Such a view exonerates God. It removes Him from the ken of man and turns His world into a hell. The world and the things in it are vile beyond the possibility of becoming sanctified.

Another view divides evil into two categories. One is natural evil, such as the kind of cataclysm that insurance companies blame God for. But the is also another kind of evil that is incurred by man as a form of punishment for his transgressions of immutable cosmic laws, be they natural or moral. Natural evil is justified as a bitter pill, a temptation, an opportunity for heroic generosity and sainthood. The other evil, which comes as a punishment, is the response to man, like a ricochet bullet that is deflected by the target and hits the man who pulled the trigger. Natural evil then comes as a *grace*. Moral evil has the rigor of *justice*.

Evil as *Kelippah*

There is much to be said for these views, but there is no way in which the truth of any of these propositions can effectively be demonstrated. Yet in a pragmatic way one could perhaps show that there is some "cash value" in the hasidic system that combines some of these, adds depth and relationship to them, and comes out with a system that is not as simple as any of the other views and still bears in itself the seeds of deliberate action that help man to "turn from evil and to do good." This is the doctrine of the sparks — *nitzotzot* — and of the two energy systems, the system of *kedushah* — holiness — and the energy system of *kelippah* — shell — husks — or *tumah* — the defilement.

The world can in this system be the place where God is truly present, so that "in their oppression is He also oppressed." A person can, by taking a physical object, fulfill a commandment and do God's will. In this system man is also able to do *teshuvah*, turning, and through an act of *teshuvah* man can convert past evil into meritorious good.

We are aware that the presentation of the hasidic system may raise many more questions than it answers immediately. Moreover, few if any of the subtle points could be made without the use of concepts, each of which needs prerequisite concepts. So we cannot really promise to give a complete account of the hasidic view. At best we can tease the appetite of those who may be called to delve deeper into these teachings with the help of a hasidic guide.

GOD, IT EXISTS; SO WHAT?

We seat ourselves at the feet of the sainted masters of Hasidism and the Kabbalah. They invite us to start with the promise of an Infinite God in an infinite number of coordinate dimensions. Three of these infinite dimensions are: the dimension of IT, the dimension of the HE, and the dimension of the THOU. By calling them "coordinate dimensions" we indicate that we are dealing with conceptual tools whose descriptive utility helps us to systematize our thinking.

We define the IT dimension of God as the concept of the Supreme Being, the philosopher's God, all powerful and all fulfilled. This God of consummate Equilibrium, not needing, not seeking nor wanting anything, is traditionally called *Ein Sof* (the Endless) in the Kabbalah. In the *Ein Sof* there is no distinction between Creator and creature, since in IT neither of these terms applies. There is no differentiation between "space" and "time," since the Infinite fills and is all. The *Ein Sof* existed before the "Prime Mover" moved anything, for in movement time began and space was "made"; the endless remains the very same *Ein Sof*.

The simplicity of the One rules supreme; He is the God who was and who will be, without change and without peer. This is the God of the mystic and the atheist. While the atheist insists that the God in whom he does not believe could only be an IT, the mystic is intoxicated with an Absolute that the IT concept of God implies.

HE CREATES THE BEST OF ALL NATURAL WORLDS

The HE of God stands for the Creator of Nature and the universe, the Prime Mover, the Planner and Originator of space and time. To the HE of God we can give a name, the biblical name *Elohim*. *Elohim* is a plural form and provides room for the plurality of existence and for a God who emanates creation and who is omnipotent. We refer to Him as a divine object, as a Someone who is not turned to us but who is busy creating constantly. So preoccupied He seems, and so turned away from us, that He is not to be influenced by any one of His creatures and therefore He cannot be reached by any of our prayers. There is no way of making Him change the laws of His creation. As a result, He is "blamed" for permitting suffering.

But HE is the God who causes evolution and being, without Himself becoming involved. HE exists without being and relating. HE is a permissive God who cannot be said to care. Moral and ethical criteria do not apply to Him. HE creates man only to forsake him, as it were. HE is the scientists' God. HE is the expert Designer whose mind is discernible in His works. But in our human predicaments, we have no concern for the purposes of His plans. HE overwhelms us as HE squelched Job. We stand in awe before His unbendingness, and cannot do anything but submit to Him. We conclude that HE has some purpose, but this purpose cannot be discerned by us. And, just as we cannot reach Him, we cannot elicit a response from Him. Consequently, other than realizing His plan and design, an intellectual need (or luxury?), we as human beings have no need of Him.

The God who can help and who relates to us cannot be found in the HE dimension. We must look for him on a different level, the level of THOU. Consider the apparent contradiction between chapters 1 and 2 of Genesis. First we hear that in the beginning *Elohim*, or HE, created the heavens and the earth. Later we find *HVYH-Elohim* made earth and heaven. Rashi informs us of the opinion of our earlier sages that "in the beginning HE wished to create the world with His attribute of law. When HE saw that the world could not exist in this manner HE wedded the attribute of mercy to it."

GOD, THOU ENTEREST INTO THY WORLD TO BE WITH US

God as THOU is Father and Helper. HE needs us as much as we need Him. HE is the moral God who cares enough to reveal himself and to relate to man. HE wedded mercy to justice as part of His original creative plan. Once man exists, God is not only an IT and a HE; HE has become a THOU.

THOU is the One who even redeems.

THOU is the One who redeems, for THOU is also called into exile. THOU redeems man and man redeems THOU. Relating to us as THOU may seem to lessen the majesty of His omnipotence, but HE restricts his power because HE as THOU so loves us that HE joins us in our limitations. Jewish tradition identified the THOU with the *Shekhinah*, the Divine Presence that we are capable of encountering. THOU is the God whom our grandmothers addressed as *Gottenyu*, of whom the Bible says, "In all their oppression was HE oppressed" (Isaaih 63:9). All our striving, our life and our love, relates us to THOU. Whenever we cry out "God" and wish to reach Him, we seek Him as THOU, as One facing us and hearing us. Whenever the answer comes forth from the depth within us, it is the THOU who answers "that Thou harkenest to the prayer of any mouth"; "before we call Thou answerest us." Without us as persons who face Him as THOU, He could never be a THOU. To angels He is always a third-person entity. Only as THOU can He enter relationship.

Since THOU relates to us, THOU demands a THOU-like life, and sets conditions for His dwelling with us. THOU is the loving Father who hears the prayers of His children and helps them. THOU is the Benign King who directs the lives of His subjects. THOU is the Teacher. THOU is He who remains forever our Father. And THOU is person, if by person we mean will, drive, intelligence, feeling, joy, and empathy.

THE LORD OUR GOD IS ONE

A prayerful approach now yields the attitude in which it is possible to think of IT, HE, and THOU as One.

The motive of the personal THOU and the infinite potential of the transcendental IT explain why HE creates the actual universe. In the HE-created universe, the IT cannot be met save as THOU. The THOU and the HE derive their divine transcendental value from their identity with the divine IT.

The existence of evil in the universe filled by God is a philosophic scandal, but we can now begin to see that the scandal was of our making. Because we flattened (at least) three dimensions into a one-dimensional line, we created "scandalous" contradictions. Perpendicular concepts relate in a "plastic" manner. Their angular coherence constitutes no inner contradiction. Besides resolving the "scandal," this approach helps us in other ways also. An absolutist's concept of God leaves little room for man to act. His questions are often answered, "My thoughts are not your thoughts" (Isaiah 55:8). A purely immanentist relativism leaves us without the "Highest." For the traditional THOU, one claims on the one hand utter transcendence — "I, *Adonai*, have not changed" (Malachi 3:6) — while at the very same time, His transcendence *is addressed to man*.

INFINITE MINUS ONE

THOU is the Infinite-minus-one, never quite finite. THOU makes room for man in the cosmic scheme of things. THOU challenges man to add his own *one* to the Infinite-minus-one. THOU is the self-limitation of the IT-HE, in whom we see ourselves as true partners sharing with God the anticipation of a blessed state of things; his efforts to bring about this state; and His care for the conversion of evil. But in giving room to man, THOU has, by allowing non-THOU, given up His omnipotence. Man suffers as THOU suffers also, and THOU suffers because of His forgoing the IT imperturbability. Only when man makes the great unification—by sanctifying every life aspect—by filling all his life space with only THOU, not leaving any life space at all to non-THOU, then, at least for him, THOU has all the HE energies, from which union all "miraculous signs" come. Thus, the *tzaddik* decrees and God fulfills. Man has so joined with the divine IT that in the unification he becomes oblivious of the non-THOU and suffers the "pangs of love." Such a man has merged with the "being of the King" so that the THOU-HE-IT are again unified.

For the whole world this unification comes only with Messiah. Then the "whole world will be filled by the glory of God as the waters cover the sea." It is only when one realizes the identity of the waters and sea (trees: woods) that one is rid of non-THOU and there is no longer IT-THOU-HE but "on that day *Adonai* will be One and His name [all outer conceptions] One." But as long as non-THOU exists for man or mankind, evil is starkly real. The root of real evil (not merely the evil that results from an absence of good) inheres in His self-limitation to become a THOU. IT is not opposed by *non*-IT; HE is not opposed by a *non*-HE; IT and HE are Infinite. But THOU is THOU only when faced by the "I" (of man). When man does not face THOU, he faces "non-THOU," another side of reality, the *Sitra Achra*.

ONE MAN'S MEAT MAY BE ANOTHER MAN'S *KELIPPAH*

There are two kinds of *kelippah*, absolute and relative evil. Acts forbidden by the Torah bring about complete enslavement to *kelippah* that yields only to the most drastic measures of *teshuvah*, turning. Relative *kelippah* energizes all "permitted" acts. It depends on intention, which can turn the permitted into good or into temporary evil. By THOU-ing, man can eat and sleep, enjoy physical pleasures, and complete the circuit, for the immanent and the transcendent release sparks from bondage and brings about God's *Nachat*. By not THOU-ing, he temporarily enslaves these energies, which can be freed only in the next *mitzvah* or *teshuvah*. Dialogue is not limited to speech but functions in dialogic *mitzvah*-action (contrary to Buber?) in which the whole man speaks through actions.

The energy systems of non-THOU hold us in defilement. On the one hand, holiness may be commonplace, for the most commonplace act can be sanctified and serve to close the circuit between the Infinite-minus-one and the One. Thus it is in the commonplaces of life that God can be freed, rather than in an ecstatic flight to a transcendental realm where

God needs no freeing. On the other hand, evil is as much at home in the commonplace as in the ecstatic.

On the ontological level, however, non-Thou is a vast energy system in its own right. While boldly real (on the Thou continuum), it has no transcendental reality of its own. Its main function is to energize the man who chooses not to face the Thou. It is dynamic because when enough men yield to its charms (and these are great because they allow man to live in self-centered conceit not answerable to a Thou) it grows to catastrophic proportions. Man is the cosmic valve that can divert He-energies to the "other side." Or, if man chooses to yield his will to the Thou, the slow redemptive process of *teshuvah* begins. Not only is man redeemed in "turning" to face the Thou but God is also extricated from the energy system of non-Thou.

All this has social consequences. We are not in isolation when we work with other "ones" of the Infinite-minus-one equation. "Love thy neighbor"—who "like Thyself" is capable of redeeming me, "I am *Adonai*" who stands in need of being redeemed by man. The Torah is not only not man's theology, but it is the guide to God's anthropology. It shows how man, facing a chunk of reality, can call the Thou into the four ells of *halakhah*, which our sages termed God's sanctuary in an upset world. In the face of such divine need, Israel has no choice but to say, "We shall do and obey" (Exodus 19:8). Were it not for the messianic hope that "on that day He shall be One and His Name One" (Zechariah 14:9), one would despair. The hope that the non-Thou will ultimately be annihilated, the growing joy that little victories gain by *mitzvot* against the non-Thou afford, are, to one sensitive to the Thou's plight, reward enough.

JOB AND EICHMANN

If God exists, and if He is what a God is supposed to be, how could He permit Hitler, Eichmann, and the death camps?

Hitler and Eichmann represent an accumulator for the discharge of non-Thou energies that potentially suffuse our corner of the universe. A saturation point was reached. Jews, the most vulnerable people in this universe, were an opposite pole, attracting discharge like a lightning rod. The highest positive potential was in Russian and Polish Jewry, because they were suffused more than anyone else in *kedushah*, holy energies. It is not for us to estimate the amount of spark liberation that took place as a result of Jewish Thou-ing in death. Only Hiroshima and Nagasaki remained as the pinpoints of discharge of non-Thou energies on the side of the Allies. With eastern European Jewry no longer a lightning rod, with non-THOU energies daily mounting in furor, what awaits the world now is far worse than the Second World War, unless we can manage by a mass *teshuvah* to neutralize non-THOU energies, to free them, and to convert them into THOU energies.

This may represent the metaphysical fact, but it is psychologically inadequate. The Holocaust could also be explained as a premessianic necessity. But to the individual in *Todesangst* such views will be inadequate. Rabbis have often pointed to the Book of Job as an explanation. Job may not explain very much, but it offers an example of yea-saying in the face of a terrible God whose ultimate purpose is not conceived but believed. "Even though He slay me, still do I trust in Him." A well-fed rabbi to a well-fed and well-cushioned congregation may "holler like hell because the argument is weak," and achieve a momentary nod of agreement that says nothing more than, "Here is an explanation so that we don't have to be uncomfortable."

I, THE MAN, SAW PAIN AT THE ROD OF HIS ANGER

But Job is no answer because, unlike us, he had no guilt whatsoever. Both the prologue of the book and the development of the theme past the comfort point to this. But we do have guilt. There is much in the "empty" consolation of the comforters that applies not to Job but to us. We have presumed, we have sinned, and we do not deserve to fall under the category, "Hast Thou considered my servant Job for there is none like him in the world"! There are many sinners like us who require comfort.

Jeremiah did not console by preaching the Job ethic. He introduced us to a sentiment of the deepest religious significance, the sentiment of lamentation. We do not have much lamentation today. We do not sit on the floor, shoes removed, ashes on the head, admitting our shame and guilt, exclaiming, "How hath this faithful city become like a harlot?" Sackcloth and ashes are outer manifestations of the sentiment of lamentation. But lamentation cannot be assumed; it must be experienced in terms of real grief and pain, accompanied by cathartic weeping, with pain, "abreacting" sinful pleasure in mournful distress.

CRY FOR YOUR TEETH

To lament is not merely to cry over one's own woe. The sainted Rizhiner once asked a person who wept bitterly after reading the Book of

Lamentations on the Ninth Av of his motive for crying. The man replied, "Why should I not cry if the Temple was destroyed?"

Said the Rizhiner to him, "What does that really mean to you?"

Embarrassed, he answered, "I am a *Cohen*—a priest."

Said the Rizhiner, "Is it merely a question of meat, that you now have less to eat? Stop crying and I will buy you ten pounds a week."

Further embarrassed, the man replied, "But, Rabbi, is it not written that since the Temple was destroyed all the taste that was in the meat is now in the bones?"

"So I will buy you a whole heap of bones. Stop crying!"

Even more embarrassed, the man replied, "But my teeth are gone."

Said the Rizhiner, "Then stop weeping for the sanctuary, weep for your teeth!"

All lamenting must be personal, must be sincere and self-referred. But even that is not enough.

In the lament one must be able to sympathize with the *Shekhinah*, for she too suffers, and her suffering is not finite. Hers is not limited to only one body, one place, or one time. Her pain is in everyone who suffers, for "in all their oppressions was He oppressed." Those who shake an accusing fist toward heaven and cite the 6 million arrogate to themselves, a position where they claim that only they suffer, forgetting that all the agonies were felt by God. Unless *Shekhinah* is redeemed by us and by Him, and the redemption redeems not only the future but also the past in one retroactive jubilee, God's spirit is in agony.

Perhaps we have managed to understand evil somewhat; understand, that is, but not condone it. For no matter what paradoxes inhere in the ambivalences of choice, we must confront evil and contest it. Moreover, we must lament evil and join it in its own lament. For, as the *Midrash* perceives it, the "lower waters" constantly raise their lament to God saying, "We who could have been before the King have been set below the firmament."

If we are to confront and contest evil, there are two kinds of evil that we must clearly separate. While one type demands that we contest it and redeem it through our involvement with it, there is another kind that becomes more and more tenacious and substantive the more we become involved in it. The second kind must be unmasked, confronted, and abandoned. Hasidism calls the first process *birrur*, clarification, and the second *nissayon*, temptation.

ISRAEL — THE WRESTLER

Birrur means clarification and separation, analysis. It describes the manner in which we are to deal with a nature not yet committed to evil in its essence. To reject the world because it faces us unsorted would mean the cowardice of escape. Usually the *yetzer hara* seeks to prevent us from grappling with it and tells us to be humble; not to attempt a job that is greater than our capacity; to leave well enough alone; to seek tasks that, though not ours, are easier to bear. It is precisely in the uncommitted social sphere that evil that challenges us to *birrur* resides. To be responsive to the outcry of the oppressed, to seek equity for them as well as for us, to work at one's profession or trade in a manner befitting one who has become a THOU-ing partner with the Infinite, to live with others and their weaknesses, to try to help them transcend themselves without being censorious, in other words to be active in a sphere where one can reply to one's own question, "Is this my real place and task?" with a yes that nevertheless is uncomfortable and would much rather be no: all this is *birrur*. *Birrur* is the way in which the vanquished faces the victor and the way in which the victim faces the oppressor, too.

The death camp inmate had a responsibility toward his executioners. Seldom did he discharge it. He escaped into terror rather than facing the oppressor and saying to him, "What you are doing is wrong. I submit not to you and will not be coerced by you. My responsibility is to God, and I am responsible not only for myself but also for your spark." He would have been put to death just the same or, what is worse, been made to suffer for speaking in this way. Passive nonresistance is escape and not *birrur*. Violent resistance seldom is good *birrur*. Nonviolent resistance, which speaks with compassion for the oppressor's spark, with concern for that one's soul: this is *birrur*. *Birrur* would have said to the oppressor, "I cannot cooperate with you; neither can I resist you, for I have not the means of resisting you; nor do I consider it my task to resist you with violence. *Birrur* is not only my task but also yours." We have no way of estimating the spiritual salvage that could have been accomplished through such words.

Birrur is a freedom ride, for it represents a sorting, an imposing of pattern on the crazy quilt of prejudice. *Birrur* is a peace corps, for there too it sets the pattern of good on a haphazard crazy quilt of raw need.

Birrur is eating the permitted in a sacrificial manner. It is begetting children and making love in honor of *Shabbat*, it is plucking what is good, delightful, and useful and offering it to God. But *birrur* is never the responsibility of man to the matter that he must separate and sort, not even to the spark hidden in that matter, but always only to God.

The neutral is no longer neutral after *birrur*; it is now good. *Birrur* does not handle opaque evil in which God is negated and blocked. Opaque evil is essentially evil *kelippah*. Neutral, translucent evil yields to *birrur*—and when transformed into good it becomes transparent, not merely translucent, to God's radiance and light.

NISSAYON

One way of translating this word is to call it temptation. Another way would be to call it an uprising, an ascent, "for the Lord your God tests you, raises you up." The evil one faces in *nissayon* is absolute. It is reinforced by an absolute arrogance that claims: "Even this can be redeemed and you are the man to do it."

The Baal Shem Tov said once, "Shabbetai Zvi had a great soul: I once tried to redeem him but his pride was so great that he wanted to swamp me with it too." *Nissayon* arrogance would say, "Everyone could not possibly redeem evil such as this. It would be very dangerous for others but not for *you*. Not only are you an exception, but it has been waiting for you all these years."

The truth is that absolute evil that disguises itself in a tempting form *cannot* be redeemed by man. Its residual reality is anchored to the pole opposite holiness. It must always be there to leave choice open. It is there also for those who have transcended themselves and entered into the universe of the One. For as Reb Nachman tells us, "Even a *tzaddik* has a *yetzer hara*, but his is a holy angel." It is basically fantasy and not reality which one faces in *nissayon*. It is a fantasy rich and seductive for the person tempted. It is also a fantasy in that it claims that it would yield up its sparks if treated in the same manner as *birrur*. Such evil is real enough if man rejects it as "fantasy," for it is then that he is capable of redeeming the lofty sparks inherent in it.

The arrogant would-be redeemer of total evil suffers from a Messiah complex. He thinks that he can grapple with it and redeem it by his own promethean powers. Poor Rabbi Joseph de la Reina, who chained a phantasm and lost his mind!

The true *tzaddik* is not a heroic redeemer; he is content to serve God. Whatever is not part of his service he is content to leave for God. But a manic-depressive Saul, whose head is higher than that of everyone else among the people, knows — so he thinks — better than a Samuel who says that God seeks humble *birrur*, obedience, not unbidden sacrifices. In a *birrur* or a *mitzvah* God inheres as Helper as well an immanent Animator. The promethean hero tries to do it all alone. Man can redeem the *Shekhinah* only with God's blessed help.

Fantasy becomes as real as man allows it to be. Once it has energized man, it cannot be shaken; like pitch, it sticks and defiles. The promethean hero is chained to his fantasy and cannot be freed. He will be damned before he calls on God to help him, and so he remains damned.

But *Teshuvah* and *Tefillah* and *Tzedakah* Remove the Evil Decree

He who, out of his fear and anxiety, returns to God, can turn the evil willed into a forgivable unintentional act. Out of anxiety for a sin one comes to realize that one lives a driven, nondeliberate, unconscious life. This realization thus has the power to transvaluate the past; but not completely. One is transported to a less incriminating category before God, but the past is not yet altogether redeemed. The palliative was not a cure.

But if one faces God in His utter preciousness, if one does not care so much for one's own safety but rather is utterly contrite at having offended Him, and if one anchors himself and his deep will in a passionate reparative love relationship, then the very passion of sin is transmuted into the present passion to be at one with Him. The passionate sin of the past becomes present merit.

This doctrine is less antinomian than it seems. If one is passionately lost in God, one cannot deliberately expose oneself to sin and hope to do *teshuvah* afterward. He who sins deliberately finds the passionate return not at hand. The cool sinner may become nothing more than a tepid penitent.

But the man of passion is redeemed by his passion when his object is God. And with his love he can turn back time, turn sin into merit. To this love even the fantastic evil yields. The *baal teshuvah* has as his wedding gift all the gems of the sparks in his soul, which now knows that the It, the He, the Thou, and he himself, with God as his own Self and Center, are One.

For the passionate *baal teshuvah*, the Messiah has come—alas, only for himself alone! For he is lonely, the *baal teshuvah*; the righteous do not stand with him; they are scandalized by his "merits." The *tzaddik* still lives in a dualistic world. He too loves God, but in a premessianic, historic, exiled way. The *baal teshuvah* has transcended history, joined It and Thou to He, abolished polarities. Like the *Shekhinah* on Sabbath eve, he is the one facing the One.

But there is more than this. Opaqueness is not altogether bad. Metal allows no light to pass, but if burnished and polished it not merely reflects a few rays but mirrors the whole sun. The passionate *baal teshuvah mirrors the whole God*, while some *tzaddikim* are at best transparent only to a transcendent It, a harsh impersonal He, or a less-than-infinite Thou. The light that is mirrored back to God by the penitent who holds the polished and burnished opaque mirror toward heaven brings Him to resplendent joy.

But Until You Get to the Inn, You Still Need a Little Bit of Gin

What the *baal teshuvah* feels is a private experience. Matter is still recalcitrant, and mirrors sometimes rust. Evil is still very much with us, both as *birrur* and as *nissayon*. The work of *birrur* is difficult, and the withstanding of *nissayon* takes every bit of our sanity. Death is close, and loneliness is the price of becoming a *baal teshuvah*. Probability seems more real than conviction. What are we to do until the Messiah comes, when even the inanimate world will awaken into organic oneness?

Let this be our consolation: We are able to do *mitzvoth* and may leave cosmic politics to God. We are able to fight evil in *birrur* and free many a holy spark. We are able to play our part in the game of *nissayon* hide-and-seek. We are able to beg God humbly for everything we need. Even if He wanted to forsake us, He could not; for as long as we are, He makes us be and inheres in us. We can love Him not only as He can be loved in this world, or in the next, but as He will be loved in the time of the Messiah.

If the way to the inn is obscure, and we do not know how much farther we must go, there is always a bit of gin available on the way. There is a *Shabbat* every week, when we princes can choose life, be armed for the next week, and dwell in Him Whom we love in His domain of the One. For on *Shabbat* the tensions cease, the wicked are released from hell, and the Voice teaches Torah distinctly and clearly. On *Shabbat* there is enough hallowing—*kiddush*—to allow us, even after the "separation," to enter the world of *birrur* and *nissayon*, to forage through patterns of good and evil seeking gems for the crown of our Beloved.

10

THE CONDITION OF JEWISH BELIEF

This symposium was gathered for Commentary *magazine and published in August 1966. Milton Himmelfarb, the editor, called my response "wild." It did not fit the usual orthodox-conservative-reform pattern. Game theory and the psychedelic experience were the challenges to which my Jewish commitment had to respond. I was beginning to understand things about the universe and* halakhah *in a new light that received its impulse from Hasidism and its direction from what was happening in the world of current thought.*

THE QUESTIONS

1. In what sense do you believe the Torah to be divine revelation? Are all 613 commandments equally binding on the believing Jew? If not, how is he to decide which to observe? What status would you accord to ritual commandments lacking in ethical or doctrinal content (e.g., the prohibition against clothing made of linen and wool)?

2. In what sense do you believe that the Jews are the chosen people of God? How do you answer the charge that this doctrine is the model from which various theories of national and racial superiority have been derived?

3. Is Judaism the one true religion, or is it one of several true religions? Does Judaism still have something distinctive—as it once had monotheism—to contribute to the world? In the ethical sphere, the sphere of *ben adam lachavero*, what distinguishes the believing Jew from the believing Christian, Moslem, or Buddhist—or, for that matter, from the unbelieving Jew and the secular humanist?

4. Does Judaism as a religion entail any particular political viewpoint? Can a man be a good Jew and yet, say, support racial segregation? Can a man be a good Jew and be a Communist? A Fascist?

5. Does the so-called God-is-dead question that has been agitating Christian theologians have any relevance to Judaism? What aspects of modern thought do you think pose the most serious challenge to Jewish belief?

*   *   *

Shammai was a great Zen master. The person who sought to learn the entire Torah while standing on one foot did not get the message. Shammai in good *Rinzai* fashion [the Zen school of abrupt enlightenment] had hit him over the head with the builder's rod. Had he gotten the point, he would not have had to go to Hillel, who managed to hook him and hold him to "the rest now go and learn." The symposium questions beg the writer to hit the reader over the head in 2,500 words or less, to enlighten him abruptly. But the questions also hit the writer over the head and here are the sparks he saw. He who needs more must go to Hillel and learn the rest.

(1) Orthodox, perhaps better "orthoprax," is a definition I'd like to have of myself—that and *hasid*. In this, the assertions I make about Torah and *mizvot* must be in consonance with the normative standards of orthodoxy—only being modified by Hasidism. However, if only this were the case, my personal reply would not be quite relevant. By aligning myself with normative opinion, I would not do more than give witness to a series of acts of faith without stating what they are and how and why they are made. That would make only another vote for tabling the issues at hand. It would also not be honest because, if I left it at that, it would not be quite true.

The questions that initially brought me during my teens into opposition to Orthodoxy, and hasidic answers I received that reconciled me again with it, have now shifted. The dialectic of my inner life has exchanged vocabularies and focused on different problems but—thank God—the noise is still great with question and answer clamoring for the floor of my awareness. What is disquieting is that the tenor of the *shegetzy* questions—the kind asked by outsiders or unbelievers or skeptics—is often more serious, more devout, holy, prophetic, and divine than the patness of the *Sha!* be-quiet-and-gorge-yourself-with-the-answer stance of the righteous one in me. At best I can sigh with R. Moshe Kobriner's *hasid*, *"Halevai she'ani maamin*—Would that I believed."

Standing on such shaky ground, how can I address myself to the question of the bindingness of the Law on others? Let them suffer their own suffering and let them as honestly as they can answer their questions. But this attitude I cannot permit myself either. Before I talk to another Jew about his bond with the 613 commandments of the Pentateuch and the seven of the rabbis and the many of the rabbinic fence-making plus the Gaonic institutions and the many beautiful and not so beautiful customs—before I talk to another, I must see how I talk to myself.

I want to be included in God's normative plan for souls and thus in the normative statements of our tradition. All the *oughts* that my master, the Lubavitcher *Rebbe* (*Shalita*)[1], my repository of the faith, prescribes for me are my *oughts*. Thus all the commandments of the *Shulchan Arukh* are equally binding on me (and my fellow Jews) as *oughts*. This is without distinction of ethical or doctrinal or deuterotic: "you shall teach them diligently" content. In fact I believe that the *hukim*—those commandments inaccessible to my own ethical and doctrinal apologetics—are more filled with heteronomic divine content because they ask for a more total surrender to God's will than *edot* (doctrinal commandments) and *mishpatim* (ethical commandments). The latter two give wider scope to inspirational motives.

The reason I believe this is that the *hukim*, as I have sometimes experienced them, touch much deeper, preverbal levels in myself than the more easily verbalizable *edot* and *mishpatim*. Therefore they bring me closer to the realization of God. But this is on the level of the *ought*.

I know also how terribly far I am from the *ought* level and how recalcitrant my nature, my crooked heart, is from God's taught and revealed will. I could, I suppose, make the leap to full obedience, to the *ought* that I know of, but there is something not quite unholy in me that stays on the level of my *is*, with all its hang-ups. Being vulnerable to world and persons, to inner and outer conflicts, I believe that there is a sliding hierarchy in which I move from *is* to *ought*. It is so dynamic that it defies analysis and justification by reason. The metatheory behind the calculus of this hierarchy, which sometimes makes me lax in the service of something more immediately compelling and of higher priority than *Avodat HaShem*—the service of God as defined by the tradition—other

---

[1] A Hebrew acronym meaning, "May he live a long and good life."

times makes me forsake the subjective standards and scramble back into the objective standards of the consensus of the pious, is not accessible to my own definition. Rather is it rooted in the subjective self that makes these decisions as part of the calculus of its covenant with God. Yet it has the power not only of shrewd calculation but also of reckless love of God. This recklessness is closer to the great *Maggid's*, "Now that I have no more part in the world to come, I can serve You the more lovingly," than to Calvin's being damned for God's greater glory. Some of R. Zussia's readiness to go to hell because "in this I can fulfill one more *mitzvah*" is stronger than a Kierkegaardian suspension of the ethical.

This metatheory is inaccessible to my own critique. If I get pushed very hard I take refuge in some vague and despairing outcry that this constitutes not the normative rule but the more and more invading "teaching of the hour" that demands exception to the rule. The rule applies to those times when the majority is ready to live by it, and it demands the excommunication of those individuals who want to dissociate themselves from the majority. However, in our day when the majority of the 11.5 million Jews do not see themselves as living under the rule, it seems the teaching of the hour has become more the rule than the exception. It is for this reason that it becomes necessary for me to realize how the dynamics of the teaching of the hour operate to me. The rule in a sense convicts me by its *ought*; it becomes so pressing that I have difficulty in locating even half of my *behavior* within it. The teaching-of-the-hour clause threatens in all reality to supplant the rule as a guide. I often see that I err in the teaching of the hour, that there is more wisdom (considering the probabilities) in the normative rule than in my own deviations. The tension between *ought* and *is* makes me wish for the unthinking and unstruggling repose that can be won by conforming to the consensus of the pious. Yet as soon as I yield to the consensus of the pious and to unthinking repose, I miss the pain of striving and the very intimate guidance of Him who imparts the teaching of the hour.

In the end I find that the sliding scale does have a rhyme and reason to it and it presents itself not in the antinomian abrogation of all Law — but in a not-so-antinomian way of keeping it.

When someone who eats in a nonkosher restaurant orders beefsteak instead of pork chops because he "keeps kosher," I can no longer laugh at him. His choice was occasioned by a sort of low-level yet very genuine concern not to eat of "impure beast." When he asks that his steak be well done — so that he can obey "eat no blood" — I respect him even more. When he refuses butter on it and milk with his coffee because of "seethe not the kid in its mother's milk," I respect him still further. And if he orders a scale-bearing fish instead of meat, I see him struggling honestly to do God's will.

Now I notice that my own sliding up and down is also based on a continuous scale rather than on an abrupt break. The deviations of the hour are not aimed against the structure of the Law. They represent the accommodation of a struggling person to a poor but living compromise. This is not hypocrisy in the usual sense. There is no pious pretense in public, with a frivolous breach of law in private. On the contrary. In private, where the environment that I create helps me to deepen my observance, I often do more than in public. The sliding scale works the other way.

In making a rule for others, I must be guided by the same scale. If the other is informed, committed, willing, and capable of observance, then the ontologically projected objectification of God's will in *halakhah* holds to the fullest. I cannot invent theological tricks to save me or him from our moral bankruptcy. I don't want to mitigate the *is-ought* tension. I also want my fellow Jew to experience this tension, for out of it new guidance arises that informs the "crooked heart," and through the multiplication of this process, the consensus of the pious (who are by and large not immune from the same tensions) is modified. This is how the *halakhah* progresses, and in this lies its viability. I must insist on the bindingness of the 613 commandments as an *ought* and yet with the compassion of one whose *is* is far from the *ought*, I must feel with others and I must not lessen the tension.

The questions of authority and historicity are for me quite beside the real point. The covenant and the Law are what they are among the pious, and it is this that creates the real tension. I cannot live in a vacuum no matter how well documented its existence be. I need the fellowship of my fellow Jews, my fellow *hasidim*, and our constant anchoring in the norms of the *Shulchan Arukh* and the *rebbe* to produce this tension I feel. But since this is not a verbal thing, the dichotomy between the deuterotic and ethical as against the nonrational commandments makes no difference. On the contrary, here too the rationals become nonrational because of the nonverbal tension. But because of that tension I return to rational concern.

Let me take up some of your questions in my own order.

(5) Nietzsche's Zarathustra is glad to announce the death of God. Prometheus is no longer threatened and all of God's fires are now available for man's use (abuse?). To Sartre this is no occasion for rejoicing. Sartre must take on infinite responsibilities. There is no exit; and looking at those who take no responsibilities at all, he is filled with

nausea. This is no problem for me. *Halakhah* limits my responsibility. I am not infinitely responsible. In responding to God through the *halakhah* my responsibility is finite, but once I fulfill His command He takes infinite responsibility. And when I implore Him in prayer He gives me His fires as a gift, and there is no Promethean cost involved. Yet even so, I must at times kill Him in me. When a heroic act or an act of help is required, I must, according to R. Moshe Leib of Sassow, not say, "God will help you, trust!" At that moment I am an atheist; God is dead and only I am available to help. This is not a theological but rather a functional way of dealing with the problem of the suffering of others and the arrogance of my offering help.

However, in this a new aspect of "God is dead" challenges me. God's will having been so clearly defined as to be capable of being printed in a *Shulchan Arukh*, He is no longer necessary. It is all cut and dried. And a cut-and-dried God is dead. To be overly concerned with Him who commands rather than with the product of His commandment is generally not *de rigueur* in the circles of the shapers of the consensus of the pious. Only by deviating from this consensus do I admit God to live in my tensions, to shape the mute, still voice that issues from my subjectivity and moves me up and down the sliding scale. Where the halakhic behaviorist kills God, so that He need no longer live among His subjects (except to keep score), the crooked heart revives Him in the battle to please and love Him. *Teshuvah* — repentance — the tension between *ought* and *is*, is the arena of His manifestation in me. In a circle of others who struggle in the same way, He becomes palpably present. A *minyan* praying, "Pull us back to You, oh Lord, and we will come back," makes Him manifest.

Speak to those who either by their fulfillment of the Law or by their complete disregard of it ignore Him, mention His blessed Name to them and there is no movement, no vital reaction. In this sense "God" is dead indeed like any other word of power that has become impotent. No longer does the word *God* compel moral choices; often the words *halakhah* and *Shulchan Arukh* still do. Civil rights and Vietnam are alive and God is dead in this sense, a dead issue for too many of us.

God is also Death. Where He fully lives I do not. To see Him from the inside is to see His face — no one can survive this. Even a short glimpse of God's own atheism is an immense shock from which one can hardly recover. He has no God: no one to judge Him and, alas, no equal to relate to. To feel God's absolute loneliness is to despair absolutely. I help him bide His eternity by contending with Him. He helps me by playing God to me. And I in return reflect back to Him my trembling fear and longing love — "for all is in the hands of Heaven but the fear of Heaven" and "what does the Lord," so bored by His Supremacy, "require of thee" — "but to" borrow some "fear." This deuteronomic covenant we promise one another, "The Lord bespake you" and "You bespoke Him." We agree to play a cosmic game.

The most serious challenges to Judaism posed by modern thought and experience are to me game theory and psychedelic experience.

Once I realize the game structure of my commitment, once I see how all my theologizing is just an elaborate death struggle between my soul and the God within her, or when I can undergo the deepest cosmic experience via some minuscule quantity of organic alkaloids or LSD, then the whole validity of my ontological assertions is in doubt.

But game theory works the other way too. God too is playing a game of hide-and-seek with Himself and me. The psychedelic experience can be not only a challenge but also a support of my faith. After seeing what really happens at the point where all is One and God immanent surprises God transcendent and they merge in cosmic laughter, I can also see Judaism in a new and amazing light. The questions to which the Torah is the answer are recovered in me. There is a new and transcendental luster on the answer, and having seen that there is little else I can do except play this game or another, having seen that this is the game to which I was chosen, I choose it in return and decide to play it with delight — what else am I going to do? Hope and despair are end-game moves.

(2) For Judah Halevi, chosenness implied being the "pick" of the nations, the best: the *Kuzari* has strong racial leanings. To Samson Raphael Hirsch it was something quasi-chemical induced by kosher food. Whenever there is a group that survives in its ethnic character one can make a case for chosenness on evolutionary grounds, and an application of the Jungian collective unconscious can help locate chosenness even there. To me chosenness implies a part in the game — the play of history. When the play is over both villains and heroes are eligible for applause.

For me the problem constitutes itself as follows: is it possible to raise people to high levels of religious intensity without the accompanying fanaticism? My working hypothesis is that this is possible — against all the evidence of the past. This means holding to a view of the cosmos as a stage for many actors. The "villain" who opposes me, "the hero," is also deserving of love since my own role is utterly dependent on his. Knowing that behind the phenomena portrayed on the stage there is a dressing-room comradeship, I can manage to oppose him on stage and love him too. "He who separates the holy from the profane . . . Israel from the nations" makes each dependent on the other. I can't do away with my chosenness, nor can I permit that violence "acted" out on the stage to be real and fatal. My mission is to convince my opponent that we are actors on life's stage, and while we must "act," we dare not resort to violence. My enemy and I must be able to congratulate each other for the good show we put on.

Prior to the Holocaust we lacked—and indeed still lack—a viable theology of the Gentile. Some liberals do not want to maintain the distinction between Israel and the nations, and the archaics take it too seriously. A realistic theology of *goy*-versus-chosen people keeps the distinction to the stage.

Once more we are involved in game theory which, in challenging us, offers us a new potential for the service of God.

(3) Judaism stands between the fatal seriousness of the West and the dreamy frivolity of the far East. It is not just a dream of Brahma's mind, it is a covenant—a collusion between God and man. There is a game in progress, and it has rules—*and here is our emphasis on Law and rules*: every move counts and God is the Scorekeeper, and the game has a terminal point at the end of the sixth millennium and the judgment will be offered, yet the players will all be rewarded for the way in which they played their respective roles. In Christianity there is only one player—the Christ. In Islam surrender is demanded and not covenant. There is no structure to the Hindu game and there is no scorekeeper in the Buddhist one. This, then, is our contribution: We give the world a metatheory for religion that at once moves it out of a purely objective and ontological realm and at the same time out of a purely subjective and psychological one. Buber's intuition that the message of Judaism to the *world* consists in just this—the I-Thou relationship that contains no special dialogue words—is correct once the basic ground rules of the seven Noahide laws are accepted by the nations. For Jews who have the full covenant and all the rules, Buber's insight is feeble when compared to Franz Rosenzweig's *do*-ability—the *could* relating to the *ought*—and growing-in-commandedness game. Rosenzweig, who includes Christianity and excludes Islam and others, is too particular. Rav Kuk saw further.

In this too the believing Jew is different from all the other knights of history, past and present. The covenantal game *ben adam lachavero* is part of the total game and the divine scorekeeping.

(4) Therefore the political framework that will permit the greatest freedom to various constituents of the game population to play the game is the one that can claim to represent the "one Torah you shall have for the citizen and the stranger." The citizen and the stranger do not play the same game, but they have a common civic framework—a metagame that

protects all games so that they do not interfere with one another. This does not mean a homogenized democracy of tyranny by the majority establishment, nor the Fascist one-game-for-all, nor the Communist one-game-for-all, nor a western one-world-game-for-all policy. Hence a man cannot be a good Jew who will not fight for the game-freedom of all men, who will not safeguard the game-freedom for others, who will not insist on the "natural law" that makes all sorts of covenants simultaneous and compatible and that pledges itself only to one basic principle—to paraphrase Hillel: "The game you don't want to play, inflict it not on someone else."

Perhaps this is a new *ought* toward which we must flex in the tension of the *is*. In responding to the challenge of this *ought* we might be able to respond to the other challenge of "Those who say unto me day by day 'Where is thy God?' " Perhaps we *could*.

11

NEO-HASIDISM AND RECONSTRUCTIONISM: A NOT-ONLY-IMAGINARY DIALOGUE

Dedicated to Rabbi Mordecai Kaplan and Rabbi Aryeh Kaplan O.B.M.

There are two ways in which a Kabbalah-informed person may look at ideas: from above to below—as in the Passover seder, *where we move from the highest level of the* Kiddush *to the lowest level at the* Had Gadya—*or from below to above—as in the* Shacharit *prayer ("the ladder stands on the ground its head reaches the heaven and the angels of God are ascending . . .") where we move from the grounding body blessings to the higher worlds of the* Shema *and the* Amidah.

The hermeneutic of PaRDeS *parallels the latter of these two models.* Peshat—*the simple meaning, is the lowest rung. It is followed by* remez— *the deductive hint. Then comes* derash—*the inductive and creative interpretation in myth simile and paradoxical tale. Finally there is* sod— *the highest anagogical, arcane, esoteric, mystical, and hidden interpretation.*

This method of expressing ideas on multiple levels of understanding works to clarify "in what universe of discourse" a thought was expressed, so that what might initially seem to be a contradiction is often a confusion of levels.

In this piece it was important to show not only the content but also the form that was needed to free Reconstructionism from its earthbound Peshat-*ness. By opening the conversation to other and higher levels, the methods of Reconstructionism and of* PaRDeS *could be made more compatible to encompass the content of the merging ideologies.*

R'UVEN: Where do you *davven*?

SHIM'ON: Sometimes at the *Havurah Minyan*, sometimes at *B'nai Or*.

R'UVEN: All my life I have been looking for a *shul* where I could both talk and *davven* with the same people. At times when I was hungry for heart I went to *davven* with the *hasidim* and I found a warm *shul* but the folks there could not share my headspace. At other times I found the people who shared my philosophy, but *davvenen* there was cold and my heart went hungry. Now I can *davven* and share both heart and head with the same folks.

Such is the marriage between neo-Hasidism and Reconstructionism in many *minyanim* and *havurot*. And it is not only a marriage of convenience. There is something organic and inevitable about the *shiddukh* that is akin to deep love.

To explore the many levels of the issue and to check on the rightness of the mix as well as looking at some of the tensions, I would like to follow the pattern of the Holy Name, my clearest map of reality, and begin with the realm of *hokhmah*, the intuitive inner-truth, right-hemisphere mode, the world of the letter.

*Y*UD

This is the level of the world of *Atzilut*. On this exalted, cosmic and holy level both neo-Hasidism and Reconstructionism have yet to become aware of themselves. This level of "*advaita*" as the vedanta refers to it, of *Yichud*, radical monism — while it is present in the inner witness of many individuals who *davven* in *minyanim* and *havurot* — is not yet part of the consciousness and the free expression of it in the social world of the movement.

The causes for this are many. Among them an embarrassment with spontaneity and the unprecedented. Many have just learned the subtle codes and the tacit game rules of the group, have just learned a traditional and soul-satisfying form that they would like to co-form, at least for a while. Others are weirded-out by associations of the holy and other-than-everyday-real with cult, madness, and the past partnerships of "consciousness" and drugs. Still others associate higher experience with charismatics whom they suspect of manipulation and want things predictable, relaxed, and *shabbes-dik*.

Still there are individuals in those groups who are hoping that a breakthrough might soon happen because their thirst for the transcendent is not dealt with. And there are outside of the usual religious channels some that offer access to *Atzilut*, but they are not Jewish and not in harmony with our life or with the Jewish calendar. With whom else and when would we want to open to *Atzilut* if not with the folks with whom we *davven*?

Another sigh for the breakthrough comes in me from the frustration that despite the fact that we all share on the level of talk an appreciation for the state of the art of holistic living we are reluctant to bring this into our *minyanim* as socially experienced realities. It would take a lot more of silent sharing to get to the place where we could be comfortable in *Atzilut*. (Much of this also pertains to the world of the *Vav* — see the following.)

Things are different in the world of concepts, *Binah, understanding and verbalization the world of the*

Upper *Heh*

The definition of Judaism as a civilization is the key here. In a faith community the deviation from the consensual *ani maamin*, the credo, constitutes a break. Not so in a civilization where diversity of opinion is part of the rainbow.

There is Reconstructionism — the philosophy, and there is reconstructionism — the method. The philosophy is to be dated, or as semantics would express it, timebound to the thirties. The method, on the other hand, is now a tool in the hands of our civilization. Like the knowledge of the hundredth monkey on the next island, it is mediated by the mind space of the *zeitgeist*. Given a transpersonal psychology, we need to expand it into a transpersonal sociology, so that the sum of shared consciousness becomes much greater than its parts. As we ascend to the aggregates of the higher levels, some Kabbalistic/Fechnerian formulation helps us to make sense of these higher levels and fields of consciousness. In midrashic/aggadic terms this would be described as the great collective of souls, *Knesset Yisrael*. Such a reconstitution of the Jewish people, as desired by M. Kaplan, cannot be separated from our universe of discourse.

Even those who hold the most antipodal attitudes to Reconstructionism as a philosophy have used this method to reinterpret and reshape their own brand of Judaism. In this sense, for Judaism to live as a civilization, reconstructing processes occur organically and constantly. In the past these could go on as an unconscious organic necessity, unreflecting on themselves. Not so after Kaplan. We cannot escape taking the responsibility to own our reinterpreting and reconstructing. Everybody is doing it!

I do not yet see a movement in neo-Hasidism. I see a trend that has components of nostalgia, as well as a search for roots and authenticity and most of all a search for vision and awareness, for the integration of all the parts of our life. The *Besht* message that came to us via Peretz and Buber promised to us a path straight to the heart of things.

The neo-*hasid* may be closer to a Jamesian pragmatism than to Deweyan, but we, as survivors, are pragmatists. Something works for us in Hasidism, and as pragmatists we don't sneer at what works. And in the word *neo* there is the pragmatist who had to hyphenate himself to Hasidism but also needed the hyphen to separate him from some of Hasidism's other features.

Besides, much of Kaplan's vision is present to the praying person. Life, God, does manifest to us the power that makes for salvation. We experience the force that keeps us working at improving the quality of the experience of living for us and for those whom we love.

Look at the interpretive versions in Kaplan's *Siddur* and you see through his mind a vision of a faith, vast and universal. Those who studied under him testify how he would begin his classes with a prayer, though not in the sense of a petition to the old monarch with the white beard for capricious favors. There is a tension between the *peshat* hermeneutic of Reconstructionism and our search to find again in our traditional sources the traces of the presence of the transpersonal. These traces become very bold figures of speech in the Kabbalah.

In Kaplan's seminal days the psychological frontiers were at Watson's and Pavlov's behaviorism and these in tension with Freud (and Jung). Rationalism was the *lingua franca* of the media and academy and the Weimar Republic. The Holocaust shocked us into descending into the hells of ego, hunger, and aggression and to look for meaning in the absurd existential commitment, the Kafka, Buber, Zen, and Sufi tale. Only later still did we get to discuss altered states of consciousness. So in the light of the paradigms now current, the hermeneutic of those who hold the most enlightened conversations on these subjects, we too need to reshape and reconstruct our reality maps to fit our experience. So we have begun to do this at the forums of the Havurah Conference, the CAJE conference, the Ruah gathering, and we continue to do this in this medium.

Hasidism and Kabbalah provide us with a terminology and a depth language with which we can do some of the homework. We can explore some of the "worlds" that we can best enter via the techniques of a *davvenology* that was raised in the *shtibel* and further educated in the *ashram*, the *zendo*, and the growth center.

This brings me to the world of relationships, emotions, esthetics, the one known as the world of *Yetzirah* and in the divine name the letter

V_{AV}

Here is the place of heart, *tiferet*, and *rachamim*. Liturgy, *Midrash*, poetry, *niggunim*, *maassiot*, and the romance of *hasid* and *rebbe*. Here Judith Eisenstein drew fully and freely from Hasidism and brought life into Conservative and Reconstructionist congregations. The sound and color of Hasidism furnished every other "Eternal Light" program with dramatis personae, story motifs, and music. The alliance of this level is not new.

Young Israel before it became over-*frum* must not be forgotten here. Much of what we use in our liturgies was shaped in *minyanim* of the Young Israel of the forties and the fifties. The Ramahs and other camps have shown us models of compatible peer groups taking Judaism more seriously than our experience with other synagogues led us to see.

Our mobility and the openness of Chabad and some other hasidic groups to accomodate visitors made for fruitful encounters. Sometimes we shopped for something there and when we found it brought it to our egalitarian settings. Instead of sermons we took to giving *divrei* Torah often patterned after hasidic teaching. Sulzer's fin-de-siecle Viennese temple chants, modeled after Gregorian, gave way to *niggunim*.

About three out of every four *niggunim* sung at the last *Havurah* institute's services were composed by Shlomo Carlebach. While he openly declares his sources to be in Hasidism, he nevertheless is the connection of the hyphen between neo and Hasidism for many of us. Basking in the glow of his *niggunim*, we formed friendships as warm and affectionate as one can see among the insiders in hasidic groups.

Things separating the neos from the Hasidism show also in relation to the connections between *rebbe* and *hasid* in the populist neo-hasidic camp. *Rebbe* is here seen as a function in the process rather than the permanent attribute of one male person. Each one, at times, serves in either position. The democratic rhetoric is not in favor of archetypal models.

The charismatics of neo-Hasidism are addressed by their first names. And they in turn make their counsel and teaching not into unalterable ukases. They suggest and share, they serve as accessible models and resource people, and they do not pose as "holy" men and women.

Reconstructionists, too, preferred the Jewish Center model over the temple and synagogue. Still, the professionalism in vogue up to the sixties demanded a rabbi and a cantor to do the official stuff. Only now in the *shiddukh* of the two is Reconstructionism coming into its own, finding a more organic way of expressing itself in smaller units.

The critical mass of doing *Shabbos* has become smaller and thus more grass rootsy. The greening of America and the tribalization McCluhan wrote about have replaced the professional caterer in favor of the *parve-milchig*-veggy potluck. There have been other forces from our environment at work as *shadkhanim* to Reconstructionism and neo-Hasidism.

Another reason neo-Hasidism is so handy here is that the circle, the singing and the dancing, all forms of rhythmic doing-together, give us access to the *we* experience. This is in harmony with the intuitions we have that world peace depends on finding better and more energizing ways to we-together.

The way our values become energized so as to really manifest in our lives depends much on our emotional investment in them. The social game rules are relaxed under the name neo-hasidic and given scope as a result of contacts with T-groups, group therapy, rap sessions, etc.

What are the action directives here? For this we need to get grounded on the level of the world of *Assiyah*, the realm of the letter

Heh (Ahronah)

The Kaplan *siddur* has been dated by time. It is on many levels still the best model for a liturgy for contemporary grown-ups. Nevertheless, if it is to serve this new constituency, the Reconstructionist movement needs to provide resources for the network of the *havurot*. Loyalties come these days not along institutional lines but are engendered by tools for living.

There are a host of other tools that need to be provided for the American Jew who will now need to have them in media other than print. Between the new electronic cybernetic and psionic technologies and our tradition there are bound to be created a series of contemporary sancta that will help us be more aware as Jews. Some of these will shape us differently and with us the entire Jewish civilization. Some old Reconstructionists might not recognize the new forms—neither will the *hasidim*.

I am not really sure that there are such beings as classical Reconstructionists. Classical Reform maybe, but not Reconstructionists. There is an attrition by age and death, and another crew is coming in. This is clear to anyone who visits the college these days. The amalgam that will emerge in the future may see its neo-hasidic and Reconstructionist phases as parts of its growth. It is bound to be post and transdenominational.

Elsewhere I wrote that Hasidism is perpendicular to all other movements, from ultraorthodoxy to humanistic agnosticism. It gives access to other dimensions of reality and adds an empirical dimension to those of theology and organization. That Reconstructionism enriches itself by opening to this transpersonal dimension may give it the vitality it needs for the next century.

12

WHAT CAN ONE SAY ABOUT GOD?

Kerry Olitzky, David Kasakove, and Steve Rosman asked me to contribute to their book, A Jewish Child's Book of Why: Questions Children Ask Parents. *This book is geared toward helping parents learn ways to respond to children's questions about God and the universe. My contribution represents another example of the four-worlds approach. This time, however, it is in ascending order.*

What can one say about God?

Shema Yisrael, Y-H-V-H is our God, YHVH is ONE!

The Hebrew for the Name of God is *Yud Heh Vav Heh* and is not pronounced, yet each one of the letters has meaning. And all these meanings for each letter, separate and then together, make for the simultaneity that is the most goddest God godding endlessly. So it is better not to look for God as a noun of something that exists but as that infinitely-inging, the never-ending process of being and not existing.

The aspect of God that we most often mean is that of the Creator whose work is perfect.

Heh! It is perfect.

God is the answer to the big "W"s, What, Who, Why, Where, When. God is a constant making, what made us be, whose designs we can only guess at, who must be underneath what is and makes it BE! That one is not apparent to our sight. But at special times we can see how together-fitting, how perfect it all is; even with what we think of as "flaws," irregularities. How come everything that gets cold shrinks and gets heavy, and water, when it freezes, expands! Figure what this world would be like if water, in freezing, shrank and sank to the bottom. There would be no life as we know it. So the perfection of the design points to a designer. This then is God the Creator, the *Bore Olam*. The more science finds out about how this universe began, the more closely it gets to what our religion teaches us and what our souls' intuition teach us, inside tuition.

Shema Yisrael, YHVH is our Creator, YHVH is ONE.

Vav, You are loved!

In our hearts we crave to hear one message—are we loved? Times occur when we know that there are no accidents in the world. God is a loving that is vaster than a parent's loving. This caring One who holds us in pleasure and in pain, who wills us to grow toward Her/Him-self. This is God, the *Ahavah Rabbah*, the great love.

That two bodies attract each other in space, the law of gravity is God, the loving, the flow in which people care for each other, the flow in which a cat licks her kittens clean, the flow in which if you ask a question "Why?" and there is another person caring enough to respond and to provide an answer. And the "Because" that makes sense because answering is a basic form of caring, which coming from God we call revelation. And when we pray and we feel we are attended to, that loving is God. So too is the wanting to make babies, and willingness to labor in giving birth, and the nursing that comes from close to the heart, that is the loving godding. The arms that wait to receive one old and worn, one fatally injured and dying, that too is that divine loving.

Shema Yisrael, YHVH cares for us, YHVH is ONE.

Heh, All is clear.

That we know anything at all is a wonder. That we know so much is overwhelming. That it all fits together is even more amazing. And that when we really know something well it also teases us to know what we don't yet know at all really. The clarity that makes sure that despite not knowing fully we know enough to do the right thing here and now, that also makes it clear that what we think is so, is really not so. That which is present to us in Torah and to other folks in the revelations addressed to them, that is God the TRUTH, the Source of all knowledge.

God is an awareness that spans from knowing psions and muons, quarks that live nanoseconds and are gone, and at the same time being the awareness that contains a solar year, one in which the sun turning once around the galaxy takes 360 million years. This awareness embraces all life and permeates each cell, each microbe and virus, beehives and anthills, rain forests and oceans. This awareness knows all, not by "thinking" them but by being them—us, and not being—at least 18,000 times each second. We are cells of Mother Earth's global brain and her knowing, and her knowing is the knowing of God, the *Melekh Ha'olam*.

Shema Yisrael, YHVH is Aware, YHVH is ONE.

Yud, I am holy.

Deeper in me than my own knowing, my "I-am awareness" and your knowing your "I-am awareness" there is something vaster, more precious than existence, than love, than knowledge. We call that "holy," sacred, a kind of God-special, enduring beyond what changes and enduring changes beyond our habits of enduring. That is sacred.

That I—am—that—I—am is

deeper than deep,

higher than high,

tinier than infinitesimal

and bigger than infinite,

older than ever

and younger than now,

beckoning and unapproachable,

judging with utter truth

and totally forgiving

longed for, adored, and dreaded

avoided and ultimately embraced

with the deepest surprise

"Hey, I am That!

You are that

and this is That too!"

Shema Yisrael, YHVH is HOLY, YHVH is ONE!

So this is why we cannot say the word YHVH. We can't do it with our mouth and mind, with our words and thoughts all at once.

It is perfect—the last *Heh*, You are loved, the *Vav*, All is clear, the upper *Heh*, and I am holy, the *Yud*,

Shema Yisrael

Yud Heh Vav He is

Our Creator,

who is aware of us,

cares for us,

is holy,

YHVH is ONE!

YHVH your God is Truth!

13

WHEN I USE THE WORD *GOD*, WHAT DO I MEAN?

Barukh Hu
IT is perfect
You are loved
All is clear
AND I AM HOLY

In the recent, rationalistic past people talked about God as a Being. They used a noun and implied some substance, albeit omni-omni and infinite. In the tradition of the medieval theologians, they sought to define the word in some ways in which the questions about the existence and nature of God could be answered in a philosophically self-respecting way.

The arguments for the existence of God; teleological (somebody had to make the world, it shows planning), ontological (one could not conceive of a God unless there were one), helped give a person a good and decent God idea.

But, upon deeper reflection, one realized that all one had gotten was a regression stopper. The best way not have to continue raising questions was to answer with God. Once the trump card "God" was played, one could not take another step behind the answer and raise a further question.

This recognition itself made it useless to engage in God talk. Not being under philosophical compulsion, we were also not under social compulsion. The power of the consensus of the pious had become weakened in the two world wars and the subsequent breakdown of the surface tension between Jews and the rest of the world.

On the ethnic home front they had said that there is God Torah and Israel, but God was the great backdrop for Israel, and if you could not claim chosenness from a transcendental source, a *Bialik* and *Ahad Haam* could still claim it for us on the basis of our Torah.

Our contact with God came largely after a spell of some sort of atheism, a process of adolescent debunking, getting high on the *chutzpah* of our iconoclasm.

We did not need to become believers in God because of the big questions, nor did we have to—especially after the Holocaust—look for the God ideas of the past. We could have chucked it all. It still is fashionable to be, if not atheist, then Buddhist-agnostic.

But we had experiences. They were so close to madness that before our time few people talked to each other about them to compare notes. The climate of what is plausible in an ordered universe did not admit that an infinitesimal chemical substance should alter perceptions so that the worlds for which we had no words could manifest.

Or the sexual and the divine had been divorced so long from each other by that repressive consensus that the transcendence of the boundaries of the skin, the physical, erotic, as well as the mental and the psychic and the cosmic telepathy experienced could not fit into anything we had been taught in any serious way. Here and there some words used by the mystics seemed to echo with significance, but what came in a decisive way was that experience.

Still, as we had shared in the experiences, we also talked about them. It had been "far out," "too much." We had to talk about the way time had been observed as flowing and with it the sameness and the differences were organically connected. We described to each other how we had "gone through the changes." And we learned some basic mind-soul disciplines, and when we focused on the experiences, that had gone deeper, way deeper than the disciplines took us by our effort—and here the word *grace* seemed to fit well—we became aware that other words could better express our experience than those that we got in translating our tradition into the terms of the *Zeitgeist* just running out of steam.

We also saw that we came back to the same reality we had left, though with an altered perspective. The tension between the perfections experienced and the mess in which we lived and breathed served as an immense goad to reshape our reality maps and our reality. We simply had to improve the quality of life and learn to make harmony and peace on the planet.

Part of that process was making new words that expressed the dynamism. Not for the noun God do we look. What we had experienced was not a static ENTITY. So VERB and PROCESS are
words that are better. Infinitely — inging
what ever was do/act/pass/happen — ing.
And that infinite/inging was the most
pervade/ing, sustain/ing, create/ing
love-ing, care/ing, feel/ing
understanding, image/ining, integrate/ing, conceptualize/ing
BE/ing
blowing our minds with identity beyond belief
shattering our concepts as inapplicable to that reality
rebirthing us as loved children of the universe who have every
right to be here and now and for all the devastation of that
living through it also gave us renewed life, vigor, energy, zest.

Godhead, Eyn Soff, Brahman were closer to the reality than Lord, Father, King, Judge.

The sense of Identity of that Being with all the roles assigned to HIM? HER also came through, yet because of the Be/ing behind the roles we saw them, names, metaphors, masks, Sephirot, Archetypes, the reality in the great conjunctive, the holy AND became the strongest paradigm of our theologies.

So the And between good and evil, Jew and Gentile, *Shabbos* and the week, holy and secular; this And, the infinitely *And*/ing ONE to serve that *Aleph* means to let oneself become aware of one's identity with the *Aleph*, to map reality in harmony with the *Aleph*, to be attuned to the compassion of the *Aleph*, to function in the flow of that *Aleph*.

So the *partzufim*, metaphor, and archetypes are the clothes *Aleph* wears.

When I speak of God's Name I mean all there is in that holy AND.
All nominative being, totally intransitive I AMming endlessly.
All times and spaces, everything dative integrating endlessly
All beings related by the gravity-Love-attracting each other
endlessly, holistically cognitively AND
All objects discretely unique existing excluding all others.
AND the name is all these four in the same HERE AND NOW
and when I become aware of what I just wrote
I, the servant in the accusative,
I, the child in the genitive

I, the conceptualizer of data
I am that I am
I experience *Barukh Hu uVarukh Shemo*.
AND I SERVE YOU
AND YOU CARE FOR ME
AND WE MAKE IT UP AS WE GO ALONG
AND THAT GOD IS *Aleph*
YUD AND *HEH* AND *VAV* AND *HEH* AND . . . THE ANP

14

REFORMATTING OUR THEOLOGY

Arifa Goodman, editor of Emergence, *a literary organ of the Sufi Order of the West, asked for an interview for an issue dealing with Embodied Spirituality. My partner, Eve Ilsen, participated in the interview, which took place in Colorado the summer of 1989. Much of our work in the* P'nai Or *Wisdom School is reflected in our responses. The interview contained more than what was transcribed and published at that time. Especially regarding the issues around* eco-kosher, *much can and needs to be said and will find its place in other forms.*

REB ZALMAN: We are getting to know God now not in the spirituality that's differentiated much from matter — not separated and etherialized — but in the concrete where the life is burgeoning. The emerging theology of *Gaia*[1] is the embodiment of spirituality for us. In Judaism this shows itself in the commandments and *mitzvot*, in the resurrection of the planet that is happening now. We are organs of that renewal.

For hundreds of years we prayed: "God, enter into our lives, descend into this world, make Yourself manifest, rule over this world in all Your glory." We asked that the transcendent might come and join us and become available. Our prayer has been answered in a way that we didn't expect. We had expected that this wonderful transcendent God would be

---

[1]*Gaia* is the Greek word for Earth.

with us and that in all that immanence we would still have the transcendence so that we can call SOS: "Would the transcendent please manifest now because we need something from outside of this world." But in the descent into immanence, our connection with the transcendent was lost to us on the outside. The divine is now in us, through us, and we must find it there. Let's take that word "indwelling presence" as it is at home in Judaism: *Shekhinah*, the Divine Presence. When one spoke of the Temple in Jerusalem or any other sanctuary that was before, the notion was that there the *Shekhinah*, the Divine Presence, would manifest. Although God was known to be beyond any particular location, that specific manifestation of the Presence would happen in this place. The Temple was destroyed and a lot of the things that had to do with holiness in *space* began to now manifest as holiness in *time*. So *Shekhinah* was no longer in space. We experienced the holiness in time, on the Sabbath. We spoke of her as the Queen of Sabbath and as the Sabbath Bride. Another form of *Shekhinah* manifestation and embodiment was in Torah, the presence of God in the *word*, so that when one carried around the scroll people would hold it, reverence it, kiss it, and read of it. The sense was that in this book, between the first letter and the last letter, there was contained divine totality. They spoke about this focus, this specification, as *tzimtzum*, the divine self-contraction. Think of the vastness of the cosmos and space. Think about Earth, how small and infinitesimal she is in comparison with that vastness. Think of God making Himself/Herself available to dwell now with us on Earth; that is *tzimtzum,* a very strong contraction and focus. The more there is immanence, the more the divine is hiding. It doesn't manifest except through that in which it inheres. We realize that in the fullest way in our own being.

So that leads to some very important questions and causes some confusion on the part of people. How do I know whether it is God stirring in me, or if whether that which stirs in me is merely my own ego program, my inclination for evil, my search of comfort? How do I know that this is God in immanence? When the notion of God's transcendence was the great paradigm of religion, you also had laws that came from that God (*nomos*—law). Heteronomy means that the law is given by someone else, an other. Whenever we would take refuge in heteronomy we would say, "It is written here in the book; it says so; we received it from tradition. I didn't make this up myself."

One of the worst things that you could do in Islam is *bidda*, make up something of yourself, to claim that this is holy tradition. At least it has to be *hadith*, it has to be Quran and so on. In Judaism it's the same way: "Did you make this up or did you receive it?" And the very word

Kabbalah, which means "to receive," has a sense that "I didn't make this up. This is not merely my insight." So you see a devaluation of insight and intuition, the teaching that takes place inside. The notion that "that which I receive is separate from myself; it comes from an exalted place" shows itself now in channeling. People don't want to allow for their own higher self to have said it; it has to be given from someone else. There's a notion that it has to be ancient; that it has to be from elsewhere; that it has to be different. How did we know it was God? It was different — the holy other. The numinous, divine quality, how did we deal with it? We said it was so totally different. Then comes the esoteric teaching and says: It's inside and you can be open to it, be host to it. Underneath your own consciousness is God, and that which "be's" you into being is God. So who is doing the talking? I'm a voice for that divine embodiment at this point. I can't take credit for it.

What's strongly coming down now is the awareness that we are part of a larger organism. The age of the focus on the ego, on the individual self is over; that has been fulfilled, that's done. We have to start considering a transpersonal sociology: who are we when we are more than one? This again has something to do with embodiment. In a group that is harmonized and that shares a rhythm, that begins to do, feel, know and intuit together, there is a plenary being inherent in that group and each individual contributes something to that being. When you take this to the next level then the ecology and the groups that live there form an aggregate being. What we used to call angels before, and principalities and powers, seem to be those aggregates of life and consciousness of which we aren't necessarily aware in our own encapsulated, single-person ego understanding.

What is coming down now is the issue of ecology and the awareness that this Earth is not a dead hunk of matter. The Earth is alive. Our destiny is completely tied to life on this planet. We are the mirror for that awareness that is Earth. That is how a planet becomes conscious and knows itself. The planet needs people to bring about that consciousness. This self-awareness is now happening. People are plugging in more and more and there's a heating up of communication. The globe is circled by communication systems; the proliferation of that is exciting. As long as Ma Bell was the only official phone company, the next step could not happen. Now that other companies proliferate, it is a step toward the next level of complexity that is necessary to make the next quantum leap. So the same way as in brain development, a quantum leap was made to connect more and more synapses; in social and *Gaian* development, we are at the quantum leap that is happening right now. For instance, if my cells were to meditate they would get the image: "I'm not just a cell but

I belong to this total body." It would for the cell be an expansion of consciousness. In the same way, there is an expansion of consciousness for us when we don't see ourselves as individuals anymore but as part of the total, larger picture. These peak experiences seem to increase now in frequency so as to reach toward a steady state. When that frequency hits a certain level, then the total awareness of people on the planet is likely to reach the point of global telepathy.

ARIFA: Could you talk about this in terms of what the Baal Shem Tov called the holy sparks of the *Shekhinah* that have become scattered throughout the universe? That it's the actual purpose and goal of a human life to reunite those sparks so that the *Shekhinah* may become liberated, may know herself.

REB ZALMAN: I feel the doctrine of the sparks has to be brought up to the current perspective. The teachings of the Baal Shem Tov are based on the teachings of Rabbi Isaac Luria, which are based on the teachings of the Zohar: there was a cosmic cataclysm in the beginning of all creation where God, wanting to create with grace, created the vessels of grace. And then it was necessary to add rigor and power and specificity. The vessels of grace couldn't take it so they shattered, they were too brittle. All the vessels of grace, of rigor, of mercy, of endurance, of the power of technology, of elegance, and of connection and procreation, and empowerment of all these were broken by the subsequent light. And that was seen as this calamity. Some souls, according to this doctrine, volunteered—and that's part of the chosenness that's seen here—to look for those sparks embedded in everything physical. According to this doctrine, the sparks are important and the physical embedding is not. It's still a holdover of the separation of matter and spirit. It says, "You can't help but get involved with matter because the higher the spark, the lower it has fallen." So the physical is the lower into which that higher light has fallen and from which it needs to be liberated. I feel that what is coming down now is not that we are dealing with a calamity, an "oops" that happened that shouldn't have happened. We are dealing with an unfolding. Creation is not best understood in terms of fiat, the king saying, "Let there be!" and *abracadabra*, there it was. If instead we start looking at it in terms of begetting and generating, then that which leads to incarnation is not an accident and is not a calamity, but is a love act. It is an intention and a deep connection. So therefore, we have to reexamine the doctrine of the sparks and speak of it better as seeds, spores. There was a moment when the spores of life were generated. Some spores wander around for eons until they come to a certain place where it is right for them to grow. So start looking at this not as sparks that have been in exile but as spores that were waiting for their right time.

That's the teaching of *kairos*, of the right time: *Shaat hakosher*—the kosher time.

ARIFA: Do you see in Judaism a return to an Earth-oriented spirituality in a parallel way to Matthew Fox's creation spirituality in the Catholic community?

REB ZALMAN: Yes, this is what is now coming down. This is what we have been experiencing and experimenting with at Wisdom School. This has to do with the paradigm shift. When you take a tradition from one paradigm into the other you can't take it raw because it's going to get rejected. The old cosmology is breaking down. And many of the traditions are hooked to reality maps that are the old decaying cosmology. You now have to reexperience the traditions in a new form in a group with people of sufficient earnestness and concern. They can then say of the values that we are carrying in the tradition from the past, which ones can be reformated to fit our new situation. The new situation is egalitarian—women have an equal, strong, and complementary voice without which the world is bound to kill itself by its technology alone. There are certain truths that prepatriarchal Judaism—which scholars called paganism—had, and for reasons of growing up, becoming spiritual adults, we had to leave them temporarily behind. These truths were still hanging out there so we find out that whatever was thrown out by the door came back by the cracks of the wall or through the window. The Goddess for whom we made no place when this split happened appeared as Torah, as *Shabbat*, and as *Shekhinah*. Now that we have become aware of awareness and how awareness operates, we have to be aware of what we have to put into our awareness. So our responsibility has become so much greater. Therefore we can no longer reject or repress or push things out because now we know that we are doing it. Before, when you repressed you weren't aware that you repressed. Now we are aware that we are doing the repressing. So everything about theology now requires a recasting.

At the same time we need to respect the process that has produced tradition. Tradition isn't something that somebody imposes on us. Tradition is a deposit we made in the last incarnation so we wouldn't have to learn from scratch in this one. I don't want to throw tradition away but not everything in the Bible can be adopted whole as it is. Very often we have to ask, what was the intent then that produced such a law and how do we best fulfill the intent now?

Now comes the question, what in tradition or what in religion is transformative? You have a bifurcation: on the one hand you have fundamentalists who say that every word of scripture is literally true and inerrant. What they have done is created a template for Bible that has become so rigid that it couldn't breathe any more. On the other hand we know that in Bible is contained much of the mythic life of the Western world. By cutting ourselves off from that we have become to some extent spiritually impotent. Is there a way of reopening the Bible to us in such a way that we can deal with the newly emerging *Gaian* issues? One of the issues that comes up is the programs that evolution put into our body take eons and eons of time. We do not have so much time because of the destructive technology we developed. So we now need to shift those instinctual, almost biological programs about territoriality, about sibling rivalry, faster than it could be done by biological generations. This is where we have to look at the transformative stuff in order to be able to deal with what is without repressing it.

EVE: And of course you see that in many of the mystical sects of all religions and certainly in Eastern religions and in the yogic traditions, it's well known that there are very precise things you do to accomplish a sort of mutation within one generation and they're all embodied, for instance, changing the electrolyte balance, changing the nervous system. . . .

There are groups of people all over who are hearing the same message and trying to accomplish the same thing. When we dip into biblical material for a basis, there are some interesting things that happen. Zalman, as a superb linguist, can bring out the inner meanings of the words that have been misinterpreted and misunderstood. The idea that the world is made for human beings and we're supposed to "have dominion over" it, in the sense that everything must be here for our use and for our service, is based on the misinterpretation of a word. This is never what it was meant to say. Would you speak about *Uredu*?

REB ZALMAN: It says *Uredu bidgat hayam*, and it is transcribed, "And you govern, subdue the fishes," like power over. But the word *redu*, from *yored*, means to descend, and it has the sense, "Go learn from the dolphins, go to their level to learn from them."

There is a beautiful statement in the Talmud: "If the Torah hadn't been given at Mt. Sinai we would have had to learn from the cats and from the dogs and from the horses." The point is that you might even say that there is a new dispensation happening that requires that we learn from other species and with it comes the recognition of the indispensible need for other species.

EVE: In the Wisdom School we're taking the outer wrappings off what is really the basic story. We are reseeing what is really there, and finding that it's saying something quite different and much more conducive to life than we've allowed it to be for us for the last long time. Then we also have to ask, as Jean Houston says, whether some part of the myth has to be redreamed, whether the thing-as-it-is at its best is no longer functional for evolution except as history. And that is a little tougher; it's a little harder to do and a little harder to swallow when you've been trained to believe that this is the last word and you better find what you need in it.

ARIFA: That goes back to what Reb Zalman was saying about restructuring the whole cosmology to fit the needs of our time.

REB ZALMAN: When we talk about God in the past still we were in the ptolomeic universe, which means that the Earth is in the center, the sun and the stars and the planets all revolve around the Earth, and God is the infinite, omni-this, omni-that of the universe. Most traditional theology has not been fully reformatted to the picture that emerged after Galileo, Newton, and Copernicus. Now after Einstein we surely haven't reformatted our theology.

Then you start wondering, at which point is human life and human awareness and our contribution and even this planet important? Let's just get some time pictures. It takes the sun 360 million years to go around the galaxy one time, a solar year. In comparison a psion and a muon, those little tiny newly discovered particles, have a life that's in nanoseconds. The whole eternity of that is a millionth of a second. Now the experience of God "Godding" that is the entire range from nanoseconds to billions of years. So what do I know of a cosmic God? A cosmic God is bigger than a galactic God, so the infinite number of galaxies are included in there. That which is going on is so beyond my awareness and the noticing me, so what's my life and death on such a vast scale? Having said that, there emerges now for me an understanding that the God that I worship is the God of *Gaia* (is not *Gaia* but is the God of *Gaia*). It's like saying the range of "Godding" to which I can address myself as a human being is a range of "Godding" that goes from the lifetimes of the smallest beings inside me, and molecules and atoms, all the way up to solar and galactic cycles, and so on and so forth. These are huge, huge cycles from my lifetime. So if I adore God and I praise God, the God I adore and the God I praise is the God who makes me and this happen. So look at the Hebrew formula: "Blessed art Thou O Lord our God, *King of the World*." When I can praise God as King of the World, the responsibility I have is to this King of the World, and so all this world is the palace of the Kingdom of God that's coming. The Kingdom of God is arriving now. The arriving of the Kingdom of God has to do with the resurrection of Earth, the physical sense of resurrection. What do I mean by resurrection? I mean not only that it comes to life but it becomes conscious.

We are the brain cells of this globe becoming conscious of itself, just as the mitochondria are doing their stuff inside my cells. So we are the brain cells of the global brain, and I believe there are larger aggregates and awarenesses yet. We are participants in the resurrection of the planet and anything that will help to make more consciousness fed back to that is the task of the current religious work. Sophia is the consciousness that God dreamed of prior to world. "I was with Him before He made the world." Sophia is seen as a daughter. Some women are saying this is *the age of God, the daughter* and, in a sense, this is what *Gaia* represents: Sophia coming out from prior to creation. According to Teilhard de Chardin, first it becomes alive [the biosphere], and then it becomes conscious [the noosphere], then it becomes divine. Being conscious is a way of becoming divine and here is where the myth of resurrection begins to have a whole other feel to it.

On Sexuality

REB ZALMAN: The strongest form of embodiment that creates embodiment is sexuality. If you check out the literature that's available in most traditional religions, you will find very little that will say what is the "yes" of how one does it in a sacred way, but you find a lot of the "no-no." This is not the right time, this is not the right setting, this is not when you must do it, and this position is no good, or what have you. I have the sense that we are coming to the end of the adversarial way of thinking.

In the same way, my sense is that the problem that the world is now having with drugs is being tackled from the wrong end. They're doing now the no-no but nobody is saying a responsible yes. We all want from time to time to change our consciousness. Besides the drive for food and drink, there's a drive for altering one's awareness. Because it's outlawed, you can't go to a health-food store and buy coca leaves, so you refine it. In the refinement of coca leaves we created cocaine and crack; and in the refinement of wine we created spirits. What would be available to give gentle euphoria, we have refined and we have outlawed. My sense is that the same applies to sexuality. We're dealing with prohibitions that did not recognize the drives that people have and didn't sacralize them.

I have a sense that *Gaia* is protecting herself from overpopulation by reorienting a large number of people to sexual partnerships that are not heterosexual. And when people will get to understand this, it's a whole other thing. For instance, I feel that the souls of the people who have contracted AIDS need to be honored in a great way; that in some way they were the people who were acting on "Make love not war," and yes, in an indiscriminate way perhaps. It was the burgeoning thing that was coming through at that time, and so now we're learning something about immunity; I can't mix body juices with too many people or my immune system gets down. Now all this needs to be spiritually looked at and honor needs to be given to the people who are bringing us, by their sacrifice, to our senses.

EVE: A big question for those of us who wish to embody our spirituality in this life is, how alive do we allow ourselves to be at all? How embodied are we; how much vitality do we allow ourselves to experience, and how do we allow it to direct our lives and our impulses, and with what kind of sensitivity? Last Rosh HaShanah, as a result of a great release through one of the ceremonies of releasing of vows, we began to dance, and one of the women really began to dance deeply in her body and heard immediately a voice saying, "You don't do this in synagogue." And what came from that was many people speaking of the distress they felt at the separation and the gap between their erotic lives and their spiritual lives, which I think is a misunderstanding and a false separation. When I say erotic, I'm speaking of eros in the broadest sense—of that vitality and love of life that perpetuates itself. What happened then was that we separated the men and the women so that an experience of our erotic selves in the context of our religious and spiritual lives wouldn't get caught in the level of habit or the level of being aware of ourselves as objects of observation. When the women were alone I began asking, "What were your true religious experiences, your sacred experiences that you may not have talked about?" And almost every one was body based in one way or another. And then one woman said, "Enough talking, let's dance." We found a samba beat and began to dance deeply into the ground, and when we were really engaged in dancing we began with the liturgy. It was an entirely different experience and a transformative experience for many of us because we were there with our whole selves in praise and in connection with each other and with that which was larger than ourselves.

ON THE NEW ASCETICISM

REB ZALMAN: Saints in the past were able to achieve what were seen as exemplary forms of their sainthood by repressing other parts of their being. So that part that was dealing with commerce and body and so on was repressed. All that energy was used to push things higher. Our understanding of the asceticism that is emerging is, first of all, holistic. It is rounded; it is also body based, it does not ignore the body. In fact, it is responsive to body. The body is smarter than we are; the body does not make generalizations and say, "That's policy forever." There will be times when the body says, "Now I need some of this; now I need something else." What we're now discovering about *Gaia* is that it is a body that will say, "Now I need this and now I need that." The asceticism is a lot more body referent than what we had before.

EVE: The new asceticism has to do with mindfulness, so that what happens in terms of gratification of desires has reason behind it. It has to do with the fullness of appreciation for what we use for our living and the mindfulness to be living in such a way as to perpetuate the richness of the planet rather than destroy it. So the new asceticism might include, for instance, that rather than throw away quickly when we're in a rush, we throw away so that it's easily recyclable, already in categories. An entirely new ethic—which is a necessity for the planet—includes scrupulously looking into the content and the effect of the products we use. Zalman refers to this as *ecokosher*. It has to do with the products; it has to do with the ways in which we use them.

15

PRACTICE OF SPIRITUAL ELDERING

Several years back I participated in a gathering of about 150 people in the Sinai Desert: Moslems, Sufis, Christians, Copts, Palestinians, Israelis, Americans, Japanese, and a Native American shaman named Richard Deer. We began our climb of Mt. Sinai at one in the morning, an old Japanese fellow and I helping each other over the tough places. There was such fellowship that we didn't need to talk to communicate. We climbed until dawn arrived as we reached the top. Then, when the sun rose over the horizon, we began our worship, each in his own way: the Japanese shouted "Banzai!" in greeting, Richard Deer offered prayers, the Moslems offered prayers, we sang Halleluia . . . it was an amazing thing. Somebody brought a stone laser-engraved with the words Dona Nobis Pacem *(Grant Us Peace), and we left it there among the other stones at the top of the mountain.*

I sat with the old Moslems and listened. And it came to me that just as male and female are more different than are Sephardi-Ashkenazi, young and old are more different than are Christian-Jewish — and how we need some unique kind of dialogue across this age gulf just as we do across these other pairs of "opposites"! But in order to have such dialogue, we older ones must learn to be and to speak as "spiritual elders."

Spiritual and Elder

The word *spiritual* repels many people because they don't understand what is meant by it. Maybe we should use another word. Perhaps the word *philosophical* is more appropriate. What does the word *philosophy* mean? — the love of wisdom, SOFIA, the Greek goddess of wisdom, she who now appears to be living and breathing in our midst. The current concern with the earth spirit, with the rising spirit of women, the witnessing to *Gaia* — it's all Sophia's work. The earth is awakening, becoming wise to itself, witnessing itself.

Now, what do we call a wise one — a sage, one rich with wisdom, one with a philosophical outlook born from the distillation of life's experience. I prefer to say these elders are "sage-ing," not "aging." It's so important for all our aging ones to learn to become such sages, ones who live the wisdom of their aging.

A sounding board or, occasionally, a father confessor, that's what an elder is — among other roles assumed. *Staretz* is the Russian word for Father Confessor, spiritual director. Father Sosima in *The Brothers Karamazov* is just such a one, a patient, holy person. *Staro* means "old" in Russian, *staretz* means "old one," or elder — elder as wise one.

Similarly, the word *senator* originally referred to an aged counselor. The word *senior* is also derived from the Latin, the original forms being *senatus* and *senex*. The elders with greater wisdom and experience would hear what the lesser assembly was considering. They would then offer their own suggestions: "Yes, in our opinion, this is a good thing," or, "You need to consider this possibility and that."

Were we to engage in similar dialogue, we could create an aging ecumenism through which older citizens could get inspiration and energy. They'd feel the urge to continue expanding, rather than contracting, shrinking from youth and lost vitality. And younger people could gather this wisdom, counsel, and sage juice from our seniors.

In a TV presentation by Bill Moyers, I saw Robert Bly working with a group of men. Bly talked about how older men used to be the initiators — sort of male mothers — to the younger men. That's what I'm talking about, too, the way the older Levites used to train the younger Levites in service to the Temple. When a young person perceives an older one seeing them as who they are to become, there is a great empowerment. That's the initiation Bly was talking about.

One of the reasons this is so urgent is that we don't live under the same roof with grandparents anymore; the nuclear family has become socially dysfunctional. Do you remember that wonderful film, *Lies My Father Told Me*? It was about a junk dealer in Montreal and his grandson. It's a very, very beautiful movie; the love that's between the two of them is extraordinary. The grandfather can teach his grandson values as an ally. Parents can't do that because they are experienced as the child's oedipal enemies. When we lived three and four generations under one roof, parent and child might be enemies, but grandchild and grandparent were allies.

When extended families split, we moved out of the nuclear family as fast as we could and we never got grandparent juice. Because of this, the cultural, ethical, and moral crisis now is extreme. If my parents were, in the absence of my grandparents, the transmitters of my values, and I had to reject them in order to become free, I also rejected the values they represented. And if there was no grandparent to provide me with moral and cultural stability, values couldn't be transmitted at all because they had to be rejected.

Many people come and tell me what they've discovered about Judaism and talk of this or that. I look at these, my students, and I can more easily see their Higher Self than who they are as persons at the time. When I look love-with-love at this Higher Self I am facing, the person gets connected with his/her Higher Self. Let's say you're a young person and you've discovered something and you'd like to have an opportunity to put your thoughts together. The best service a grandparent, an elder, can offer is to listen, maybe to remind you of your Higher Self. But where can we find them now?

THE SEMINARS

By the spiritual eldering project I mean the creation of a series of seminars designed to help people make the transition to eldering. Generally, people want to make the elderly comfortable. But it's not enough to make them comfortable like slightly mobile objects; we have to treat them like conscious individuals. We have to help them regenerate the limberness of their bodies and minds.

In order to do this right, we need more research and development. At this point I'm asking more questions than I have answers, though I do have a good idea of how to achieve the results I'm hoping for. Doing it right calls for pilot programs to evaluate, to see what needs to be refined to move toward what is envisioned. This is not solo work: I need to connect with people who are willing to help create what's not yet available. When the R&D is complete, we will have separated the chaff from the wheat, and we'll know what works best, how, and in what order.

Presently, I see four seminar units, each 3 to 5 days in midweek so people can be at home on weekends. We will initially make a plain "vanilla," so that we can always affix "Jewish" or "Catholic" if we choose to. But basically, the differences don't really matter because, as I said before, elders have so much in common just being elders. While Jews are saying, "*Adonai Melekh, Adonai Malakh, Adonai yimlokh le'olam va'ed* (The Lord is, was, and will be Sovereign)," Moslems can say, "*Ya Rahim, Ya Rahman Dhul Djalal w'al ikram,*" and Christians can say "Glory Father, Glory Son, Glory Spirit, Three in One." These seminars will be full days, with sessions in the mornings, afternoons, and evenings, rest periods in between, and body work with trained facilitators. Perhaps we will be able to franchise the program.

BECOMING AWARE

Insomnia troubles many older people. Most of them just toss and turn and reach for sleeping pills rather than sit up and meditate. Their bodies are calling, Become aware, become aware. But what makes it so hard for many older people to meditate? Sitting cross-legged on the floor in the so-called "meditation position" is not the only way to context the body, particularly if the bones ache or the muscles feel rheumatic.

One day I noticed how good I felt sitting in the tub, and it reminded me of the old Roman baths. People sat comfortably, socially, in the nice warm water, talked with each other, contemplated life. I began to understand that an older person can sit in a warm bath and with the right kind of music and the body's natural buoyancy can follow a thought for a while. This may be a place where the necessary contemplative homework and life review is more easily done. But this is not to be merely a situation where we chat with our fellows. We need rituals and initiations to deepen the process, to open up new dimensions of the inner life.

Let's consider another group, girls from age 12 to 14. Andy Gold does something parallel and very wonderful with them. Their parents bring them to Rose Mountain, his growth center in New Mexico. In a beautiful Aspen grove, the girls and their parents are tied together with a white ribbon. Then the girls cut the ribbon and run into the forest. Three women wait for them—a young woman of 18, a 35-year-old in the middle of her child-bearing years, and a woman of 50-odd, what we call a "crone." (Crone means an older woman, one who is no longer in child-bearing mode.) The girls spend a week being initiated into women's mysteries. Then their parents come back and meet their daughters as young women rather than as the girls they left a week before. It is clear that the girls experience an initiation into their woman lives. This is the kind of experience elders also need.

I know a psychologist who told me how tired she is of working with people with all the youthful Freudian, early sexual stuff over and over again. I asked her whether she was finished with her menopause, and she answered affirmatively. Then I asked her if she could have used some help at that time, and she replied, "Absolutely. Except, there was no one around." Perhaps she could become a menopause counselor, doing "cronework."

At a recent retreat we did a wonderful meditation with the Book of Job. We were awakened in the middle of the night and gathered in a dimly lit room. While we sat in a circle, the suffering of Job was recounted in dramatic fashion: the loss of his possessions, friends, family, health, and ultimately, the loss of his sense of purpose and justice in life. Each of us then imagined suffering those same losses. We were then asked, in our humbled state, "Who are you?" "What do you believe?" The exercise revealed how powerful the meditative/imaginative approach can be in examining what we really believe and understand.

That's how we can approach the issues around aging—entering into the mysteries of our lives consciously and intentionally through guided practices and new rituals.

ELDER MEDITATION

We begin by giving people the basic tools for meditation. In the earlier stages of life, people need more active forms of meditation. In the life stages we're talking about for elders, centering prayer works best, such as sitting in deep silence and simple mindfulness of the presence of God. We don't need very much else, just to be ushered to the place where we can do this comfortably and learn a few techniques to take us there.

One of these techniques is what I call "socialized meditation." Most people do meditation solo. When I ask, "What's your practice?" there's a whole spiel—"I've got this great practice; I do this and I do that." When I ask them, "How often do you do your practice?" they say, "Well, I don't often get around to it. You see, my family needs me and I have to do quality time with the kids." "Da da da da da da." My next question is, "Okay, how often do you do quality time with the kids?" And they say, "Well, I'm not centered enough. If I meditated more I'd be more centered." So they're not doing their practice, and they're not spending quality time with their family, and on and on. We take meditation out of solo and socialize it, so that people are encouraged to meditate in twos and threes. This way the meditative process itself becomes a way to spend quality time.

There is another technique I call "making credo." If I were to say what I believe, and then you were to say what you believe, sooner or later we'd find ourselves in adversarial positions. "No, I don't believe what you believe. You believe in a different . . ." Instead, if I say, "I believe the purpose of life on earth is . . ." and you finish the sentence and then you start a sentence and I finish it, we can get excited just sharing this spiritual intimacy with each other.

There's a whole range of spiritual techniques we are introducing, some of which are traditional, some new, and some an amalgamation. We're training people in these techniques, which, like everything else, will take practice to perfect. The project is a grand and timely one, and the resource of our elders too precious to lose by not working to develop a process that will best serve to bring them "From Aging to Sage-ing."

IV

DAVVENOLOGY: THE ART AND SCIENCE OF *DAVVENEN*

Introduction

An important note: This is the second time I am attempting to write this piece, an introduction to the section on davvenology. I had a few good pages written and "saved" the file in my computer and something went wrong; it was not saved. I lost it all! One gets frustrated, and I did. I asked WHY? and the answer came, "If you are going to write about davvenology, you'd better pray first."

So this is my prayer:

May these words written to help souls to make a vital connection with You, the living God, come from You to us who seek You!

After the Holocaust it seemed that the gates to God were shut. When most of us were introduced to *davvenen*, it was to recite the Hebrew with an urgent and pressured pace that bypasses understanding. I sought to find someone who could teach me what I surmised was there when I saw my Papa *a"h davven*. I saw many a person *davven* with serious intent and fervor. They told me that one must *davven*, that one ought to see God, that it was wrong not to *davven* and a wickedness not to honor the Creator. This did not help me in my quest to learn how to *davven*. In my heart, as I remembered moments of higher connection, I had a feeling for that which was genuine and holy in it. I also had a good sense of what makes for an elating aesthetic. I had had the good fortune to be a choirboy in the Polish Temple, as that *shul* was known in Vienna, under

Cantor Fraenkl and could recall moments when the sound of the *chazzanut* assisted by the choir was heavenly.

These were my questions for which I sought answers. This then is davvenology. It is the art and science of *davvenen*. And what, pray, is *davvenen*?

Some derive this word from the Aramaic *d'avinun*, which means that which we received from our parents. Others derive it from the Lithuanian word for gift, a translation of the word for the *minchah* prayer. My take on this is that the word is of Latin origin and came to us as a translation of the Hebrew *Avodat HaShem*, the Divine Service (*Opus Dei*) and in the same derivation as the Frankfurt Jewish-German *Oren* from the Latin *orare*. Our way of saying Grace after Meals we call *Bentshen*, a contraction of Benediction. Hence *davvenen* is doing the divine-inging. It differs (as I discussed at greater length in my article "Prayer as a Resource for the Rabbi") from both prayer and worship.

Prayer (derived from the Latin *precare* to be, a synonym for the Hebrew *bakkashah*, *atirah*, *tzaakah*, etc.) is making requests for help from God. We who are in a precarious, beggarlike position, pray.

Worship is celebrative, joyous, adoring public acclamation of God as sovereign. At different times and occasions we worship in the celebration of year-cycle and life-cycle events.

Davvenen is living the liturgical life in the presence of God. It is transformative of the individual, the group, and the situation. It takes us through the changes, past our tentative following, assured in God's taking of our hand in Hers/His.

There is a literature in which davvenology is rooted for me. Beyond the obvious sources of *Siddur*, Talmud, and the Codes, I draw from the teachings of the Baal Shem Tov (see especially the *Midrash Besht*, vol. 1, *P'Noah*, which gathers his teachings on davvening and much of which is found in Green et al., *Your Word is Fire*). The teachings derived from *Chabad*, Bratzlav, and other hasidic lineages were also of great importance to me. Many of these are well presented in English by Y. Buxbaum in his excellent *Jewish Spiritual Practices* (Jason Aronson, 1990).

But as the Apter *Rebbe*, Rabbi Avraham Yehoshua Heschel, stated, one cannot learn *davvenen* from books. One needs to learn from a *davvener*. My first mentors were the members of a *Havurah* in Antwerp in 1939–1940, headed by Baruch Mersel, who were guided by the late Rabbi Mosheh Tchechowal *ob"m h'i"d*. They taught me some of the basics. My "prayer coaches" in the Lubavitcher *Yeshivah*, the *mashpiyim*, Rabbis Avraham Paris, Elie Simpson, Israel Jacobson, and Shmu'el Levitan ob"m also taught me a great deal about *davvenen*.

In addition to learning about hasidic masters from their teachings as

Gershom Scholem insisted we must, and from their tales as Martin Buber held, it is also necessary to understand them via their *niggunim*, music, and their mode of prayer, the *nusach*. Only from these four dimensions does it become clear what a rebbe teaches and stands for.

Over time I have come to understand that the impulse to *davven* is generic. The birds and animals do it as in Psalm 148 at dawn and at dusk in a palpable way. Humans the world over, of all persuasions and ethnic backgrounds, *davven*. And thus I have found that there is much to learn from other praying people. I was blessed in being led to the late Dr. Howard Thurman of Boston University. He gave a course in spiritual disciplines and resources. There I was introduced to a literature and "ology" of practical prayer. So I learned from him and subsequently from others; Catholic and Orthodox monks, Sufis, Yoga-Vedantists, various Buddhist teachers of meditation, and Native American elders.

The pieces in this section reflect the ideas I have developed on davvenology. A few words on some of them follow:

My first manual was published in the *First Jewish Catalog* under the title "A First Step." Much of the material in it is discussed in "On Mystical–Empirical Jewish Prayer — A 'Rap,' " an interview conducted by Jerry Diller.

Much of what we developed in Jewish Renewal in a variety of settings, including Havurat Shalom of Boston, the Aquarian Minyan of Berkeley, the National Havurah Institutes, and *P'nai Or* Religious Fellowship, we hoped to form into a new *siddur*. A number of our pieces of work became part of *Sim Shalom*, the *siddur* of Congregation Beth El in Sudbury, Massachusetts, of *Kol Hanshama*, the *siddur* of Reconstructionist Movement, and of other significant small editions of *siddurim*. Finally, we included them in our own *P'nai Or siddur* project, *Or Chadash*. The introduction for the *Or Chadash siddur* is found here under the title "Introduction: Davvenology and the Four Worlds."

Also offered here are several selections of *davvenen* poetry taken from our *Hashir VeHaShevach*. This project reflects efforts to address the needs of those who want to *davven* but cannot do so in Hebrew. Therefore, I translated sections of the High Holy Day *Machzor* with the intent that people could recite them in English along with those who recite them in Hebrew. And everyone would use the same *davvenen* melody. I paid special attention to maintain the structure of the poetry so that even in translation, characteristics such as acrostics and meter would not be lost. For example, someone singing, "You who love my soul" alongside someone singing, "*Yedid nefesh*" will feel included; and the one who is reciting in Hebrew will "give the ear to hear what the mouth expresses."

Early in my work, when I served a congregation in New England, I was
made painfully aware of the inability of those who had become members
of the Kaddish College, the mourners who attended daily to honor the
memory of their loved ones, to read Hebrew, some because they had not
learned or forgotten the alphabet, others, because they could not keep up
with the *shaliach tzibbur*, the prayer leader. In either case they knew little
of the content of the prayers and were infantilized by those who had
made it their task to instruct them. I had been asked to lead some parts
of the service in English and found myself reciting, declaiming, in what
I thought was the proper (sepulchral) pulpit voice. In "responsive
readings" we unconsciously tried to copy what we thought was the style
of Episcopalians, making the best of such words as "bestow" and
"vouchsafe." We were self-conscious and we deep down knew that I did
not *davven* and neither did the people in the pews.

I began to *davven* my own prayers in English so I could sense that I
was talking with God. Rabbi Nachman of Bratzlav had urged his *hasidim*
to *davven* in the Yiddish vernacular. English was ours. I noticed then that
I began to chant when I used English, and soon enough began to do this
with others who then got to feel that they too were *davvenen*. Since those
days, more and more people have managed Hebrew and feel deprived of
it when it is not used. Yet often they do not understand what they are
saying. So I began to encourage people to *davven* Hebrew and English
simultaneously. There still was a problem; often the meter and rhythm
were out of sync. At that time I found Franz Rosenzweig's *Birkhat
Hamazon*, the Grace after Meals, which he on his honeymoon translated
for his bride into the German *Tischdank*. I was delighted to see how well
his German phrasing matched the Hebrew. This has served as my model
for a translation of the grace as well as for the selections included here.

A few years ago, with the help of Jonathan Rose and Gerd Stern, I
produced an audio *siddur* (available from P'nai Or-Aleph). It is a
stereophonic, bilingual Hebrew-English weekday morning service that
can be *davvened*, hands free and with a Walkman and earphones. When
the English text is heard on the right ear it engages the left hemisphere
and the Hebrew the right, which then makes both parts of the brain
perform in harmony.

The text is laid out with the Hebrew on the left and the English on the
right, both justified at center. In trying out a number of layouts, I
designed this arrangement. It is more ergonomic than the old one and
allows the reader who focuses on the Hebrew to scan the English with

ease. Several Jewish Renewal *siddurim* that have recently appeared have used this layout with success.

The symphonic nature of prayer becomes apparent when one takes pains to observe the various aspects brought to bear on prayer. Hence one comes to realize that Body, Heart, Mind, and Spirit each contribute to effective prayer. Feeling that the simultaneity of the various levels activated in *davvenen* needed to be expressed, I wrote the symphonic score for the first blessing of the *Amidah*. One who practices this can then easily improvise on other sections.

A description of body movements to go with prayer phrases, and redesigned *hakkafot* based on the teachings about the seven dances of *Simchat Torah* can be found in "A Meditation for Simchat Torah," *New Menorah*, Rosh HaShana 5750, p. 7.

NOTE ON AFFIRMATIONS

Rabbenu Bachya Ibn Paquda, the author of the *Chovot Hal'vavot*, teaches that one can observe some of the core *mitzvot* simply by being conscious of them. For instance, if I think at God "I love You, I believe in You, I affirm Your oneness," I in this way have fulfilled three of the commandments that are the "Duties of the Heart" (the meaning of the title of his book). I trained myself to fulfill one of these each time a little bell, suspended on my rearview mirror, rang as a result of an unevenness of the road. I began to share these affirmations with others, especially R' Ahrele Roth's list of 32 of these (reminiscent of the 32 Paths of Wisdom and the numerical value of the word *Lev, Lammed Beth*, which means heart. (The text is part of the *Siddur Or Hadash*, published by *P'nai Or*.) As I proceeded in Kabbalistic meditation on the *sephirot* it became clear to me that the petitions of the *Amidah* had been designated positions on the Tree of Life. These were then arranged to comprise the Affirmations on the *Amidah*.

In the inner work of transpersonal psychology, affirmations have won a place as a powerful tool for transformation; hence these and other affirmations.

A GUIDE TO THE USE OF THE SHIVITI

Shiviti comes from the sentence, "I have set (*shiviti*) the Lord before me always." Looking at a *Shiviti* is Name-gazing; it is akin to icon-gazing:

concentrating on the symbol of the Deity with a focused gaze, until the distance between inside and outside becomes obliterated, and what was on the outside (the *Shiviti*) becomes internalized. Looking at the *Shiviti* we view the world from God's vantage point. *Hesed*, God's right hand, as it were, is on our right, not opposite our left hand, as it would be if we were facing God. This is connected to God's words to Moses, "You shall see my back, but my face is not to be seen." So one walks, as it were, into the YHVH, facing in the same direction, becoming one with it.

It is of great value to color the *Shiviti* in such a way as to make it a more personal aid to prayer. In fact, the wonderful Swiss artist, Henri Mugier, who created this *Shiviti* for *P'nai Or*, left the spaces open precisely for this purpose.

On the top of the *Shiviti* it says, "*Mimizrach shemesh ad mevo'o mehullal shem* (YHVH)." This section can be colored with rainbow colors. The sentence means, "From the rising of the sun to its setting, praised be the Name of God." The Name of God, YHVH, is the object of *Shiviti*. "*Shiviti YHVH lenegedi tamid*," "I have placed YHVH opposite me always," also involves the Name in the *Shiviti*.

The Name is written in such a way, top to bottom, rather than right to left, to create a hierarchy and also a figure: *Yud* is the head; the upper *Heh*, the arms and shoulders; *Vav*, the heart, spine, and genitals; and the lower *Heh*, the legs and pelvis. These are the four levels: The top of the *Yud* is *Keter* and the rest of it is *Hokhmah*, the two *Hehs* are *Binah* and *Malkhut*. The *Vav* contains the *sephirot Hesed*, *Gevurah*, *Tiferet*, *Netzach*, *Hod*, and *Yesod*.

The *nekudot*, the vowels, also represent the ten *sephirot*: The *kamatz* "ah" is placed in *Keter*; *patach* "ah," in *Hokhmah*; *tzereh* "ey," in *Binah*; *segol* "eh," in *Hesed*; *sheva*, a glottal stop, in *Gevurah*; *holam* "oh," in *Tiferet*; *hirik* "ee," in *Netzach*; *kubutz* "oo," in *Hod*; and *shuruk* "oo," in *Yesod*. There is no vowel in *Malkhut*, which is the silence under the final letter of a word.

If you want to make the *sephirot* explicit, you can color the *nekudot* to bring them out, or leave them faint, so the YHVH stands out clearly. A color scheme for the *sephirot* that you may use for the *nekudot* is: white for *Keter*, gold for *Hokhmah*, silver for *Binah*, purple for *Hesed*, blue for *Gevurah*, green for *Tiferet*, yellow for *Netzach*, orange for *Hod*, red for *Yesod*, and black for *Malkhut*.

To color the YHVH, make the *Yud* white, the first *Heh* yellow, the *Vav* (the six *sephirot* that represent the perceivable aspects of God) all the colors of the rainbow, and the lower *Heh* black, the absence of color, which absorbs and is receptive to all colors.

In prayer, one sits in front of the *Shiviti* and stares at it to ascend to

God's Presence, and then to descend. The four letters represent the parts of the prayer service: in the morning prayer, one looks at the lower *Heh* during the *Birkat HaShachar*, the opening blessings that address the world of *Assiyah*, the world of our bodies, our environment; getting ready in *Assiyah* requires doing an inventory of the body: what tensions are my muscles holding on to, what messages is my body telling me that I have been too busy to pay attention to? To place oneself in the presence of God is to let the body out from any compulsion it is under.

We turn our attention to the *Vav*, representing the world of *Yetzirah*, the world of feelings, emotions, affect, during the *Pesukey Dezimrah*, the prayers and psalms of thanksgiving. Here the grateful mentality reigns. We are thankful with humility, because we know we are receiving love without having had to earn it. And we are thankful, equally, for the tribulations and pain we have suffered that have enabled us to grow and learn.

In the world of intellect, *Briyah*, which we enter after the *Barekhu*, with the first of the blessings of the *Shema*, ". . . *yotzer or* . . .," our focus turns to the upper *Heh*. Here we want to be open to any truth that wants to burst forth, without predilections. So we let go of our expectations that reality will turn out this way, or that cosmology will turn out that way. If we do that, then what will come to us will be precisely what this moment requires.

And now, the goal of the *Shiviti* is realized as we come to the world of *Atzilut*, being, with the *Amidah*, the silent standing prayer. We look at the *Yud*, and the *Shiviti*, which we initially placed opposite us, moves from the outside to the inside, through our skin, so that we become one with the divine. The *Shiviti* is no longer external; it burns within us. Stay in this state as long as possible.

Why do we do the *Amidah* silently? Because the greatest thing we can do is to offer our stillness to God, to make ourselves so transparent to the Infinite that the ego doesn't offer any resistance. But since this is so difficult, the *Amidah* consists of all of the things that come up in a person's mind: "I am so blessed to have had ancestors that created and passed to me a tradition of seeking God." "I am aware of the cycle of life and death." "When I still myself I feel holiness." "I am trying to quiet myself, so that I can place all of my awareness in the right place, so that I can harmonize myself, so that I can be forgiven my sins." And so the *Amidah* unfolds. But better even than just the recital of the individual prayers is to return after each one to the stillness, and then resume the formal prayer only when you can't hold the stillness anymore. It's a very strong thing to do.

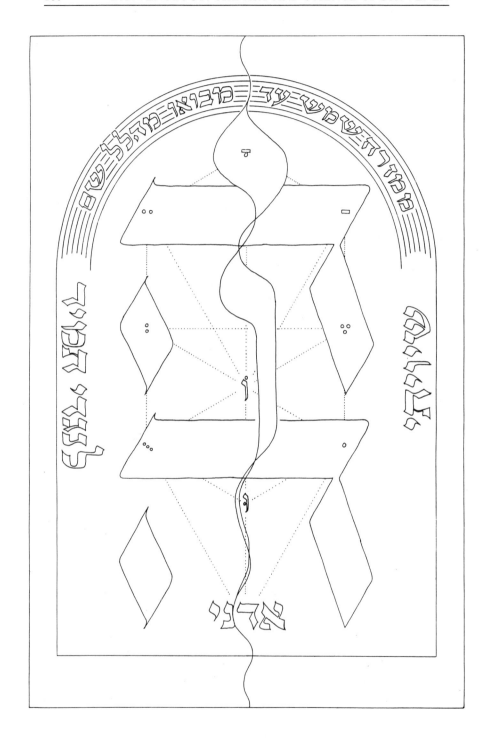

16

ON MYSTICAL-EMPIRICAL JEWISH PRAYER — A "RAP"[1]

If I were to make a distinction between mystical and dogmatic elements in religion, the distinction would boil down to the issue of how much empirical stuff there is behind it. How much can be checked out as living reality. Mysticism says you can experience the Infinite right now, that beneath the surface of the obvious, there exists the Divine. The dogmatic approach, on the other hand, doubts the possibility of experiencing God on this plane and with our present consciousness tools and contents itself with belief in revealed principles, reasoned theology, and outward observance and ritual. It sees little purpose in looking below the surface for hidden meanings and experiences.

People seem naturally drawn to one of these two positions, to the exoteric or the esoteric, using Frithjof Schuon's categories. This distinction underlies the old arguments of the *mitnagdim* against the *hasidim*, of the Aristotelians against the Platonists. Some people are content to be the exoteric folk, to settle for a certain level of observance and insight and just leave it at that. Others cannot stay exclusively on this level. They feel it is just not enough and that they must move in search of the esoteric. They say: "I must know" and "I must get down to it." These are

---

[1]This essay is based on a taped interview with Zalman M. Schachter, edited by Jerry V. Diller.

the people who come to mysticism. Since we have ways of making this kind of experience accessible to them, doing so is very exciting to me.

For many years now I have been introducing young Jews to the empirical experiences behind Jewish mysticism as well as more satisfying ways of relating to the exoteric elements in *Yiddishkeit*. Before going into my method, a little of my personal background and history may be useful in understanding how it evolved.

I was drawn to Habad Hasidism, especially Lubavitch, because of their promise that one could attain certain mystical experiences in this lifetime. The various tales told by the *hasidim* about their *rebbes* concern the attainment of such experiences. I also liked the nature of the relationship between the *rebbe* and the individual *hasid*. Rather than saying that the person must allow the *rebbe* to do the spiritual work and just hang at his coattails, Habad's basic notion was different. The *rebbe* is just going to show you the way, but you have to do the work yourself.

I remember once bringing a group of young people to see the present *rebbe*. When the *rebbe* invited questions, one young man, the president of my Hillel group in Winnipeg, raised his hand and asked: "What is a *rebbe* good for?" Instead of being put off, the *rebbe* said: "It is a very good question. Let me tell you. It is written: 'You will be unto me a land of desire.' The Earth contains in herself all kinds of treasures, but you have to know where to dig. If you do not, you will hit either rock or mud or whatever. But, if you ask the geologist of the soul where to dig, you might find silver, which is the love of God; gold, which is the fear of God; or diamonds, which is faith. All a *rebbe* can do is show you where to dig. You must do the digging yourself." That was a beautiful answer and invited the young man to do further work.

I experimented with all these methods, having in mind the idea of bringing them out of the doors of Lubavich and into the camps, like Ramah, into the conservative and reform movements, and even into Orthodox circles. It is strange how so many Orthodox people are vaccinated against Hasidism. As long as there is dogma and specific behaviors to perform—as long as they put on *tefillin*, keep *kosher* and all that—what more is there to want?

At this point in my life I had the good fortune to meet and study with Howard Thurman, then dean of the chapel at Boston University.

I learned a great deal, especially from his use of labs. In his labs we experimented with various spiritual exercises. People seldom have the primary experiences in religion that William James, Aldous Huxley, and others make reference to. Without this firsthand knowledge, the study of religion is poor in meaning. Such labs allow the student to understand what is being taught. This is now part of my method, providing these primary experiences. They turn out to be very, very important in the spiritual growth of the individual.

In time, people started to ask me questions about these primary experiences, about what it is that we do in meditation. I started my first instructional group in Winnipeg, which we called the Chapel Group for lack of a better name because we met in a chapel. In it I introduced the students to various hasidic methods of meditation and inner exploration and awareness. As a result of the instructions that were given to the Chapel Group, I wrote the little booklet "The First Step."[2] That was in the late fifties, before acid made the scene and before the whole consciousness explosion. I probably would not write it the same way today, given the changing needs of young people. But at the time it came almost as a result of automatic writing, as if I were merely a vehicle for the expression of hasidic voices from the past.

Another aspect of my method came out of my previous work as a rabbi in Fall River, Massachusetts. People would come to the synagogue to say *Kaddish*. When I would ask them to put on *tefillin*, they would say: "I don't believe in it." I wondered where they had learned not to believe in it. When visiting their homes while sitting *shivah*, I would again ask: "Do you have a pair of *tefillin*; let me show you how to put them on, here in privacy." All of a sudden people started to believe in it. So I realized what they did not believe in was making an ass of themselves in public. What most people lack are basic skills in Judaism. So I showed them how to make *talaysim* and how to do *mezzuzahs* and all that. I found that the more skills people could gain, the happier they were and the more they were able to relate to *Yiddishkeit*.

This attitude, together with the primary experiences, provide a perfect complement, a way of getting the outer and the inner parts, the exoteric and the esoteric elements, going at the same time.

Young people come to me most typically having first explored other non-Jewish avenues to mysticism. It is very seldom that I find a spiritual virgin saying I would like to get more into *Yiddishkeit* or learn about Judaism or learn about spiritual things. A lot of the people have smoked dope, which means they have experienced certain expansions of the mind—certain openings. They come looking for a map to help them make sense out of these experiences. Others come who have had Transcendental Meditation. They say: "I am happy doing TM; it is really great. I have gotten many benefits from it. But it is a little too foreign for

---

[2]"The First Step" appears as "A First Step: A Devotional Guide" in *The Jewish Catalogue*, ed. Richard Siegel, Michael Strassfeld, and Sharon Strassfeld (Philadelphia: The Jewish Publication Society, 1973).

me, not Jewish enough. What can I do about it? Can you give me a Jewish mantra?"

Still others come a more circuitous route, beginning at a place where they are very suspicious of anything having to do with religion, especially with Judaism. Not only Judaism, but all Western religions are suffering from having become ververbalized and underexperienced. Eastern religions, so popular today, come on with this fabulous propaganda that they have a "high" you will never come down from and find a receptive audience. So, for many a Jew it happens that he has to come to us via Eastern religion. It is in the nature of the situation that people will turn away from something that is not satisfying to them. When I am being manipulated by my religion and do not like that manipulation; when I am not being given decent answers to my questions; when the people who teach me at my *bar mitzvah* do not know; when my teachers do not speak from firsthand experience; when they really do not know who God is and can only tell me what others have said about Him; I will surely turn away. On the other hand, there is this Zen master who says: "Come and sit and experience for yourself." So I go there and I find out.

But paradoxically, once I go and sit and meditate for a while, I find that a lot of Jewish stuff starts coming through — *Bubbeh, Zayde, Torah, Shabbes*; all kinds of stuff buried deep inside that both resistance and the normal pressures of everyday life does not allow to come out. But, if I do *zazen* it all starts. The pressure is off; it starts coming out and has to be dealt with. So many young Jews involved in other movements that call for Sunyata, the void, for psychological emptying, find themselves in this crazy position, confronted once again with their Jewishness. They may want to cut off this Jewish stuff, but in order to do this, they have to choke off the Eastern goodies as well. What happens is that these Jewish elements take on a different perspective when viewed from this Eastern viewpoint. They realize that what they so despised before as *schmaltz*, they now like when seen as nectar in Hinduism, for example. They begin to ask questions and eventually turn to things Jewish.

I am not upset by the fact that many young people come back to *Yiddishkeit* through Eastern religions. I do not believe that anyone has the exclusive Truth. What we have is a good approximation, for Jews, of how to get there. But even that is inexact. Each person in his own life has to create the exactness that fits his situation. While there are many differences between Jewish and non-Jewish approaches to mysticism on the exoteric level of methods, there are few on the esoteric, in regards to the experiences themselves. When it comes down to what I call the "heart stuff," all approaches overlap.

In fact, I find these comparisons and parallels interesting and useful in communicating with the young people who come to me. Let me describe a particularly exciting example. Psychologist-guru John Lilly in his *Center of the Cyclone* talks about a number of spaces – inner spaces borrowed from Sufi mysticism – that he calls 48, 24, 12, 6, and 3. These descriptions are amazingly parallel to the Kabbalistic teachings concerning ways of experiencing God. Level 48, called physical *Assiyah* in the Kabbalah, is the designation for this physical world. Level 24 or *Assiyah* is a place of spiritual action or the spiritual ground upon which we stand. The inner experience of feeling or deep emotion is *Yetzirah* or 12. The world of thought or contemplation where we want to understand the blueprint of the universe, what it all means and what its significance is, is 6 or *Briyah*. Finally, 3 or *Atzilut* is a deep or divine intuition that participates in the thing it intuits about. Within Jewish mysticism these inner spaces are represented by both parts of the body and letter in the holy name of God, YHVH. My head (3) is the Y; my arms and shoulders (6) are the H; my spine (12) is the V; and my pelvis and legs (24) are the lower H. Spiritual man is thus made in the image of God. Each of these inner spaces has different laws and potentialities, each related to its particular symbolic location.

Now, if you have this schema, a whole bunch of things will start making sense. Many religious rituals, for example, are really journeys through these inner spaces. In Hinduism the various yogas each relate to a different and higher inner state. Hatha yoga is body yoga; karma yoga is 24 stuff; bhakti yoga is oriented toward #12 experience; Jnana yoga is 6 stuff; and raja yoga is #3.

The davvening, or daily prayer in Judaism, is also built that way, as a journey up through these spaces and down again. In order to heighten this realization I often combine davening with other spiritual practices, some Jewish and others non-Jewish. The davening begins with various *berakhot*, or blessings, oriented toward the physical body. With this in mind they unfold naturally: "Blessed are you Lord God, King of the Universe, who takes those who are bent and straightens them out, who opens the eyes of the blind, who gives me firm ground to stand on, who girds me with strength." I accompany these blessings with appropriate yoga postures, and they serve to bring the *berakhot* into sharp focus. Another *berakhah* says: "O God, the soul you give me is pure." But in Hebrew the word for soul in this context means breathe, so I do some breathing exercises in conjunction with it. I particularly like an exercise I found in the writings of Rabbi Joseph Ibn Gikatilla. All of the breath expelled, the sound of the Y; breathing in, the sound of H; holding the breath, the V; and exhaling, the sound of the other H. So I have the rhythm and awareness of YHVH as I breathe.

The second part of the davvening is called the sacrifice of the *korbanot* and is focused on the plane of 24. This part of the service encourages me to begin exploring inner spiritual spaces, to make sure that the places from which my psychic energies come are still alive. I must be sure that there are coals burning on the inner altar. Sometimes I just feel what is going on in my body; other times I add to that energy through yoga breathing exercises. Reb Nachman of Brazlav said that if you want to know God, you need only listen to His voice within, the pulse. One need never be lonely for Him or out of touch with His inner spirit; you can always touch your pulse and say: "Oh, there You are."

The person moves from this place into the world of V or 12. That is what the *Halleluyas* and the *Ashrei* are about. They focus me on the feeling and emotional side of my being. So it begins with an emotional plea: "God, what good will it be if I go down to the pit? Will the dust praise You?" And so forth. "I praise you God for all the good that You have done . . ."

Then I go still higher into the place where the *Shema* is located. This is an invitation for meditation, for the H or 6 space is a level of contemplation of God and His Universe. At this point my prayer is less loud, more gentle; the melodies become more head melodies.

After this I move into the highest point of the service and get in touch with a level of deep intuition with God. This calls for a different kind of meditation, one in which I try to become one with Him. It begins: "Lord, open Thou my lips and my mouth shall show forth Thy praise." Rather than seeing myself as a supplicant before God, I try to visualize myself as seen by Him saying these prayers. I become object and He subject, rather than remaining a subject opposite and apart from him. This merging with Him is what the Y level of consciousness entails.

Finally, after the *Shemoneh Esrei*, I do all my private praying, for all the needs that I have. "God, I need this today; I need that today." And then coming down again, I bring back all of the spaces I visited on the way up. Periodically throughout the day I reflect back on each of these as a means of keeping myself spiritually alive and focused. Now you have a sense of the journey up and down that the davvening was meant to be and how the schema I described here makes this process clear and understandable.

I believe that much of *Yiddishkeit* has become elite religion: highly prescriptive, oververbalized and intellectualized, and underexperienced. In order to overcome these trends I first introduce young people to the meaning and experiences underlying Jewish rituals and observance, to their psychological and emotional intent rather than to their outward manifestations. People must realize that religious acts are no more than natural unfoldings of the human condition. In order to do this I show the person how to re-create these acts, beginning with his own experiences in living. By replicating the process, he moves naturally closer and closer to the ritual itself, becoming aware that the ritual is a tried-and-true means of accomplishing the same human ends.

Let me give you several different examples to make this point clear. First, let us look at the blessings or the *berakhot*.

Traditional expectations hold that the person repeat those *berakhot* that the rabbis prescribe. According to the *Gemara*: "Everything of the world belongs to God—the earth is the Lord's and the fullness thereof." But He has given the earth to man. The *berakhah* is a means of restriking this bargain, of feeding coins of the realm into the permission machine to secure something from God. Now this is a nice legal move, but it is not a heart move. Ultimately, this approach cannot help but turn many people off.

If a person wants to learn how to say the *berakhot* and what they are really about, I say to him: "Every time you feel something good happening to you or even something tough or painful say: *Barukh atah Adonai* . . . You make the sun shine. *Barukh atah Adonai* . . . it is a beautiful day out today. *Barukh atah Adonai* . . . the air is so polluted it is amazing that I am still alive." Each time a person focuses in this way, *berakhot* become a reality, and the person really begins to learn about prayer and life.

In a similar vein, when a person asks me how to start davvening, I suggest he not use the *siddur* for a while. When you come to the *Shemoneh Esrei*, for example, let the meaning of this unfold itself within you. First, recognize the chain that connects you to God through your ancestors. Make a *berakhah* and thank God for that. Then recognize the chain that connects you to life and make a *berakhah* over that. Then recognize the chain that connects you with holiness. Now, begin asking for the things you need. The first thing you need is to have the good sense to know what to ask for. Ask for *sekhel*. You get some common sense; the next thing comes in: "Who the hell am I to ask anything of God?" Why? Because I am so far away from him. OK, now pray to get closer. The next thing you realize: "Did I do this? Did I do that?" So pray for forgiveness. "It is such a struggle to live." So pray over the struggle. "I have got so many things that are sick inside of me." Pray for them. "I have got to make a living." Pray for that. So, as you watch the *Shemoneh Esrei* unfold, you see it is a very natural unraveling of the human being and the human situation. Once a person learns how to make a request and seal it with: "Thank you God," he gets closer to the design of the prayer. Once he replicates the process underlying the prayer, he will be appreciative of having the *siddur* as a guide.

Now, the *siddur*, or prayer book, has come to be highly misunderstood today in most Jewish circles. As a result, many people have become alienated from it and what it represents. The problem goes back to the nineteenth century and its overemphasis on rationality. The nineteenth century was so smart it was stupid. It outsmarted itself. To many Jews of that time period, as is now true today, the prayer book became a book of information. Whenever it said: "Say this three times," they did not want to do it. One time is enough they reasoned; for information, one time is enough. But the prayer book is not a book for information. Approaching it as such cannot help but turn you off and distort the experience it is meant to convey.

Let me give you an example. I am settling down to sit and read in the synagogue, to sit and read a book of information. My body goes into the posture I would assume if I want to read a novel. I look in the front of the book to find out what committee worked on it. I look in the back to see who the contributors were. Very quickly I become bored; I do not know what to do with it anymore.

Now, if I relate to it in a slightly different manner, the whole thing changes. I sit more grounded, with a kind of body eagerness. I hold the *siddur* in the left hand and begin to look at it only with one eye. I do not *davven* into the *siddur*. Rather, I pick out a phrase, look away from the book, focus toward the Presence, and repeat it. Every time I look in the *siddur* I do not talk; everytime I repeat the phrase I do not look in. I project a bit. I try to get into the feeling of the phrase. I breathe in a particular way; I *shuckle* with my body, make gestures, and try to give the feeling a total scene to develop in.

In this way I can say the same stuff I said last week. I can say it again. It is like when a husband says to his wife: "I love you." What is he talking about? He is not giving her new information. If she sees it as information, she says: "Stop, you told me already, enough." But he says: "I am not telling you this for information. I have a feeling and this is the best way I can express it. We are not in a place where I can kiss you or make love to you. But I can say: 'Dear, I love you so much.' " And when he does this it is not a vehicle for information. It is a vehicle for feeling. Davvening and the *siddur* are vehicles for creating these feelings and not for information. How many times can you say: "I love you?" As many times as I have the feeling and energy to put into it.

Even the prayer language chosen by those of the nineteenth century reflects their bias against feeling words. Sanctuary is for the head;

holy place is for the heart. I encourage young people to make their own translation of texts, into a language they understand and to which they can relate. When they can pick language from the *Zeitgeist* and at the same time retain a faithful translation to what the Hebrew says, people can get off on it, and the process will have real significance for them.

The *Keriyat Shema*, the traditional prayer said before retiring at night, provides yet another example of how Jewish ritual can function in one's life. The problem of how one lives deliberately underlies the intention behind the *Keriyat Shema*.

Most of us have trouble distinguishing between living for ourselves and living for others. While a lot of people think that they know how to live, in reality they are being lived. They are being lived by their parents, by the school, by the draft board, by everyone else. They are consistently ripped apart trying to live up to each demand made upon them and never get a chance to live deliberately, for they are too busy living up to someone else's expectations. The first move toward living deliberately entails assessing where you are each day and initiating whatever changes are necessary, reprogramming for tomorrow.

But having an insight is not enough in itself, I must also spend some time erasing all the other tapes that do not connect with the new insight. If, for example, I have been overeating for many years and get the insight that it is not good for me, I have only begun the process. Now I have to learn something more about why and where it came from. I may find out that when I overeat, I am hungry, but not for food. I may be hungry for meaning, or love, or knowledge. I learn that I have lost the ability to discriminate between hungers, that my appetite thermostat is not working. I may be able to trace it back to my mother. She may have said to me repeatedly: "Eat for your father; for mama eat a spoon; one for *bubbeh*, one for *zayde*, one for your teddy bear." And I did not even feel like eating. In this way my appestat was overridden, and I can no longer make the distinction between different kinds of hunger. But with this awareness I can begin the change process, the reprogramming necessary so I can once again be able to make the distinction between what I need and what others wish for me. If I do not take the time out to learn to make these discriminations, I will eventually need a shrink.

Late evenings, before going to bed, provide an excellent time to do this work, to develop such awarenesses and to set up strong anticipations for changes in my behavior for the next day. And this is what the reading of the *Shema* before retiring at night is all about, a time to ensure deliberate living in our lives.

I also encourage my students to develop a more personal interaction with God. Good communication is based upon giving clear and honest messages and receiving in return good feedback on how well we are being understood. Only by making our needs, expectations, and feelings clear to another person, can we avoid misunderstanding and miscommunication.

17

SPIRITUAL FORMATION IN JUDAISM

In this I trace some of the history of spiritual formation in Judaism. In this part I want to emphasize that Judaism as an evolving spiritual civilization has undergone many shifts. Spirituality in the deistic patriarchal-biblical period had other connotations than in the theistic rabbinic-medieval era. The reality model in our day is more pantheistic. This difference may also show in the way halakhic and posthalakhic Jews perceive the divine call to them and the literal-specific or general and model-in-situation nature of the commandments.

Kohlberg/Gilligan and Fowler have offered developmental stages for moral and faith development for the individual. I believe that they describe a process in ontogeny that is replicated in the evolution of religions in philogeny. It is inevitable that, given this, there are also different models of the spiritual ideal on each of the stages.

In the second part I deal with the subject at hand at times descriptively, at times prescriptively. This confusion cannot be helped. It is part of the fabric of such discourse. What a person experiences on the path becomes in his/her description also prescription. The scholar who describes what he reads in volumes of spiritual direction/prescriptions is then read by the spiritual aspirant as if she/he had offered prescriptions. I too cannot divorce myself from either the descriptive (I teach religion at Temple University) or the prescriptive (I am a rabbi who has deeply and variedly experienced some of the paths that lead to God). The motivation to describe would have been insufficient to take this task on during a very

pressured time in my life had it not been for the motivation to inform
seekers by this means and also to prescribe.

THE SOURCES IN THE PAST

The Bible gives us the basics of the spiritual life in the injunction
(Deuteronomy 13:5) "Walk ye after the Lord your God." This commandment takes for granted that the person who wishes to follow it will have
no difficulty other than getting his will and disposition to conform with
that commandment. The roles are apparent and clear. One emulates the
patriarch (Genesis 18:19 "for I know that he will command his seed after
him") or the prophet (Deuteronomy 18:15 "A prophet from among your
brethren like me"), one follows the injunctions of holiness (Leviticus 19
"be ye holy") and makes the words of the models (as in the psalms "a
prayer of Moses," "a praise of David") one's own, and it is simple.

Prophets and the Sons of the Prophets

In the formation of the spirituality of the sons of the prophets, shamanic
transformations seemed to play a large part. They seem to have been
engaged in thaumaturgic practices, some of which were dangerous and
could be fatal. Physical prowess was connected with the practitioners,
and music played its part in rousing the latent spirit to manifest in
prophecy. (See the Elisha cycle 2 Kings 3:15.) The literary prophets were
of a different nature. We know little about their development and
formation. For them it was enough that they heard the call ("Whom shall
I send and who will go for us?" Isaiah 6:8) or that the "heavens opened
and I saw god-visions" (Ezekiel 1:1).

Avot

In the time of the intertestamental period there are further counsels such
as these of Ecclesiasticus and the Manual of Discipline. The Manual of
Discipline called for a shared commonwealth of the spirit. Any adept
who did not share his visions was shunned for a month. There were some
hermits who were the models of the desert fathers and stoics.

The classic of spiritual formation of rabbinic Judaism is *Avot* ("One
who aspires to be pious let him busy himself with the words of . . .
Avot," *Bava Kamma* 30.a) and later *Avot d'Rabbi Nathan*. Here, we find
not so much action directives as attitudinal injunctions. "Said Antigonos

of Sokho: 'Be ye not like servants who serve the master for the sake of the bonus, instead be like servants who serve without expecting to be rewarded' " (*Avot* 1:3) and contemplative considerations "Said Aqabya ben Mahallalel: 'Contemplate on three things: Whence comest thou, whither goest thou and before whom wilt thou have to give an accounting' " (*Avot* 3: 1).

Musar *Classic*

In the eleventh century the rabbinic instructions became systematized in works such as the Duties of the Heart by Bahyah Ibn Paquda and after him spiritual directors such as Rabbenu Yonah Gerondi, etc. Their injunctions were aimed at helping the penitent to make his peace with God, to help the ascetic with his work, as for instance the counsels of the Sepher *hasidim* of the school of Rabbi Samuel, the *hasid* and his son Judah, the *hasid* of Regensberg and others. Their hope was to achieve in this life the purgation that would otherwise await them in the next. (This was parallel to Friends of God of the Rhineland and the other great penitential pilgrim movements that built the cathedrals and recruited for the Crusades. Indulgences were granted to those who in this life practiced such austerities as would clear them from the punishment of the purgatory.)

Parents and Masters wrote ethical wills directing their children or disciples to the virtues of humility, to the practice of prayer and compassionate acts of charity. The acquisition of virtue and the avoidance of the vices was the main purpose of spiritual formation at this stage. *D'vekut,* adsorption to God meant mostly the emulation of His attributes.

Kabbalah and Its Musar

With the advent of the *Zohar* the cosmic contribution of the faithful was stressed. It was no longer just the fate of the individual that was imperiled by his sin. Sin caused a cosmic catastrophe. "The *Zohar* often states 'Woe unto the sinners who sin by . . . for they cause the destruction of the world,' and conversely 'Happy are they who . . . for they make peace above and below and bring the King and the Matrona together.' "

The geography of heaven and hell and the conditions of those assigned to them were described in the literature in lurid detail. Directions for the acquisition of the infusion of the Holy Spirit contained injunctions for radical metanoia. *Tikkun*, the restoration of the balance of the cosmos, was no longer a matter of the individual or his immediate societal group. It had become the culmination of the process of history. The most heroic measures to restore the fallen sparks to their pristine place had become the goal of the elite of the initiated. Despite the grave dangers that this entailed, some heroic souls made attempts to hasten the millenium. Shabbetai Zvi and Jakob Frank were two examples of promethean failed attempts to bring about the redemption of Israel.

Hasidism and Its Zettels and Prescriptions

With the advent of the *Besht* and the founding of Hasidism, the base of people involved in the pursuit of their spiritual growth was widened as the numbers of the adherents to the new path increased. Prayer, now linked to the devout heart, was accessible even to those with less education. Spiritual direction now dealt also with reincarnation. Instead of demanding that the *hasid* follow an abstract and ethereal scheme of contemplative symbol-manipulation gymnastics, the masters after the *Besht* prescribed for their *hasidim* procedures that were individualized to their specific needs. To us who read such *zettels* (literally, billets, notes) of spiritual prescriptions these injunctions offered, along with severe, ascetic formulae devout, warm, and inspirational guidance. Before we look to the current injunctions, we need to look at our relationship to God.

Upayas and their methodology

In the East one speaks of two types of teachers: the *sat guru* and the *upa guru*. While the former must be a person of exceptional attainment, one who has transcended all illusion, the *upa guru* has only the task to teach his disciples some methods in psychotechnology. *Upaya*, skillful means, are well suited to a more modern temperament. Prescriptions and recipes for one's spiritual cookbook allow one to be independent of a guru's hegemony while at the same time making available such injunctions, which, if followed, will lead the aspirant to spiritual attainment. These *upaya* injunctions for body, heart, mind, and soul can be found in hasidic collections of *etzot* (counsels), and there are such for every level.

In Our Time, Where Are We with God?

Opus dei, Avodat HaShem, liturgies, the work of the people, worship— all of these have connotations that put us into some conflict. On the one hand, we wish to be maximally involved with God—to adore, celebrate, be consoled by Him/Her and to give with all our heart, soul, and might that which our intuition knows God wants from us. We want "not to withhold our son, our unique one, the one we most love." On the other, we also intuit that there is another order, one less feudal, not liege and serf, but a collaborative flowing with growth and process. God as Mother, as *Shekhinah,* addresses us differently.

Without contemporary models showing us contemporary prayers, many of us, feeling the conflict, withdraw from prayer. It takes some God wrestling to check a little deeper into the unease, to forge ahead past the conflict and to ask what outcome do we seek. There the answer presents itself: we want to be attuned to God, experience a closeness to Him/Her, collaborate with Him/Her entelechy as it unfolds His/Her design, become one-d with others who mind as we do, become aligned toward oneness and organicity, to receive the revelation of planetary telepathy with all the other sentient beings who form His/Her embodiment, to be instruments, limbs of God.

Our questions are not so much what can we say about God's existence or the nature of His/Her Being. Beyond all our definitions we are challenged by the ground of our being that lives and breathes, thinks and feels in us.

The Siddur

Compare this sense of the cosmic with "Master of the Universe! Not in the merit of our righteousness did we cast our supplications before thee but in the merit of Thy abundant mercy . . . Man is not much more than beast, all is vanity . . . nations are but dust on the scales . . ." and you see clearly that among other things we are plagued by an anachronistic *siddur,* a prayer book. That goes for all of us, Christians as well as Jews.

A regular diet, exclusively aligned to one kind of worship, feels wrong to some of us. The surface tensions that separate between religions, confessions, creeds, liturgies, rites, and congregations that served us well in previous eras seem wrong today. Most of us get inspired and refreshed by attending services of others who celebrate the Presence in their midst in styles, languages, symbols, and rituals that differ from our wont. We at *P'nai Or* are now at work on a new *siddur.* It is clear to us that surface patches to placate the feminist voice in us are not enough. We are not even sure that the best way to do a restructuring of the prayer resource is to produce another "book" anchored in the Gutenberg technology. Other media, designed for an interaction that takes us deeper than books do, may be needed to carry the message. We look to the deep structure of the process of prayer in order to redesign the resources.

The **Minyan**

Jewish worship demands the presence of a quorum of ten males past puberty. As a sort of minimum requirement it looks to the thrice daily visit to the synagogue and participating with the minyan as the right model. To be among the first ten to assemble is a matter of increased merit. Part of the reason given for the need to worship with a quorum was "the glory of the king is enhanced by the multitudes" (Palms 14:28). This feudal throne-room image needs to be replaced by something more organic. Certainly, we do not wish to continue to make a quorum of ten adult males the only option for public worship. We have experimented with other forms and found encouragement there for growing our souls.

Solo **Davvenen** *and Meditation*

Many of us have found that most of the *public* worship services available to us in the suburbs are not conducive to spiritual growth. Most of the *Upaya* recipes available to us promote solo meditation. Besides, our work schedules keep us from thrice daily attendance at synagogues. So many of us have our own sacred routines for morning and evening that do not quite parallel the surface structure of the regular liturgy.

According to the deep structure of the Kabbalah we are able to attune in ascending order:

1. our bodies to God in action,
2. our emotions — in devotion,
3. our intellect to reality maps based on our understanding of God's plan, harmonizing the value complexes of our traditions with the clearest view we have of how what is works, and
4. our spirit as an organic part of the "body of God" and
5. to ground this attunement in our being as a prelude to "know Him/Her in all your ways." Action directives received as a result of this grounding have the flavor and urgency of divine commandments.

We are helped in this by integrating the wisdom of the tradition with the constructs of psychological systems that parallel with four yogas and the four realms of the Kabbalah.

Behaviorism, **Assiyah,** *and* Halakhah

Behaviorism, seeing the person in the world of objects, what Buber calls the I-IT relationship, seeks to understand what persons do in terms of stimuli acting on organisms and, as such, eliciting responses in actions. This attitude closely parallels the mind of Deuteronomy. Draconic measures will serve to "and you will eradicate the evil from your midst" (Deuteronomy 13:6). On the most basic level, religion sought to train people in such behavior as would please God. The holiness laws of Leviticus 19 are also examples of this.

Esoteric religion favors behavior-modification schemes, and there is much evidence that in relation to habit craft much can be learned from behaviorists. Much of what happens in the formation of children is the result of reinforcement and the association of pleasant stimuli with modes of behavior. The dripping of a drop of honey on a page containing the first letters of the alphabet taught to a 3 to 5-year-old who gets to lick it after having learned to recognize it, is such an example. Other rewards and punishments are designed to modify behavior. Much of the interaction between parents and children at the Passover *seder* is based on reinforcement. Behavior modification was behind the tariffs of fast days. And austere disciplines were set by Kabbalists for making amends for infractions of religious rules that, as they taught, caused cosmic imbalances.

Most religionists opting for esoteric views and heteronomic authority admonitions employ behaviorist models. The Kabbalist reaches for behavioristic *upayas* mostly where the techniques of coping in the realm of doing/sensing (*Assiyah*) are concerned. Here habits and body issues are attended to.

Psychoanalysis, Yetzirah, *Attitude, and* Musar

Next in the Kabbalistic hierarchy is the world of *yetzirah*, the realm of feelings and the functions of emotions. Feelings come in ripples that evade verbalization and operational awareness. The domain of the affect manifests a kinship to the spirit that tends to confuse the novice. The hungers of the heart can easily be confused with the hungers of the soul. And as Maslow pointed out, lower-order needs must be dealt with before one can deal with the higher-order ones. And so too did Assagioli show us that we need to distinguish between the psychological disturbances that occur after spiritual breakthroughs and those that are the result of emotional imbalances.

We are all in Freud's debt for attaching words to the storms of feelings that are active in us from childhood on. By allowing for the existence of the unconscious he made it possible to bring consciousness to bear upon it. However, his contributions have also made holiness more difficult to attain. How is one to distinguish heroic virtue from one or a combination of defense mechanisms? Almost all the spiritual directors who in Judaism wrote on the acquisition, or better, the opening of one's being to the infusion of the *Ruach Hakodesh*—the holy spirit—ask for a spiritual cleaning in the realm of the emotions. Luzatto in his basic *Mesillat Yesharim* (translated by M. Kaplan as *The Path of the Upright*) is paradigmatic as he quotes Rabbi Pinhas ben Ya'ir's famous *beraita Avodah Zarah* 20:b: "Torah brings one to carefulness, which leads to zeal, which leads to cleanliness, which leads to abstemiousness, which leads to purity, which leads to devoutness, which leads to humility, which leads to the fear of sin, which leads to holiness, which leads to the Holy Spirit, which leads to the resurrection of the dead."

However, the purgation is not complete by following a regimen of carefulness (*zhirut*) and zeal (*zrizut*) in matters of ritual and what is between humans and God. The basic dictum: Yom Kippur atones only for the sins between us and God but the sins between human and human are to be dealt with by reconciliation and restitution.

The basic interpersonal relationship that formed us is that with our parents. Here much of the basic *yetzirah* work needs to be done. Since Freud we have become aware that we are bent out of shape by our early experiences with our parents. We so longed for their love that we tried to emulate their models or their admonitions, invalidating our own perceptions, favoring their assertions in the hope of gaining their love. By addressing God as father-parent, we transfer some of our problems to our relationship with God. We learned to take the admonitions of our traditions uncritically as if they were the means of gaining God's love and good will. Not locating traditions as the product of history and the results of the vicissitudes of persons, space, and time, we invalidated our experiences before the admonitions of those "greater and better than we by wisdom and number" (*Eduyyot* 1:5).

In the past, tradition was a stronger web than it is today. The modeling offered by the accessible models available in the community was bolder. One lived under the same roof with grandparents, who were the natural allies of grandchildren. Grandparents controlled the child-twisting on the part of the immediate parents. Then, therapy of one's early life situation was of less necessity than it is today.

With the constant use of root metaphors father, king, judge, Lord, which connect us to experiences with the authority person in the liturgy, we transfer much of our conflict to our spiritual life. This is another cause for some of our spiritual difficulties. A purgation is henceforth necessary to be done with our hankering for and addiction to negative love.

Humanistic Psychology, Briyah, and Habad

Victor Frankel in his book *The Search for Meaning* pointed out that the quest to know the meaning and purpose of one's life is a very potent drive. Roberto Assagioli, the founder of Psychosynthesis, gave us a system that could be more closely identified with the task of religion than Freud's. Humanistic psychology, continuing in their path and following also Maslow, brought into the process of therapy a wellness model. They showed how making the right affirmations, holding sane-reality maps, reframing our experiences to more mature views of reality is part of the normal growth process leading to actualization. Lubavitch Habad *Hasidim* taught that the emotions are the results of thoughts held in one's consciousness. Much of the teaching of Habad is to give the adherent a repertoire of thought to be held in his/her mind, thoughts that would in their train produce feelings, attitudes, and behaviors. Hasidic masters taught their disciples how to fill their heart and mind with content that would make them transparent to the power and the light of the soul.

Transpersonal psychology, Atzilut

Only in the last 20 years did some psychologists lift the boundaries that encased a person in his/her skin. The auric field, the *chakras*, the empirical reality behind such words as *sefirot, wazifas,* received new and scientific attention. Human aggregates and the way in which individuals influenced one another on levels that transcended behavior, feelings, and states of mind were focused on. Ideas that there are awarenesses higher than ordinary human mind states, that there are altered states, replaced psychological reductionism. Ken Wilber's important works made clear that the subtle and causal realms described in Buddhism were indeed to be reckoned with when one began to see with the eye of the spirit. When one considered the contributions of Shankara, Meister Eckardt, and Rabbi Isaac Luria as having psychological rather than theological significance, then Athman *is* Brahman, *Yehidah is* YHVH, the Eye with which God sees me *is* the same eye with which I see God.

The *upayas,* injunctions to verify the laws of the realm of *Atzilut,* are in need of updating. Yihud, Kensho, Satori, Samadhi, are nowadays being monitored along physiological lines. This is not enough. The dialogue of the devout as they share a consensus resulting from their own inner knowing is here of great help. In the West we did not trust our esoteric lore. It began to open to us anew with the influx of persons from the East who shared their light.

THE EAST AND ITS IMPACT

My friend Reb Shlomo Carlebach, in a message to a conference on "Torah and *Dharma*," put it this way. He paraphrased the Izhbitzer *Rebbe* who, in his *Mei Hashiloach*, says that "anger is a defilement. A *Kohen* is not to defile himself to the dead. How could he teach the knowledge so that they would seek the Teaching from his mouth if he is raging against God? Now anyone who faces a corpse cannot help but feel anger at the One who made it so that no one born can live and not die. This rage would disqualify him from teaching unpolluted Torah." Shlomo then said: "After the Holocaust we all became defiled by so much death. Rage at God at times unconscious and repressed was seething in our teachers below the surface. Some of us still needed access to God. The grace was that at that time there were some holy teachers who did not feel the anger we felt, they came from the East and in their thirst for God many turned to them for a word and a teaching how to be close to God."

This may not be the only cause for the phenomenon of a larger-than-chance-expectation-per-capita Jewish participation in Eastern disciplines. There was something in the air, of the religious *Zeitgeist* that expressed itself also in "Catholic Zen" and "Christian Yoga." Merton, the trappist, and Watts, the graduate of the Anglican Church, both found their way to Taoism and Zen as a balance to their Christianity.

There was a not-so-hidden revolution of the religion's entrance into the Age of Aquarius, which was accompanied by a terminology based on the Sanskrit terms of the Vedanta. Chakras, Yoga, breath, mantra, guru, samadhi, satori, koan, yin/yang have become good words to use to speak about subtle processes experienced in the Western religions. Silence, chanting, cushions on the floor and liturgies in the circle are now part of what happens in charismatic and living-room congregations and Judaism in our *havuroth*. Native American and wise women's ways have also entered into the circles, complementing that which came from the East. But beyond the ethnic and geographic origins there stands the ecological empirical imperative to shape us to live in harmony with our mother the Earth.

The know-how of the legal-rational male elite oriented to product and quantification and at the service of the industrial military complex had little to offer that was helpful. Just as the Aquarian conspiracy manifested in the *Whole Earth Catalogue* so did *The Jewish Catalog* become the collective know-how of the *havurah* movement.

THE *HAVUROT* AND *P'NAI OR*

The *havurah* movement perceived itself permitted, guided, and empowered to experiment with liturgies and seek such forms that would satisfy their needs. Networking and sharing what they had found, via *The Jewish Catalog*, the CAJE—Conference on Alternatives in Jewish Education—the Havurah Institutes. Some felt the need to respond to the calling for a world safe from war, terrorism, and ecological disaster by opening their spiritual concerns to the Jewish Agenda as it dealt with politics. Others wanted to deepen their spiritual know-how and connected with *P'nai Or*, planning and running retreats, designing liturgies and training liturgists for their new understanding of the spiritual process.

Between Solo and Minyan

The quorum of ten was not always available. The usual way in the absence of a quorum was to separate into solo units for individual prayer. *Havurot* were not inclined to do this. Instead they developed strategies and formats that would allow for clearing and sharing in smaller groups.

Family people who sought to do their spiritual work found themselves in conflict over the use of time. Quality time spent with spouse and children had to come from the same time and energy budget as the time for spiritual practice. By creating forms of socialized interactive meditation one could do the spiritual practice as shared quality time of the highest caliber. At *P'nai Or* there were further developments for dyadic and triadic groups, these techniques allowed for easy doubling to fours and sixes. The model of the Tree of Life of the Ten *Sefirot* could also serve as a way to see the deep structure of the minyan. No longer understood merely as the quantitative aggregate of the ten, it now manifested the deeper structure of the ten making a process whole in which each part contributed its particular Sephirotic mode of being. There is still much work to be done in the field of social/tantric meditation.

THE PATH FOR HALAKHIC JEWS

For the Orthodox, the words are sacred and potent *ex opere*, rooted in secretly transmitted principles. What is manifest to one's human experience is but the tip of an iceberg. Since for him nothing has changed, the old formulae of the way are valid. The results are never totally accessible to experience. This approach is not empirical but anchored in a belief system.

Teshuvah, askesis as means to atonement; the full practice of halakhic Judaism; the observances of the yearly cycle and of the tasks of the life cycle; daily study of Torah as God's will and wisdom are the basic requirements. Further steps, so Orthodox teachers maintain, can be taken only once this basic level of sine-qua-non observance is reached. Posthalakhic Jews will take other dimensions into consideration. These who participate in the *havurot* and *P'nai Or* constitute a rainbow of observance from halakhic orthopraxy to Zen-Judaism. Most people who have found their way to these forms, be it from exposure on the West Coast to the Aquarian *minyan* of Berkeley, to the *minyanim* in West Mount Airy in Philadelphia, have had some form of psychotherapy to focus them on their inner life. This makes them see issues and patterns in their lives in terms of unrealized human potential—and not in terms of deviations from observance that need to be atoned for by fasting and more zealous committment to *halakhah*.

Seeing their prayers together as part of other shared life events, they feel that they can, in their relatively small and intimate groups, share their inner process and gain help from their fellows. They design High Holy Day liturgies as purgative and committing processes and share the recipes of what-works-for-me with one another (see *Jewish Catalog* and its bibliographies). Even though the posthalakhic Jew does not consider hirself bound by *halakhah* she/he will draw on the deep structures of the tradition, on expanded and adapted versions of the tools of the spirit, the chief of which is the examination of one's conscience in various forms.

HESHBON HANEFESH, THE EXAMINATION OF CONSCIENCE, AT THE BEDTIME SHEMA

"Let us examine our ways and scrutinize them and return to our God" (Lamentations 3:40). One does not wait for Yom Kippur as the only time during the year to examine one's conscience. The eve of the new moon, Thursday night, eve of the sabbath, the time immediately before the sabbath, and every night before one retires, one is to examine one's conscience. This is traditionally done by looking for infractions of/ against the Code of Jewish Law. Remorse and regret, affirmed and felt, prepare the way for making a firm commitment not to do so again. One needs to forgive others and recites the following formula: Master of the Universe! Behold I forgive anyone who has angered or frustrated me, who has sinned against me in thought, word or deed . . . whether in this incarnation or in any other, may no person be punished on my account . . ."

One needs, of course, to gain insight into one's patterns, and it may be that the intentions alone are not enough. One of the modern favorite ways dealing with self witnessing is:

THE JOURNAL

Entries here can run the range from a *"Beichtzettel,"* a list of acts to confess, to deep meditations in writing. The function of the journal is not only getting one to witness one's inner process, but also upon rereading and reconsidering the journal, for patterns to emerge. These can be dealt with more radically than our individual transgressions. Here it is not enough to offer remorse. The purgative measures sought by most posthalakhic Jews will be from the arsenals of psychotherapy and growth techniques as informed by the *Kabbalah* as well as by clearing with the members of one's reference group.

THE BUILDING OF DEVOTION

The heart needs to love, to emulate an adored model. If God as person were to face us in a tangible and sensory way we would not need to work on making ourselves present to Him/Her. In the past we looked for the highest in the models of our society and came up with parent, king, and judge. These models became the root metaphors into which we entered via emotional emulations. They took us to polarized extremes most easily available in the feudal systems. They also produced action directives most often urging our submission to God's providence. Traditional prayer was often a form of apple polishing and soft soaping of the exalted authority person.

When people signed letters with, "Your most obedient and humble servant," it fit to use such expressions. Besides, the feudal, traditional models no longer are available to us in real beings. Presidents are not kings, parents are much more fallible to post-Freudians; judges are seen often as autocratic and worse, corrupt. The devotional vocabulary is today very anemic. Without generating and nurturing a grateful attitude toward the Source of Life, prayer becomes barren. The masculine imagery connected with God is also a source of much pain and difficulty, and to this day is being used to deny access to women who wish to serve in sacerdotal capacities.

Somehow, chanting the words of the classical prayer books in one of the melodic modes of the tradition makes them more connotational and thus transparent to one's heart than reciting them as speech. Paradoxically, at times, significance and emotional focus is heightened by using the sacred language instead of the vernacular. This helps in corporate worship as well as in solo prayer. Another way utilized by some is the "arrow prayer"—short exclamations, like sighs addressed to God in one or another of His/Her Names or Attributes. This helps in directing affect focus to experienced attributes. Let's say I am in need of guidance and sigh: "Oh Guide, Oh Light, Oh Helper!" The attributes invoked ad lib in free experience or according to a traditional pattern: Oh Goodness, Oh Power, Oh Heart, Oh Order, Oh Harmony, Oh Life, and Oh Majesty, help in the arousal of affect. The psalter is still a very effective help when it is not merely recited. Each psalm is someone's experience with God. By placing oneself in the position of David upon being set free by Abimelekh after having feigned idiocy, it is easier to recite "I sought YHVH and He answered me, saving me from all my opponents" (Psalm 34).

Monists find the devotional way difficult, yet they miss the way of the heart. It is not easy to love the self in the way in which one loves another. It may be that for most souls the experience of devoutness is only accessible in the I-Thou relationship. Yet all love comes from the love of self: "Thou shalt love thy co-person—as thy-Self-I-AM-YHVH." The radically monistic realm is still too esoteric for most of public conversation.

The prayer of realm of the mind concerns itself with locating the person in the reality maps that are centered in God. In Jewish prayer cosmological considerations form the first phase of the blessings of the *shema*. Here the stars and planets, the seraphim and *hayot* call to each other the thrice holy-*Kadosh Kadosh Kadosh* YHVH *tzebaot*, the whole universe is filled with God's glory. Once this is seen by the mind's eye and gets consent and affirmation by the person, she/he moves to the next phase, which deals with revelation. The mind considers the immense love of God that manifests in the sharing of His/Her will and wisdom. This consideration prepares the person to receive the flow of continuous revelation as it manifests in "what I command you this day." The affirmation of the *Shema Yisrael*, the central unification of the prayer, leading one to "accept the yoke of God's kingdom and the yoke of God's commandments" is followed by affirmations of past and future redemption.

The weekday *Amidah* prayer contains petitions for oneself and for all of Israel and humankind. Here one sees oneself in most intimate closeness with God and invited to make present one's needs form the mundane to the loftiest concern for all beings. The *Amidah* prayer is in the realm of the divine essence, beyond mind and heart. The late lamented Rabbi Aryeh Kaplan in his works on Jewish meditation has described many helpful suggestions for making this daily prayer experience powerful and real. After the *Amidah* one tarries and brings down into the regular consciousness the sparks of holy light and insight gained in the ascent.

Of Times and Seasons

Dawn and dusk are the natural times in which we would join not only the choirs of angels and archangels but also of insects, amphibians, birds, and mammals. The sanctus is a law revealed by nature, echoed in the Bible, where in Leviticus we are bidden to offer a lamb at dawn and one at dusk. Services that begin at eleven o'clock in the morning cannot offer the same natural lift that a vigil for the dawn supplies.

Thus prayer, meditation, spiritual practice at these times are more potent. The social compulsions of commodity time are set aside, and organic time is in force. This has great healing power and realigns the person to his/her God. Once rhythms of body and soul, of person and group, of male and female within the same person, and in relationships are part of one's primary experience, the teachings of the calendar, the flow of the liturgical year, begin to make a natural sense. "Teach us to number our days that we may get us a heart of wisdom" (Psalm 90:12).

Cycles of the year and in life's stages are sure guides to the growth of the soul.

Of the Resources

People

Rabbi Abraham Joshua Heschel of Aptow taught: "Prayer cannot be learned from books. It can only be learned from a praying person." People often turn to people who can talk about prayer first. It needs to be realized that the service of the heart and the soul differs from the service of the mind. The credentials of the spirit may often reside in simple people. Many are the hasidic tales speaking of the learned who humbled themselves in order to learn from children and seeming ignoramuses.

One who looks for a model might find such a one in a house of worship, make contact with him/her and have shared prayer. One teacher of the Holy Way urged one of his disciples to share one prayer book with a simpleton. The student later confessed that only now did he understand what he found in books about prayer.

Literature

Every synagogue and church library contains valuable volumes. There are also "head" book shops full of self-help material from medieval classics to *A Lazy Man's Guide to Enlightenment*. It is essential that one find a friend with whom one can discuss the spiritual diet. People fancy prescriptions that seem extraordinary and close to the bizarre. Common sense is a better guide than exotic nostrums.

And Last but not Least, the Body

From Feldenkrais to Rolfing and Bio-energetics, from jogging to Tai-Chi and calisthenics, the testimony of the practitioners is that there are spiritual effects resulting from conscious and exerting body movement. Many who have watched *hasidim* at prayer have wondered about the function of their rhythmic swaying. The whirling dervishes of the Mevlevi order and the *hasidim* share in their appreciation of the body as it becomes reinvigorated in the service of God. Perhaps this is what Rabbi Pinhas ben Yair meant in his statement, "The Holy Spirit leads to the resurrection of the dead."

18

INTRODUCTION: DAVVENOLOGY AND THE FOUR WORLDS

The need for a new *siddur* has arisen from the times in which we live and the changes we are experiencing in our doing, feeling, thinking, and being. Certainly, after Auschwitz, Nagasaki, the Moonwalk, and our tapping into the Global Brain, we have become aware of a cosmology that is radically different from the Ptolomaeian understanding of a geocentric world surrounded by circling spheres.

The last time the whole notion of *siddur* was examined was in the time of Rabban Gamliel II, in the second century C.E. Since then, the structure of the *siddur* has been elaborated upon and content has been added, but its function, language, and relevance has not been reexamined.

Prayer in Judaism has never yielded to the usual descriptions of prayer as worship, devotion, etc. God-talk has had its theology; the psyche, psychology. But until now, *davvenen*, the Jewish liturgical life beyond prayer or worship, has not had its " . . . ology." So we have created a davvenology. In this *siddur*, the work of the *P'nai Or* Religious Fellowship, the methods and processes of *davvenen* have been analyzed and recombined to create a psychospiritual process that can be applied in social settings of *havurah minyanim*.

These methods, applied by people who have come in contact with *P'nai Or davvenen* retreats, have been tested in various settings involving people of different age groups, social status, and levels of education.

They have also been taught in rabbi-training workshops, and have been used and applied by many *havurot* in North America.

The new *siddur* is characterized by:

1. An understanding of the psychospiritual process of ascending "Jacob's Ladder."
2. A recasting of the language that, in old *siddurim*, is often gender-related to masculine elite terminology.
3. A new understanding of the human, which enables the praying person to see him/herself in terms of wellness and Creation's original blessing, rather than a worthless and sinful worm.
4. A new emphasis on our relationship to nature and the ecology, and a freeing of our understanding of God from the feudal power position so that we can perceive the Sustainer and Nurturer of the planet.
5. A reintegration of body and soul so that they are organically in harmony and reintroduction of the body into the prayer process, using techniques we have learned from Hasidism, Yoga, Feldenkreis, and Alexander Technique.

We decided to concentrate our efforts on the *Shabbat Shacharit* (morning) service, to enable us to work on a service that is both paradigmatic (it has the four levels corresponding to the Divine Name), as well as useful to the many people who wish to free themselves from the "junior congregation" liturgical style to one of empowerment and the ability to experience the full range of Jewish spirituality.

The Jewish service is intended to attune us to the four levels of divine manifestation. It deals with the person as a quadrinity: body, emotions, intellect, and spiritual-divine essence:

1. We begin our prayer by focusing our attention on the body with the *Birkat HaShachar* (dawn prayers).
2. We then open our feeling nature in the *Pesukey DeZimrah* (songs of praise) in order to celebrate, rejoice, worship, and adore the One.
3. We then give to the intellectual part of our being the inner space to stretch to cosmic proportions in the *berakhot*, the blessings, before and after the *Shema*, and in the *Shema* itself.
4. Finally, in the *Amidah*, we intuitively enter the innermost realm of private intimacy with God.

With this schema in mind, we can now focus our attention on some of the details of each domain and the considerations we attend to as we dis- and re- assemble the *siddur* for our use.

THIS IS A SHABBAT MORNING SIDDUR

We believe that there is today a great and pressing need felt by our constituency for a manual for use on *Shabbat* morning. Friday night, as it is celebrated in homes with a service preceding it, permits greater freedom; the service is not inhibited by the strong model that has kept North American Jews in its grip, starting from junior congregation and *bar* and *bat mitzvahs* led by rabbis and cantors.

Shabbat morning's shared worship experience needs more structure and modeling. We have, at services at *Beit P'nai Or*, at retreats, in outreach work, and at services at affiliated and parallel *minyanim*, followed our urgings, insight, and hearts. We also followed the guidance of masters of Jewish mystical prayer, as well as what we had empirically learned about the process of the spirit in groups, to build our understanding of the process of davvening. This is how we developed our davvenology. This *siddur* is based on it.

The *Shabbat* morning prayers have a more conceptual and intellective texture, while those of Friday night are characterized by a more affective and feeling flow. Thus, Friday night celebrates God and creation in a manner of coming home to Mother *Shekhinah*, meeting the feminine in the divine. *Shabbat* morning, on the other hand, takes us to Torah and Revelation and to God as the "Ancient of Days." (*Shabbat* afternoon takes us to "Israel," Redemption, and to God immanent in small things.)

THE FOUR WORLDS

"Behold there is a ladder standing firmly set groundward and its head reaches heavenward and God's messengers are rising up and nethering down on it."

This sentence from Jacob's vision has been used to describe the process of prayer. The *Zohar* suggests that the ladder has Four Rungs and that the phrase *olim veyordim bo*, "rising up and nethering down on it," can also be read as "rising up and nethering down on the *vav*" (*bo*). The dot near the *vav* can be above the letter, next to it, or below it, corresponding, according to R' Aaron of Karlin, to the knowing, feeling, and doing centers. The service is intended to rouse and attune us to the four levels of divine manifestation. It deals with the person as a quadrinity: body, feelings, intellect, and spiritual-divine essence.

For the Kabbalist, the four letters of the name of God, *Yud-Heh-Vav-Heh*, together symbolize a gestalt in which each letter represents a World, or rung of Jacob's ladder.

MANIFESTATION			WORLD
	Y		
	YYY		
Essence-Being	Y		*Atzilut* — Fire: I Am That I Am
	H		
	HHHHHHH		
Knowing	H	H	*Briyah* — Air: S/He-Me
	H	H	
	H V	H	
	VV		
Feeling	V		*Yetzirah* — Water: I-Thou
	V		
	V		
	H		
	HHHHHHH		
Doing	H	H	*Assiyah* — Earth: I-It
	H	H	
	H	H	

The World of the lower *Heh*, the World of *Assiyah*, is where we live with our bodies. It is this world, that of sensible, concrete facts and their data. The laws of nature as we observe them operate here. It is here that we encounter the angels on the lowest rung of Jacob's ladder, our body angels, whom we give life through the traditional morning service opening—the *birkot haShachar*, which we accompany with our movements and postures. We experience our body in its perfection, with its ducts and passages; we direct our attention to our cycling breath, our senses; and we participate consciously in healing it where it is needed, and get its consent for further prayer. We become conscious of our garments, of our freedom to move; we love the firm ground under our feet and feel the power and the glory of being one who wrestles with God, free, in the divine image, and renewed in strength and awakened for this day. *Assiyah* is the world of Buber's I-It, in which we are the objects of Creation.

The *Vav* of the Holy Name represents *Yetzirah*, the world of vital feelings, where affect works in the imaginal realm. This means more than just visualization. It includes, in addition to the visceral, the muscular, balance, groundedness, feelings of warmth and cold, etc. Here, our emotional being is attuned, the negativity of resentments, frustrations, vindictiveness, and paranoia is replaced by an attitude of gratefulness and joy. As this occurs, we open ourselves to the pain of our fellow beings, and we become aware of our own mortality and smallness in the grand scheme of eternity. This awareness places us squarely in the present. Much of what we feel, and as a result do, is energized by this world. Here we are commanded to love, to be "in awe," to "cleave to," to appreciate and be grateful. In the *siddur*, it is the *Pesukey Dezimrah*, with its singing, dancing, reciting, and chanting of psalms and outpourings of love and joy that brings us to this state. No wonder this section has become the largest one in the *siddur*! The contributions contained herein reflect the creativity of many people; we invite you to use your own creativity as well. This fluid world—the element of water—is the domain of meeting and sharing with others whom one regards as peers, as in Buber's concept of I-Thou. Here, we bring all of our warmth to God, the Eternal Thou indwelling in all of those with whom we share the prayer experience. Our meditations may here be shared with others in dyads and triads.

The upper *Heh* represents the world of the intellect, of pure thought, where the thought behind all Creation is at home. Here we are commanded to exert ourselves to know and to reach the very edge of what is thinkable and understandable. "Know the God of your ancestors" addresses us. Here we know even that which is usually accepted as tradition, as that of the "God of your ancestors," and beyond our own experience. There is a love in understanding, and a great delight in knowing all we can about the divine in our lives. Many times we turn prematurely to faith when we could reach deeply with our reason and intellect. We need understanding as we need air to breathe. In prayer there is the additional insight to be experienced in the ONE of the *Shema*, who is also the ONE of the *Barukh/Berukhah Shem Kevod*. We understand ourselves as being the result of intended, loved, and continuous creation. And when we experience ourselves as creatures, then we are in the realm of the S/HE-me relationship. So the mode of prayer in the *Shema* and its blessings is more meditative and more deeply experienced within. This is the place where guided meditation works well.

The *Yud* of the divine name represents the world of *Atzilut*, the element of fire, of intuition, of being a spark of God's fire. It is here, in the *Amidah* prayer, that an individual's I-AM is identical with the Cosmic I-AM. It is not we who pray; rather, God prays in us, in accordance with the prefatory prayer, "Yah, open my lips and let my mouth tell Your praise." Here, with God's own Eye, we see ourselves before God's own Eye. Though words are incapable of addressing the experience of being in the World of *Atzilut* and in fact remove us from the experience, they are given to us to cover our deep interior present-being with the *Shekhinah*. The *Amidah* is thus where we stand in God.

This is the scheme of the *Shacharit* as the Kabbalist saw it. It follows a universal scheme, like that of the four Yogas, where we Do, Feel, Know, and Are for God. This *siddur* will guide you through this scheme of the Four Worlds by providing several alternative approaches that you may select, according to your needs and inclinations. And it will help you to integrate your physicality, emotions, and intellect in your davvening. Each section of the *siddur* entrains you differently.

The morning *berakhot*, blessings, call on conscious focusing in the body, asking it for its messages and responses. The *siddur* will help you to become aware of what it is that your body is revealing to you.

When you move to the *Pesukey DeZimrah*, the songs of praise, with its emphasis on the affective, attitudinal and emotional, you will bring your body awareness with you and periodically attune to it in order to use it as a *merkavah*, a vehicle for the feelings to which you will now want to direct your attention.

Moving then to the third phase, the *Shema* and its blessing, the intellective level, you will want to maintain your awareness of the sensory and the affective-feeling levels in order to give the intellect and its way of being with God a good base. The amor dei intellectualis, the intellectual love of God, is seated in the warmth of the heart and its love, as well as on the vital aliveness and the sensory, close-to-ecstasy loving of the body.

Rising for the *Amidah*, you maintain that equipoise of body, heart, and mind to give the higher self—the ever God-connected spirit—the intuitive—the soul-God particle—the cosmic hologram—the opportunity to reach the rest of your awareness and to express your wholeness and needs to the cosmos in its merging-*d'vequt* connection.

After the *Amidah* there is a bit of lingering in that space that the Kabbalists called *Sheerit HaAtzilut*, the remaining imprint of that momentous and numinous encounter with divine identity. Then begins the descent into your daily life. This, too is done with slow care so as to gather from each level the insights and action-directives that constitute a part of the response to your prayer. Thus you review the concerns that you placed before God, the insights that the One of the *Shema* brought you to, what you felt you needed to do as your part in making this life "heavenly days right here on this earth." Then you hug the warmth of the grateful praises of the Halleluyahs, the moments of yearning for greater harmony with God's purposes, and you check again what it was that you promised your body to do as a response to its messages.

The *siddur* contains suggestions for the use of dyads and other small group ways of davvening. While some of us are adept enough to bypass the ego's blockade of the access to the Divine Self directly, many of us find it easier to do this by addressing the divine in each other. The directions in the *siddur* are graphic and clear. While one can *davven* the sections so marked by oneself in solo or choral fashion, many will find that it works so much better when done as dyadic I-Thou dialogues.

When you work in dyads, respond to the other focusing on the God within him/her, and recite alternately. Dyads may be used in other sections of the service than what is suggested in the *siddur*. For example, during the *Shema* and its blessings one partner may read while the other is free to concentrate on the nonverbal and visual elements of the prayer. Then they can either switch or make affirmations: you begin by stating half a credo sentence, which your partner finishes. This will open you and your partner to surprise and astonishment. Or, you can use the following form:

First Person: *Shema*, (name of partner)
Both: *Yah Eloheinu*
Second Person: *Yah Echad/Achat.*

Second Person: *Shema*, (name of partner)
Both: *Yah Eloheinu*
First Person: *Yah Echad/Achat.*

Repeated challenge and naming raises the partners to heightened awareness.

In triads, as in dyads, the partners alternate. For example:

First Person: *Yah Melekh*
Second Person: *Yah Malakh*
Third Person: *Yah Yimlokh*
All Together: *Le'olam Va'ed.*

At times, for example when working with a group composed of both Jews and non-Jews, it may be more appropriate to use a chant such as:

First Person: The fullness — God
Second Person: The void — God
Third Person: This moment — God
All Together: And eternity.
             or
First Person: It is perfect,
Second Person: You are loved,
Third Person: All is clear,
All Together: And I am holy.

At times you might form a *Magen David* of two triads, a powerful exercise.

We welcome you to explore, expand the parameters of your own ways of *davvenen*, and to approach joyfully the human-God and human-human encounter with all your body, all your heart, all your mind, and all your soul.

19

DAVVENEN POETRY

Current rendition in consultation with the spirit of Rabbi Israel al Najara.

> Yah Ribon Olam ve'olmaya
> Ahnt hu malko melekh malkhaya
> Ovad gevurtekh vetim'haya
> Shefar kadamak lehahvaya

Yah Ribon Olam — the countless worlds' Source
All the realms of life they do belong to You
wondrous are the words of Your potent force!
Delightful it is for us that we worship You!

Serenades we offer You at dusk and at dawn
To You Holy God I render them and sing
You dwell in heart of friend, in Seraph and in fawn
in lilies, in cedars tall and in doves on wing!

Raiser of the meek and humbler of proud
So varied are Your creatures — so vast is their amount
If thousands and thousands of years thousand of poets would shout?
The glory that's Yours alone they could never recount.

All Honor to You God, All splendor Yours and might!
Redeem us, Holy God, bring us home to our place
help us we are Your people take note of our plight
Let all Your created ones rejoice and delight in Your Grace.

Let Your Glory return to the all-holy shrine
To Jerusalem holy that to all of us belongs.
The place where all peoples attain joys sublime
We will sing to You hymns of love and anthems in chorus and song.

YAH EKHSOF NOAM SHABBAT
Shabbat hymn by the great Reb Ahron of Karlin, נבנ״ם זי״ע

י   א   נ

Yah! How I long for the bliss of the *Shabbat,*
united in secret with Your own fervent wish.
Give way to Your own deep desire to love us.
May Sabbath in Torah be our sacred bliss.
Share Her with us who desire to please You —
Our deep thirst for union be met with delight.

ש   ה   ה

Holy Presence that fills time and space!
Keep safe who keep *Shabbat* in their longing all week.
Like a deer that seeks water by the banks of the river,
We seek *Shabbat,* the secret of Your sacred Name!
Grant us all week long Her shimmering Presence,
So our hearts and our faith be pure service to You!

מ   ר   ו

Warmly embrace us with Your kind compassion,
Quench quickly our thirst for Your unending Grace.
Give us the bliss drink from Eden's own river.
Your praises we sing with joy on our face.
Let Jacob's gift to us — echo all week long
Infusing our lives with a Shabbes-filled trace.

ה   נ   ה

Hail Shabbat, delight of our souls and our Spirits.
Ecstasy life-throb I am awed by Your love,
Secure in Your caring there is safety and nurture —
You feed us sweet nectar from Your Source above.
As You embrace us with Mothering comfort —
In You I take refuge and pledge You my love.

אברהם בן עזרא
לבי ובשרי ירננו אל צֿ חי

א

צֿ אחד בראני
ואמר חי אני
כי לא יראני
האדם וחי

All potent God! You made me
"Alive I am," You told me
Yet no one's eyes can see Me
remaining flesh—alive

לבי ובשרי
ירננו
אל צֿ חי

my heart and my flesh
they sing to You,
to You the Source of Life!

ב

ברא כל בחכמה
בעצה ובמזימה
מאד נעלמה
מעיני כל חי

Brought forth we were by intent
in counsel and consent
yet hidden is the plan's intent
from us who are alive

ר

רם על כל כבודו
כל פה יחוה הודו
ברוך אשר בידו
נפש כל חי

Resplendent in Your glory
all tales are but Your story
praise to You who is pouring
into our souls our life

ה

הבדיל ניני תם
חוקים להורותם
אשר יעשה אותם
האדם וחי

How generous on Your side
To teach us laws which guide
those who by them abide
as sources of good life

ס

מה זה יצטדק
נמשל לאבק דק
ואיככה יצדק
לפניך כל חי

Might we be ever right
and live all in the light
what am I but a mite
and yet You give us life

ב

בלב יצר חשוב

כדמות חמת עכשוב

ואיככה ישוב

הבשר החי

Born 'though we are of passion
at times we lack compassion
if only we could fashion
a God-filled way of life

נ

נסוגים אם אבו

ומדרכם שבו

טרם ישכבו

בית מועד לכל חי

Near God to be we yearn
From wicked ways to turn
before bodies to dust return
and souls to the Source of Life

ע

על כל אהודך

כל פה תיחדך

פותח את ידך

ומשביע לכל חי

Every way will I adore You
my fervent prayer implores You
to open my path before You
to sate my soul with life.

ז

זכור אהבת קדומים

והחיה נרדמים

וקרב הימים

אשר בן ישי חי

Zeal filled our sires with fervor
do rouse us from our torpor
and help us meet our saviour
Of Jesse's stock—in Life

ר

ראה לגברת אמת

שפחה נואמת

לא כי בנך המת

ובני החי

Remember! we kept Your trust
May Your response be just
and being fair You must
decree us toward life

א

אקוד על אפי

ואפרוש לך כפי

עת כי אפתח פי

בנשמת כל חי

Awed am I, amazed at You
my arms I raise in pray'r to You
my mouth will sings its praise to You
Oh Source and Soul of Life!

Nishmat Kol Hay
נשמת כל חי

For simultaneous *davvenen* in Hebrew and English

נשמת כל חי	All breathing life
תברך את שמך	adores Your Name
יֵ' אלהינו	*Yah*, our God—
ורוח כל בשר	All flesh alive
תפאר ותרומם	is raised to ecstasy
זכרך מלכינו תמיד·	each time we become aware of You!
מן העולם ועד העולם	Beyond endless Time and Space that's vast
אתה אל	You are Divine
ומבלעדיך אין לנו	Only You are the One who
מלך גואל ומושיע	ultimately extricates and frees
פודה ומציל ומפרנס	ransoms, saves and sustains us
ומרחם בכל עת צרה וצוקה	and cares when we are in distress
אין לנו מלך אלא אתה·	You, You alone secure our lives.
אלהי הראשונים והאחרונים	You ultimate Cause and ultimate Effect,
אלוה כל בריאות	Source of all Creation
אדון כל תולדות	You manifest in all birthing
המהולל ברוב התשבחות	In every compliment it is You we praise
המנהג עולמו בחסד	You manage Your universe with kindness—
ובריאותיו ברחמים·	with compassion all beings in it.
וּיֵ' לא ינום ולא יישן	*Yah* ever awake and ever alert!
המעורר ישנים והמקיץ נרדמים	You rouse us from the deepest sleep
והמשיח אלמים	You give words to the speechless
והמתיר אסורים	You release the imprisoned
והסומך נופלים	You support the stumbling
והזוקף כפופים	You give dignity to the downtrodden
לך לבדך אנחנו מודים·	Every appreciation we offer is Yours.
אלו פינו מלא שירה כים	If ocean-full our mouth were with music
ולשוננו רינה כהמון גליו	Our tongues singing like the ceaseless surf

ושפתותינו שבח כמרחבי רקיע	Our lips praising You to the skies
ועינינו מאירות כשמש וכירח	Our eyes blazing like sun and moon
וידינו פרושות כנשרי שמים	Our arms spread like soaring eagles
ורגלינו קלות כאילות	Our legs sprinting like those of deer
אין אנחנו מספקים להודות לך	We could not thank You enough
יָ׳ אלהינו ואלהי הורינו	*Yah!* Our God, our parents' God!
ולברך את שמך	Neither could we celebrate by naming
אל אחת מאלף אלפי אלפים	the times exceeding millions
ורבי רבבות פעמים	the places exceeding billions
הטובות שעשית	the favors You did
עם הורינו ועמנו	for our parents and for us.

ממצרים גאלתנו יָ׳ אלהינו	*Yah!* Oh God! From oppression You redeemed us
ומבית עבדים פדיתנו	Now we can never be at home in slavery—
ברעב זנתנו ובשבע כלכלתנו	During famines You fed us enough to live on
מחרב הצלתנו ומדבר מלטתנו	You shielded us from wars and plagues
ומחלאים רעים ונאמנים דליתנו	From diseases of body and mind You pulled us out.
עד הנה עזרנו רחמיך	To this moment Your caring helped us
ולא עזבנו חסדיך	We never lacked Your kindness
ואל תטשנו יָ׳ אלהינו לנצח	—Please don't ever abandon us God!

על כן אברים שפלגת בנו	Our limbs want each to thank you
ורוח ונשמה שנפחת באפינו	The air of each breath You breathed into us
הן הם יודו ויברכו	Their very substance bless with gratitude
וישבחו ויפארו	with praise and celebration
וירוממו ויערצו ויקדישו	honoring that exalted holiness
וימליכו את שמך מלכינו	so majestic, that is Your fame!

כי כל פה לך יודה	Our speech is appreciation
וכל לשון לך תשבע	our expression an oath of loyalty
וכל ברך לך תכרע	our attitude surrender
וכל קומה לפניך תשתחוה	our stance before You obedience
וכל לבבות יראוך	our feelings overwhelming awe

וכל קרב וכליות יזמרו לשמך our inners singing scales of Your Names

כדבר שכתוב׃ As it is in Scripture:

כל עצמותי תאמרנה All my very essence exclaims:

יֱ מי כמוך *Yah!* Who? Like You?

מציל עני מחזק ממנו You inspire the gentle to stand up to the bully

ועני ואביון מגוזלו׃ The poor disempowered to stand up to the thug.

מי ידמה לך ומי ישוה לך No other can claim to be what You are

ומי יערוך לך הֱ הגדול No other can pretend to be THE GREAT GOD

הגבור והנורא ֱ עליון THE MIGHTY, THE AWESOME, THE GOD, MOST HIGH

קונה שמים וארץ Yet nesting in Heavens and Earth!

נהללך ונשבחך ונפארך So we will keep celebrating and delighting

ונברך את שם קדשך כאמור and blessing Your Holy Name with David:

לדוד ברכי נפשי את יֱ "*Yahhh!* breathes my soul out to You.

וכל קרבי את שם קדשו׃ all my inners pulse with You!"

הֱ בתעצומות עוזך Potent God Force!

הגדול בכבוד שמך Magnanimous in Glory

הגבור לנצח Ever prevailing

והנורא בנוראותיך Awesome Mystery!

המלך היושב על כסא רם ונשא Majestic One, who presides over all destiny!

שוכן עד מרום וקדוש שמו Eternal *Shekhinah*, Holy Beyond

וכתובי רננו צדיקים בֱ׳ Saints sing *Yah!*

לישרים נאוה תהלה In harmony with decent folks.

בפי ישרים תת רומם Good people exalt You

ובדברי צדיקים תת ברך Saints are Your blessing

ובלשון חסידים תת קדש Devotees sanctify You

ובקרב קדושים תת הלל You delight in our inner holiness.

Barkhi Nafshi
ברכי נפשי את יָהּ

Psalm 104: For simultaneous Hebrew and English *davvenen*

ברכי נפשי את יָהּ	*Breath of mine bless my* Yah
יָהּ אֱלֹהַי גדלת מאד	Yah *my God so vast and great*
הוד והדר לבשת:	*All veiled in pride and glory!*
עוטה אור כשלמה	Wrapped in Light are You
נוטה שמים כיריעה:	The sky You spread—a sheet.
המקרה במים עליותיו	*Your upper chambers water roofed*
השם עבים רכובו	*Astride You sit on clouds*
המהלך על כנפי רוח:	*You waft on the wings of wind.*
עושה מלאכיו רוחות	The breezes You send are Your aides
משרתיו אש לוהט:	Your helpers—blazing flames.
יסד ארץ על מכוניה	*You founded Earth so sound*
בל תמוט עולם ועד:	*to outlast time itself.*
תהום כלבוש כסיתו	The abyss You covered like a mantle
על הרים יעמדו מים:	Water! On mountains rests.
מן גערתך ינוסון	*You sound a roar and they flee*
מן קיל רעמך יחפזון:	*Your thunder makes them shake.*
יעלו הרים ירדו בקעות	Mountains high and valleys low
אל מקום זה יסדת להם:	their places they assume.
גבול שמת בל יעברון	*You set them them limits they cannot pass*
בל ישובון לכסות הארץ:	*Never again to flood the land.*
המשלח מעינות בנחלים	Springs—flow into brooks
בין הרים יהלכון:	and snake between the mountains.
ישקו כל חיתו שדי	*All the wild of field drink there*
ישברו פראים צמאם:	*The beast there slake their thirst.*

עליהם עוף השמים ישכון
מבין עפאים יתנו קול:

By their shores dwell birds that soar,
sounding calls through leaves and reeds.

משקה הרים מעליותיו
מפרי מעשיך תשבע הארץ:

You drench the hills from Your Upper Chambers
From your hands' fruits the Earth is filled

מצמיח חציר לבהמה
ועשב לעבודת האדם
להוציא לחם מן הארץ:

You grow fodder for the tamed beasts
and herbs with human labor
to bring forth bread from Earth.

ויין ישמח לבב אנוש
להצהיל פנים משמן
ולחם לבב אנוש יסעד:

And wine—to delight the sad ones
and oil—that softens skin
and bread—that sustains the weak

ישבעו עצי ﬡ'
ארזי לבנון אשר נטע:

Even the trees you sate with sap,
the cedars You planted on the Lebanon.

אשר שם צפרים יקננו
חסידה ברושים ביתה:

There birds their nesting find
There storks find homes to rest.

הרים הגבוהים ליעלים
סלעים מחסה לשפנים:

Antelopes bound on the heights
marmots hide behind rocks.

עשה ירח למועדים
שמש ידע מבואו:

And the moon pulls tides and seasons
The sun knows where to set.

תשת חושך ויהי לילה
בו תרמש כלחיתו יער:

You darken dusk to night
the forest's night life stirs.

הכפירים שאגו לטרף
לבקש מﬡל אכלם:

The big cats cry for prey
praying God for their food.

תזרח השמש יאספון
ואל מעונתם ירבצון:

They return at the rising of the sun
to crouch once more in lairs.

יצא אדם לפעלו
ולעבודתו עדי ערב:

While humans go out to work
to their service—up to night

מה רבו מעשיך ﬡ'
כולם בחכמה עשית
מלאה הארץ קנינך:

How many things You do
So wisely are they made.
All Earth at your command.

זה הים גדול ורחב ידים   *This vast sea beyond all grasp*
שם רמש ואין מספר   *countless are the creatures in her*
חיות קטנות עם גדולות: *tiny ones and giant whales.*

שם אניות יהלכון   There go stately ships
לויתן זה יצרת   This Leviathan You shaped
לשחק בו: to play and romp therein.

כלם אליך ישברון   *They all rely on Your care*
לתת אכלם בעתו: *to feed them well each time.*

תתן להם ילקטון   You give to them and they take it
תפתח ידך ישבעון טוב: Your hand's gifts sate them well.

תסתיר פניך יבהלון   *You hide your face, they panic*
תוסף רוח יגועון   *You recall their breaths, they die*
ואל עפרם ישובון: *they return to their dust.*

תשלח רוחך יבראון   You send your spirit and they are
   re-created
ותחדש פני אדמה: So too You renew life on Earth.

יהי כבוד יְ לעולם   *Let Your glory* Yah *fill time and space*
ישמח יְ במעשיו: *Take Joy O* Yah *in what You do!*

המביט לארץ ותרעד   You look at Earth and she trembles
יגע בהרים ויעשנו: Hills You touch and they smoke.

אשירה ליְ בחיי   *I live Your song my* Yah
אזמרה ליְ בעודי: *My* Yah *I am Your tune.*

יערב עליו שיחי   Let my talking give You joy
אנכי אשמח בְיְ:   I am so happy my *Yah!*

יתמו חטאים מן הארץ   *I wish no sin exist on Earth*
ורשעים עוד אינם   *All wickedness were gone—*

ברכי נפשי את יְ   Bless that *Yah* my soul, my breath
הללויה ::   *Hallelu-Yah!*

Yom Zeh LeYisrael Orah Vesimchah: Shabbat Menuchah

Rabbi Yitzchak Luria

This version works best when sung to the Sephardic Flamenco tune
and the English version is done simultaneously with the Hebrew.

י

Your gift
    to those who strive with You
    is joy and light
    Shabbat Menuchah

Yom zeh leYisrael orah —
vesimchah Shabbat menuchah

צ

You revealed Your holy ways
    when we communed with You at Sinai
    Shabbat and other holy days
    we are to keep as You commanded
    You send your healing rays
    accept our human ways
    Shabbat Menuchah

ח

Charm is *Shabbat* for the heart
    for the poor and broken people
    if all week we were depressed
    additional souls are ours on *Shabbat*
    to help our anxious moods
    breathe a relaxing sigh
    Shabbat Menuchah

ק

The bride you blessed and sanctified
    all other days gave her their blessing
    in the sixth and final phase
    You finished global creation
    There found the sorrowing
    calm and security
    Shabbat Menuchah

ל

Forbidding every form of toil
    You in Your kindness have commanded
    regal auras shine from us
    when we keep *Shabbat* as is wanted
    I offer holy gifts
    a fragrant sacrifice
    Shabbat Menuchah

ו

What songs of love could I perform
    with rhythm and harmony and music
    to please your presence holy God?
    My soul delights in her surrender
Do Keep that promise God
    to your beloved folk
    Shabbat Menuchah

ר

Receive my worship blessed God
    as if it was my life I offered
    This restful, blissful *Shabbat* day
    with ample joy and sweet elation
    we feel secure and loved
    in Your protection God
    Shabbat Menuchah

י

Your salvation do we trust
    Yah God most powerful and mighty
    David's heirs — do send them soon
    to those who do transcend convention
    Let Freedom be proclaimed
    and with it space that's safe
    Shabbat Menuchah

א

Awesome God who is most High
    do look for us and give an answer
    redeem this troubled planet soon
    be kind and manifest Your caring
    revive our trust in You
    with light and blissfulness
    Shabbat Menuchah

ח

Cherish and Renew Your house
    enough the years it was in shambles
    With Your compassion Gentle God
    console the grieving ones in sorrow
    who puts her grief aside
    to sing You *Shabbat* songs
    Shabbat Menuchah

ז

In merit of this holy day
    keep us well in your remembrance
    protect and guard us wondrous God
    This day and every other day
    Beloved do respond
    and grant deliverance
    Shabbat Menuchah

ק

Could celebration's welcome song
   be heard by Israel and her neighbors
   When that vast vision is fulfilled
   and all the world is safe from terror
   Our light has dawned this day
   and shines in every way
   Shabbat Menuchah

1. YEDID NEFESH

י You who love my soul,
   Compassion's gentle source,
   Take my disposition
   And shape it to Your will.
   Like a darting deer
   I will flee to You.
   Before Your glorious Presence
   Humbly I do bow.
   Let Your sweet love
   Delight me with its thrill,
   Because no other dainty
   Will my hunger still.

ה How splendid is Your light.
   Which worlds do reflect!
   My soul is worn from craving
   For Your love's delight.
   Please, good God, do heal her
   And show to her Your face,
   So my soul can see You
   And bathe in Your grace.
   There she will find strength
   And healing in this sight.
   Her joy will be complete then
   Eternal her delight.

ו   What pity stirs in You
      Since days of old, my God!
      Be kind to me Your own child
      Begotten by Your love.
      For long and longing hours
      I yearned for your embrace
      To see my light in Your light
      Basking in Your grace.
      My heart's desire is
      To harmonize with Yours
      Do not conceal Your pity
      Hide not that light of Yours.

ה   Help, my Lover, spread
      Your canopy of peace,
      Enfold all human beings
      Give all pain surcease.
      Your presence on this earth plane
      Do make known to us
      And we shall respond then
      With song and with dance.
      Rush, my love, be quick,
      The time for love is now,
      Let Your gentle favor
      Grace us as of old . . .

Beyond I and Thou

יה אֵי איכה גואלי *Y ah*, my God where are You?
I call You as if from far

שוכן בלבי ולא ידעתי and You Redeemer dwell in my heart
so close and I know it not.

הנך נוכח בתוך תוכי **H**ere You are, present in my innermost

ואף בקצוי תבל שם and so too are You at the outermost edge,

אתה גוחי both Source of mine and goal!

ובתוך רגשי אתה המרגיש **W**here my feelings rise in me
there are You stirring me

ובתוך הרהורי שמת קנך nesting in the womb of my urges

הוי אתגעגע לראותך **H**ere, in my eye's pupil are You

ואתה שוכו בבת עיני and I yearn so much to make
You object of my sight.

מקדשך אשר בקרבי **M**y innards would become—if only pure—
how I would scour them—

אתאו נקות ולהקדיש Your sanctuary in me,
sacred by Your Presence

שא נא את ברכותך **Sh**ow me how to host You,
What a blessing!

והורני איך להאריחך Your nestling in my heart.

לוא היית חוץ ממני **L**ife of my life, You are within me

ולא עצמות בעצמותי so how could I meet You on the outside?

מה ישיר היתה פולחני לך **M**y song would be addressed to You

לשיר לך קילוסי שבח were You beside me
and not hidden in my voice.

זאת נכון ועוד אחרת **Z**oned in the point of knowing,
                              You hide in unseen splendor—
כי לך יאה עוז ותפארת   glorious as I seek Your Glory

לולא יצרי יבלבלני **L**ingering on Your threshold,
                                   my ego squats claiming to be
בחוטפו לעצמו נדבות פי   the legal tenant of Your home.

מה טוב שאתה בתו **M**ore I cannot con-fuse the two
תוכיותי
איך אבחיו בינך ואנוכיותי   who shimmer as one I-AMness

נא תראני איך לצאת **N**ever can I leave this labyrinth, my self
ממבוכתי   by myself
אז נקיה תהיה תפילתי **D**o help me sortie and free me.
וברכתי   Then my pray'r will be pure for You.

אפילו דברי אלו לא אדע **E**cho—are You the call or the answer?

                              Even these words are they mine
מי אמרם אני או אתה   or Yours?
הגידה לי את שנפשי אהבה **H**elp and tell me, Love of my Heart

האם אינך גם נפשי   Are You not also
וגם האהבה   the Love and the Heart?
יה יוצרי מה יש לי לתת לך **Y** *ah*! God, adored One.
                              I want to offer You
רק הרצון שרצוני יהי רצונך   a gift You will not spurn, Your will be
                              mine—is it not already so?
הוי נפשי אייתי **H**oly solitude, All One Al-one,
בהיותי לבדי   my sole One,
כי אתה בטחוני צורו ומשגבי   My soul's One, my part(ner)
                              My wholly—Holy Other—One.
אמן **A**MEN

20

AN AFFIRMATION ON THE
TREE OF LIFE

An affirmation is a positive thought that you consciously choose to immerse in your consciousness to produce a desired result.

I affirm the power of positive affirmations.

I affirm that the *Shekhinah* surrounds me and blesses me.

I affirm the lightbeings in God's service who support and guide me.

I affirm the blessing of Abraham and Sarah in my life.

I affirm the sacrifice of Isaac and God's power over my life and death.

I affirm God's holiness and my growth toward it.

I place my Self under the protection of the *sefirah* of *Keter*, which will shield me from all harm and neutralize it.

I invoke the flash of *Hokhmah* to align my intellect to clarity and purposefulness, to inspiration and realization.

I invoke the care of *Binah* to lead me to God's heart.

I invoke the abundance of *Hesed* to bring me to atonement.

I invoke the power of *Gevurah* to see me through trouble and lead me to redemption.

I place my Self at the compassionate heart of God's *Tiferet* and affirm the healing, balancing, and integrative centering light within me.

I support my Self on the pillar of *Netzah* channeling to me all manner of blessing and prosperity, and place it at the disposal of the redeeming Messiah, unfolding to witness the *Shekhinah's* residing in Zion.

I support my Self on the pillar of *Hod*, making order in my life, gathering all the forces from dispersion and settling them in the blessed Jerusalem where I offer my thanks to God's glory.

I base my Self on the foundation of *Yisod* to act righteously and justly, to assist all righteous effort in the world and to become peace-full to work for peace.

I affirm that *Malkhut*, the *Shekhinah*, is the one offering these affirmations in me and is attracting the flow of blessing to suffuse my life. Amen.

21

A SCORE

FOR THE *AMIDAH*

What follows is a "score" with which to pray the first blessing of the Amidah on many levels of action and meaning. Above the Hebrew word are the four levels of meaning traditionally wrapped into Pardes (reading up). Below it, reading down, are the four levels of reality in Kabbalah: the physical, Assiyah, represented by the body's muscle actions; the emotional, represented by feelings; the intellectual, represented by ideas; and the existential, Atzilut, represented by union with God in "being Godded."

This prayer, the Avot or "Forebears" prayer, has been scored in its traditional form with only three "fathers" mentioned aloud, and the four matriarchs consciously understood. Current practice in P'nai Or is to say the names of the matriarchs aloud as well.

	Barukh	Atah	Adonai
Sod mystery	*B-rokh*-in gentleness *Keter's* goodwill is available	To those who as sparks merge with the flame as one substance and being	
Drush inductive	Be drawn from the High place to the here and now	From *aleph* to *tav* through the 5 *heh* modifiers of speech	Contraction, expansion connection, expansion
Remez deductive	Let your blessing flow to the world	Through the I-Thou relationship	Name of God under the attribute of Mercy (Love 13 × 2 in relation: 26 YHVH)
Peshat simple meaning	Be worshiped	You	Who causes the present to be
WORD IN HEBREW	בָּרוּךְ	אַתָּה	יְיָ (אֲדֹנָי)
Sound 48	*Barukh*	*Atah*	*Adonai (Yah)*
Body do 24	Bow head and spine	Bow knees and pelvis	Stand up straight, raise eyes up
Emotions feel 12	Wait for being in touch with generosity in self and release flow	Focus on other, "Hey There" beyond details or names	Be in touch with the eternal as remembered from past and anticipated for future, yet NOW
Think-intend 6	To channel divine energies through self	To focus on God the person	His name involves Him in your life
be-intend 3	God: I want to be with this person	This person addresses Me	He calls Me by My Name

Sod mystery	*Elohim-HaTeva* both 86 *Gematria* Our very nature as souls is divine	Hence our ancestors' nature in all its variations was also divine — His plan of reality is begotten by the parents *Hokhmah* and *Binah*
Drush inductive	He is our God as we make Him ours	Yet He is also our parents' God and He is both the same as He was with them as well as different with each of them according as his or her personality
Remez deductive	My own personhood is consciously created and formed by Him, He has unique and special insights, feelings and tasks for me in this life	As He had for my ancestors and I want to stay in the tension of both what inheres in me as well as what tradition told me of Him
Peshat simple meaning	Our God	And the God of our parents
WORD IN HEBREW	אֱלֹהֵינוּ	אֲבוֹתֵינוּ · וֵאלֹהֵי
Sound 48	*Eloheinu*	*Velohei* *Avoteiu*
Body do 24	gesture of submission	
Emotions feel 12	He is checking me out; I am embarrassed and honored at same time	I feel awed at His connection with all my many ancestors. This moment is precious as the culmination of all that happened before
Think-intend 6	Everytime I do what He wants and submit to His judgment, He becomes mine in my surrender	He became my parents' God in their submission to Him
be-intend 3	I want to be His God, especially when he talks with Me	As I was his parents' God before

Sod mystery	The divine light manifests as light	The divine power limits as vessel	The divine light is scaled to illumine (not flood) us
Drush inductive	He forever expands	He forever concentrates	He forever integrates
Remez deductive	You want this world to be generous	You want this world to be self-sacrifice	You want this world to be busy and mundane
P'shat simple meaning	Abraham's (and Sarah's) God	Issac's (and Rivkah's) God	Jacob's (Rachel and Leah's) God
WORD IN HEBREW	אֱלֹהֵי אַבְרָהָם	אֱלֹהֵי יִצְחָק	וֵאלֹהֵי יַעֲקֹב.
Sound 48	*Elohei Avraham*	*Elohei Yitzchak*	*Velohei Yaakov*
Body do 24	raise right hand	raise left hand	put both over heart
Emotions feel 12	response to grace thanksgiving	response of awe to the tremendousness	response of joy to the beauty and compassion
Think-intend 6	I will follow Him like Abraham generously	I will follow Him like Isaac to the alter, despite my fears	I will follow Him like Jacob through a busy and often disappointing life being grateful for each up and down the ladder
be-intend 3	Yes my attribute of *Hesed* was/is in him	yes my attribute of *Gevurah* is/was in him	Yes my attribute of *Tiferet Rachamim* is/was in him

Sod mystery	The divine light	that makes space	and time	and person
Drush inductive	Who causes all processes	That give and nourish	that take and de- stroy	that still make it seem as one pro- cess
Remez deductive	The indepen- dent God	Who basks in His greatness	His might	and His mystery
Peshat simple meaning	The God	The great One	The mighty One	The awesome One
WORD IN HEBREW	הָאֵל.	הַגָּדוֹל	הַגִּבּוֹר	וְהַנּוֹרָא.
Sound 48	*HaEl*	*HaGadol*	*HaGibbor*	*VeHaNora*
Body do 24	raise hands	hold up the right	hold up the left	put both over heart
Emotions feel 12	response	to grace	to awe	to mystery of both together
Think-intend 6	I will serve Him by being	gracious	strong	and open to the astonish- ment of life
be-intend 3	So my attributes will be with this one too	*Hesed*	*Gevurah*	*Tiferet, Rachamin*

Sod mystery	The grace of Adam *Kadmon*	The grace of *Atzilut*	The grace incarnate in created beings
Drush inductive	source of superlatives	Source of all action	And of all beings
Remez deductive	Source of all highs	Who gives everything away without concern to withhold (and yet)	Possesses what he gives away
Peshat simple meaning	MOST HIGH GOD	WHO GIVES FREELY GENTLE GRACES	AND MAKES-OWNS EVERY BEING
WORD IN HEBREW	קוֹנֶה הַכֹּל . גּוֹמֵל חֲסָדִים טוֹבִים . אֵל עֶלְיוֹן		
Sound 48	*El Elyon*	*Gomel Hasadim tovim*	*Koneh hakol*
Body do 24	Hands point up	Hands open palm	arms sweep
Emotions feel 12	Opposite pole—lowest in chain of being—abasement	Receiving the flow gratefully	And assigning back to God all boons received
Think-intend 6	Focus on the unearned grace of all beginnings	Focus on divine need to give all	Recognize that all divine potential realized is still divine
be-intend 3	I want to dwell with that person in *Keter*	And give my All to Him/Her in *Tiferet*	Because I want Him/Her to be mine with that one's consent in *Malkhut*

Sod mystery	From the pre-conscious realm	to the loving space of mind	He activates *Netzach* and *Hod*	to effect the Union of *Yisod* and *Malkhut*
Drush inductive	He is the male	to the femaleness of souls	when they both come	there is transcendance
Remez deductive	He reexperiences of parents	the openness to Him Him the desire	which raised in	to redeem
Peshat simple meaning	He remembers	the grace of parents	and He makes come	the redeemer
WORD IN HEBREW	.וְזוֹכֵר	לְחַסְדֵי אָבוֹת	וּמֵבִיא	גּוֹאֵל
Sound 48	*Vezokher*	*Hasdei Avot*	*Umevi*	*Go'el*
Body do 24	raise head as in trying to remember	slowly move head down as if looking past parents to Adam and Eve	raise head as if to look straight ahead	and focus through third eye
Emotions feel 12	Grateful to parents who were in contact with God		grateful to	messiah persons
Think-intend	There is a web of events and persons extending from Abraham to *Mashiach*			intend 6
be-intend 3	Each single being I am re-member-ing as if I made a string of Pearls of parts of my Self			

Sod mystery	Then maintains loving contact with begotten souls in the doubleness—Of love mutality 2 × 13 = 26 YHVH		
Drush inductive	Even for the most particular effects	So that He has an answer to the challenge His name offers to Him	In the givingness that is in the center of love
Remez deductive	The final effect's of causes	So that His reputation as redeemer and promise keeper be vindicated	This He does by loving means
Peshat simple meaning	To their children's children for His Name's sake		In love
WORD IN HEBREW	בָּנֵי בְּנֵיהֶם	לְמַעַן שְׁמוֹ	בְּאַהֲבָה
Sound 48	*Livnei Veneihem*	*Lemaan Shemo*	*Be'ahavah*
Body do 24	into the future	and visualize the complete name as the center	Radiating warmth and light
Emotions-feel 12	Love for child multiplied	And suffused with holiness love and	
Think-intend 6	Through the chain of incarnations fulfilling His Name and intention willingly		
be-intend 3	And will bring each one in the end back to My Self because we are One		

Sod mystery	King in *At-zilut*	You help us in *Assiyah*	Save us in *Yetzirah*	and pushed us in *Briyah*
Drush inductive	You rule us by taking counsel with us	but not robbing us of our initiative teaching us Torah	and still not abandoning us in helplessness teaching us prayer	and shielding us by making us your hosts and giving us *mitzvot*
Remez deductive	When we see this happen we are in awe of the amazing way He governs	And even by our distractions and vicissitudes helps us in our journey	and extricates us when we seem hopelessly captive	and surrounds us with a protective screen and force-field
Peshat simple meaning	King	Who assists everyone	and saves the helpless	and shields the able
WORD IN HEBREW	מֶלֶךְ	עוֹזֵר	וּמוֹשִׁיעַ	וּמָגֵן
Sound 48	*Melekh*	*ozer*	*umoshia*	*umagen*
Body do 24	Assume dignified posture	feel arms and shoulders	spine	back
Emotions-feel 12	Awe	Helpfulness	Compassion	Security
Think-intend 6	He governs	Aids	Rescues	And protects them
be-intend 3	Thus I rule	and assist each one who expends all his own energy	and the one who cannot do anything for himself	and protects all from dangers they are unaware of

	Barukh	Atah	Adonai (Yah)	Magen Avraham
Sod mystery	*B'rokh*—in gentleness *Keter's* goodwill is available	to those who as sparks merge with the flame as one substance and being		*Keter's* compassion infusing with transcendent love and protection
Drush inductive	Be drawn from the high place to the here and now	from *aleph* to *tav* through the *heh*—5# modifiers of consonants	*Yud*-contraction, *Heh*-expansion, *Vav*-connection, *Heh*-expansion, thus does YHVH project the flow of compassion	With the *niggun* of *Hesed Avraham*
Remez deductive	Let Your blessings flow to the world	through the I-Thou relationship	Name of God under the attribute of Mercy. Love AHVH #13 /2 in relationship - YHVH #26	in the garden of Avraham
Peshat simple meaning	Be worshiped	You	Who causes the present to be	Shield of Avraham
WORD IN HEBREW	בָּרוּךְ.	אַתָּה	יְהֹוָה	מָגֵן אַבְרָהָם
Sound 48	Barukh	Atah	Adonai (Yah)	Magen Avraham
Body do 24	Bow head and bend spine	bow knees and pelvis	stand up straight, raise eyes up	Put right hand over heart
Emotions-feel 12	Wait and get in touch with flow of generosity in Self and release flow	focus on the "other" beyond name and form	get in touch with eternal as remembered from the past and anticipated for the future	Like Abraham in the furnace shielded by the protective aura of love
Think-intend 6	To channel divine energies through the Self	to focus on God the Person	Whose Name involves Him in my life	In the role of loving protector
be-intend 3	God; I want to be with this person	this person addresses Me	He calls me by my Name	I place him in my protection

22

An Open Letter to the Honorable Teddy Kolleck, Mayor of Jerusalem, and Anyone Who Would Like to Read Over His Shoulder

Honorable Mayor!

Please, lend me an eye and an ear and some time to imagine that the year is 5752 and you read the attached announcement.

There is a *yeshivah* where the *Kohanim* study to be able to act in the office of their priesthood, learning the laws of the various animal and other sacrifices that they might bring in a restored third Temple. There are some of us who intuit that this may not be God's will in the restored Temple, but only time and revelation will tell. Until we know for sure we must prepare for the day.

So the *Kohanim* must study the laws and rehearse the actions in order to be ready. The Levites, too, must be ready to make music. They may not be prepared unless they begin to study the dinim and to practice and rehearse.

And where are they to find the repertoire for their offerings? They could choose from a number of possible musical compositions from the past and arrange commissions and competitions involving all the *edot* of Jews. Since we take seriously Isaiah 66: 20–21, even non-Jewish compositions could contribute to God's greater Glory. We have music even for the commemoration of sad events, and could set *Kinot* and *Selichot* to music for the *sefirah* period and the Three Weeks. Festive occasions could be celebrated with even richer and more colorful musical offerings.

There are no halakhic problems with such an effort. It would give

Jerusalem a constant stream of esthetic spirituality to complement all the verbal-intellectual proclamations. Levite concerti would provide harmony and common rhythm, and could be broadcast worldwide via audio and video, giving other Jews a chance to participate in this weekly island of peace and elation.

This could be a source of great *Kiddush HaShem* if done right. A source of income for the Levites could be a form of *Maassar* (tithing) that would be a more immediately real form than the few leaves of vegetables separated from the weekly purchases. This project could bridge all levels of observance and commitment.

The Levitical council could also oversee a daily minyan at the *Kotel*, run according to a seven-year *shemitah* cycle. Each year another one of the *edot* could hold services in their classical *nusach*, where all those who wish to learn the *nusachot* could study. Such services could become the bureau of standards for *edot* just as the *Vaad Arba Aratzot* set and demonstrated the standards for *Nusach Ashkenaz* in Leipzig. In the seventh year a *nusach* of contemporary forms could be offered for the sake of stimulating further development of *Nusach HaTefillah*. All this and more could well become the possible nucleus of an esthetic renaissance for Judaism and Jews.

Do you think it worthwhile to appoint a commission to bring this to life? I will offer a fervent and musical *Mi Sheberakh* for you and the members of your task force.

Sincerely yours,
Rabbi Zalman M. Schachter-Shalomi

> > > > >COME LET US SING TO HASHEM< < < < <

DUKAN Ben ASSAF,
THE M'NATZE'AH OF THE LEVITE AVODAH ASSOCIATION IS HONORED TO ANNOUNCE
that there will be a performance of the Jerusalem Levite Symphony next Thursday Evening on the
Southern steps of the Temple Mount right after sunset. Open Seating.
The programme will — im yirtzeh Hashem — consist of:

The Ma'ariv Overture in B Minor..........Felix ben Menahem Halevi
Jerusalem Levite Consortium.

Kaddish............................Maurice Ravel
Kinoryahu Ben Hefetz, Violin Soloist.
Jerusalem Levite Consortium.
Psalm 23 (Chichester)...............Leonard Bernstein
Yossele Segal, Soprano Solo.
Musical Anshei Ma'amad of Jerusalem and Levite Choir.

> > > >This segment will be conducted by the composer in honor of his 75th birthday< < < <

Alenu.........................Ernest Bloch
From his Avodat Haqodesh.
Musical Anshei Ma'amad of Jerusalem and Levite Choir.

Intermission.

{Ma'assarot will be accepted at the Lishkah during this time and for an hour after the
performance}

Mi sh'berakh for participants and donors.
Hazzan Gronam Halevi Sa't, Baritone.
Motet on the Sidrah (a capella)...........Parshat B'shallah
Yohanan Sh.Nahal, composer...Hebrew arrangement, Shirah Geshuri.

Intermezzo LIKVHOD MIRIAM..........Battei L'viyah String Quartet
Yokheved Amramit, 1st Violin,
Batyah Far'oni, 2nd Violin,
Shifra M'yaledet, Viola,
Pu'ah Magdalit, Cello.

Yonah T'mimah.............Al Shabazzi, (Diwan)
in the mode of Hadramauti Jews.
Yehoram Ga'on, solo,........accomp. by Habrerah Hativ'it

My House Shall Be a House of Prayer for All Peoples.......Spiritual
Zion Gospel Singers of Germantown, PA.

Shiru Lahashem.............Yeshivah Rock Medley
in honor of Shabbat Shirah
B'nei Qorah Collective

This evening is sponsored by the Tor'mei Ma'assarot of Philadelphia, PA, USA.

23

TRANSCENDING THE *SEFER* BARRIER

Often what stands between a person and her or his tradition is the authentic form in which it is presented. In our case it is the Hebrew of the *sefarim*, the sacred texts, in which they have been preserved. People yearning to own their heritage find themselves locked out because of the חומת הספר , the *sefer* barrier. They are intimidated and often feel anxious and humiliated by an absent and often neglected Hebrew-school education. Frustrated that they were not taught effectively, they feel crippled and shamed by their inability to read and understand the texts that are reputed to hold the treasures they would wish to enjoy. Those among the committed and traditional people who wish to help them, go back to their own youth when they learned to read Hebrew and offer their methods to the seekers. Most often they uncritically apply what is fit for children and immature minds to sophisticated adults. This helps only those who persist heroically.

We have broken many a barrier; the sound barrier in flight is one example. There are many obstacles to breaking through habitual boundaries. Several barriers stand between the Jewish tradition and a modern, concerned, and committed Jew who has not learned Hebrew from his or her childhood. The usual Hebrew *Ulpan* is not very helpful in this case. It is concerned more with helping the student to get along in Israel and is distant from what is needed for religious and spiritual applications. There are some who have broken through this language barrier, but it took them an inordinate amount of effort and time. Many lose patience and hope, giving up the intense struggle with antiquated and infantilizing methods. Those who cannot read a text by themselves are always subject to other people's sectarian interpretations and pressures, which are often intended to build dependencies and partisan loyalties. The seasoned and matured life experiences of those who wish to learn Hebrew can give a new and vital slant to renew our tradition. What the traditional teachers could not surmise in a text a physicist or poet could enhance through their associations.

Alas! Unless they break the *sefer* barrier, they will look only at the available translations, and these are often stodgy. The translators tend to filter out what in their opinion won't enhance the reader's religious fervor, or what they believe will demean the stature of the text. Look at the *Shir HaShirim* in the ArtScroll *Siddur*, and the Soncino *Zohar* for examples of this type of translation filtered for children. The more sensitive of the seekers give up their search and drop out. This need not be if we create an institute for breaking the *sefer* barrier.

I will outline the feasible steps available to us at present at the state of the art of language instruction. We now have good means at our disposal. The first hurdle to overcome is

THE *SIDDUR* BARRIER

People would like to be able to *davven*. Those who cannot read the Hebrew letters could learn to do this in about 5 to 10 hours. Given that they are taught to write and draw the vowels and letters, they will learn to read faster. If this is done with an eye to the distinctions that make for character recognition between ס and ם or ע and צ or ב and כ , it speeds the process further.

We do not read English by laborious spelling out of the letters and forming them into words. As you read this you let your automatic mind do the actual reading while your conscious mind follows the sense. The function of our connecting the letters into words operates in the background of our consciousness. The sooner this happens with Hebrew, the greater the ease of learning the sense of the words. The best methods are to drive oneself to read past the point of boredom into fatigue. Then mercifully the body takes over and one can think of other things while the reading goes on. By rhythmic chanting instead of reading in straight voice, one gets past the point of boredom to a level of fatigue in which one reaches for the second wind. In this way both speed and accuracy are improved.

Soft and hardware tools, such as a Nintendo-type cartridge, could be developed that would pace a person to greater levels of speed. This type of technology is already in use leading to increased speed and accuracy in touch-typing instruction.

It is also important to free the readers from being locked into only one typeface and font so that one could easily show them the deep structure of the letters and the patterns they make in word sets by moving them to recognize

בָּרוּךְ אַתָּה - מֶ.לֶ.ךְ הָעוֹלָם
בָּרוּךְ אַתָּה - מֶ.לֶ.ךְ הָעוֹלָם
צָרוּךְ אֹתָה -- מֶ.לֶ.ךְ הָעוֹלָס
בָּרוּךְ אַתָּה -- מֶ.לֶ.ךְ הָעוֹלָם

and other fonts.

Beyond learning to draw, write, and read, there is a swift way to word recognition. The bulk of the *siddur* becomes accessible if one but learns to recognize about 200 verbs that make up the *siddur* vocabulary. The rest of the words become accessible through the context and with the help of a dictionary. Beginning with the roots מלכ and ברכ, and their many forms, one can make swift progress.

Given the current computer capabilities, e.g., HyperCard, one could create a database around the basic vocabulary so that, for instance, the words based on a root, say מלכ, could be fitted with a different letter form or font that links the root מלכ - מלך ומלכ מלך

מלכי המלכ° ם   מֶ.לֶ.ךְ - מֶלֶךְ - °מְלִי ךְ

מלכ ומ with the letters that conjugate and specify the meaning. Just making the root letters in a strong and bold style, and the assisting articles, performatives, and possessives, etc., in a hollow style, can make a large difference in the progress to the recognition of meaning.

The rabbinic formulae in the *siddur* are simple and iterative. The sections of the Psalms and other poetic books of the Bible appearing in the *siddur* double phrases such as אשרי יושבי ביתך and עוד יהללוך סלה. The context of the first part of the sentence makes it easier to understand the second. All of this, once shown to the student, will aid understanding.

A method of utilizing videotape and computer drill could allow one to break the *siddur* barrier in 2 to 3 weeks full time, or 4 to 5 weeks of 2-hour days.

The *Humash* Barrier

This the second phase of the "break the *sefer* barrier" work. Introducing additional drills for trope chanting in the reading and expanding the *siddur* vocabulary by an additional 200 roots as well as demonstrating other peculiarities of biblical Hebrew (such as the *vav consecutive* in the imperfect-durative tense), one can make further progress in a relatively short time.

The Rashi Barrier

A person who is shown how *Chancery Script* relates to 𝔬𝔩𝔡 𝔈𝔫𝔤𝔩𝔦𝔰𝔥 can soon see the similarities between Rashi and Torah script. Given that one also writes Rashi script with a wedge pen, one can see how the פ and כ were formed from the square type. The sensory-motor and the other proprioceptive learnings will have a holistic impact. Given that one could practice with a Mac, one could read a familiar text in several different fonts. Thus, reading the *Shema* and *Birkat HaMazon* in Rashi S"TaM, or cursive script, would soon build a large area of type recognition.

The Talmud Barrier

Moving from *Humash* and Rashi to other commentaries and to *Pirkei Avot*, it is easier each time to proceed from there to other *mishnayot* and *Midrash*. Starting from the Pesach *Haggadah* one can move to Maimonides and Codes with Talmud as the last and most advanced stage.

Sacred Poetry

Shabbat Zemirot and samples from the High Holy Day hymnody move the students into the rest of the *siddur* and *mahzor*, the *Selihot* and *Kinnot* at this point.

The Kabbalah and Hasidism Barrier

Texts such as Luzzatto's *Mesillat Yesharim* are beautiful and lucid in their style. Mordechai ben Yehezkel's *Sefer HaMasiot* and some of the hasidic tales are bridges to Pertez and Agnon. After some reading in these fields, some of the better translations from the medieval Judeo-Arabic can prepare the way to samples from the *Sefer Yetzirah*, the *Bahir*, the Hebrew sections of the *Zohar* and the *Shaarei Orah*, Cordovero's *Tomer Devorah* and Vital's *Shaar HaKedushah* to sections of the *Tanya* and *Humash Peninei HaHasidut*.

Aramaic

The more adept of the students can be introduced to the *Targumim*, *Aggadta* of the *Gemara*, the *Akdamot* and *Yah Ribbon* poems and pieces of the *Zohar*. And all this can be done in one intensive year.

A "Break-The-*Sefer*-Barrier Institute"

would in my dream be arranged as follows: The students would save during six years for a sabbatical year in Israel (presumably the institute would be located there). During this seventh year they would live in an environment that would, like an *ulpan*, use only immersion Hebrew for living and instruction. They would live in some form of community. Participants would encounter a variety of Jews, traditions, liturgical rites, formats, and *nus'chaot*. They would participate in various types of *davvenen* (such as Yemenite, Iraqi, etc.). The students would live a calendar year in the basic—maximalist as to form and ritual—traditions and would perform at least twelve hours of work daily, including services. The study hall would be equipped with network-linked Macintosh computers and interactive software. For classroom use with larger groups it would also have a computer-driven projection screen and would employ the function of a "Techno-scribe" (as demonstrated by Bernard DeKoven for corporate meetings). It would have tachistoscopes for speeding up character recognition. Those texts that are to be studied the next day would be piped into the sleeping quarters for hypnotic learning.

Because teaching is also a powerful way of learning, the faster students would tutor the slower ones. I take it that there need to be sections in which all proceed together and others where individualized progress could be made by *hevruta*—dyads or triads that are faster paced.

Texts would be introduced according to immediate application in the liturgical cycle. The winter months would give the program a chance to learn to handle increasing amounts of *hok leYisrael*, which contains a section for each day of the week, consisting of *Humash* with commentaries, *Nevi'im* with commentaries, *Ketuvim* with commentaries, and

Mishnah (each day another of the six orders of the *Mishnah*), followed by a section of Talmud *Aggadah* (from the same order). This in turn is followed by a section of Codes (Maimonides or *Shulchan Arukh*) and *Musar*.

By the end of the year the students would be able to handle these and other texts with ease and be able to return to their homes with Jewish skills brought up to a level harmonious with their other competencies.

THE MARKET

There are students who would want to take a year between high school and college, and there are those who would want a year between college and graduate school, etc. Credit for such a Break-the-*Sefer*-Barrier Institute—a model for other intensive language preparation—could no doubt be arranged with a host of collaborating institutions of higher learning. Other people in various stages of life could enjoy the possibilities of such a sabbatical. They could then devote—should they so desire—other sabbatical years to deeper and more extensive studies and creativity. Seminaries for cantors and educators and rabbinical schools could send their students to be prepared in such an institute.

THE OPPORTUNITY

Such an increase of ספר ידעי is critical for the reconstitution of an informed and potent laity for the meaningful survival of our people. One could not help but wish that this be implemented. We have the best minds and the technical know-how available to do this and to do it well. It would provide a תיקון to the ravages of past "Hebrew School" education and create model Jews to inspire others.

The *Klal Yisrael* (ecumenical) policy of such an institution would have to be maintained. Just as the CAJE conference has become a כלל ישראל forum, so would such an institute have to be hospitable to all wings of Judaism. Those of strong orthodox persuasion who would not be willing to study alongside women already have available many *yeshivot* where they could pursue their studies in their cherished ways. The Break-the-*Sefer*-Barrier Institute would also serve the orthodox *yeshivot* as a model. But the institute would in a manner—while maximizing the Jewish content—have to open to women in an egalitarian manner, to an ecumenical spirit and to modern scholarship. The needs of the people who would make such a commitment for ecological respect and maybe vegetarian food and spiritual practices have to be given caring consideration.

The tools are ready, the know-how is here; needed are the financial and personal resources. We could in a short time have an immense renewal. As Herzl has said, אם תרצו אין זו אגדה.

V

PARADIGM SHIFT

INTRODUCTION

THE TEXTURE OF TIME

I had an early intuition that time has texture. The conviction that the texture of time determines what happens in her field kept growing in me. When we left Austria, where I grew up, that perspective on history sought to understand what was happening to us "refugees." People spoke of the Hitler years as the "Birth pangs of the Messiah," and all of Jewish history was for me coming to its end when the late *rebbe* proclaimed in 1943 the imminent coming of the Messiah. Yet at the same time I was also learning about the ages as seen by the rabbis of the Talmud. These teachings were further implemented by teachings on epochs, eons, eras of varying and developing God Aspects, *partzufim*.

The sense that a new time was birthing was expressed by the "birth pangs" teachings.

As I reflected on the growth of my thought from the catastrophal "end of the world" feared during the Hitler years to the birthing of the "New Age," I realized that the thoughts about these issues represent meditations between contractions of the birthing of a new eon.

The reality maps keep changing to help us survive the crisis of all these pervasive changes. New readings of who and what we are are emerging as cosmologists and other thinkers teach us about Earth as *Gaia*, a living

Being, and the human adventure as the growth and awakening of the Global Brain.

The ideas growing out of the Kabbalah and the emerging understanding of the vast shift we are undergoing interwine in the writings offered here. Focusing on various specific topics, they have teachings on the paradigm shift as their underpinning.

I am indebted to Rabbi Gershon Winkler, who served as compiler-writer-editor of "New Myths and Reality Maps," chapter 30 of this volume.

24

An Interview with Zalman Schachter-Shalomi

The year 1983 was a stressful time for me, as well as a time for breakthroughs. I sat with friends. They pushed me on questions. The talk had an intimate, locker-room quality, which was not prettied up. It still has an authentic personal voice.

Growing Up

Tell us a little about your childhood. We know you grew up in Vienna, but beyond that, what can you add? Could you say a few words about your religious background?

My father, may he rest in peace, wanted me to go to the [Jewish] Gymnasium where we learned Hebrew and Latin. It was coed. But in the afternoon I went to Yeshiva Yesodei HaTorah. It was an old-style *yeshivah*.

What was your father's religious orientation?

My father really knew about davvening. He was a real *davvener*, especially when he led the community as the *hazzan*. I remember that when I was a kid, I once said to him, "Why are you crying, Daddy? Who hit you?"

And he replied, "I just talked to God."

And I said to him, "Does it hurt?"

And he said back to me, "No, it doesn't hurt when you talk to God. You're just sad because you've waited so long." On a child that makes a strong impression.

Was he a hasid?

Yes and no. On the one hand, he came from a line of *hasidim*. On one of the latest Belzer cassettes is one of my *alter zayde's niggunim*. On the other hand, he wore a velour hat, midnight blue, so that it could go both ways. He didn't want to be identified 100 percent with any one group. Now that we're talking about this, I feel that I've taken over his style.

Don't you also have a big velour hat?

Yes, I have one too, the kind that you can wear in Brooklyn if you have to. But it's just odd enough to give it away, to say, "Don't put your trip on me, I don't quite belong, I'm just passing."

How did your family end up in Vienna?

Papa left for Vienna half a year after I was born because the Polish army wanted to induct him. Mama came with me afterward.

Did you speak Yiddish at home?

No. My mother tongue was German. Yiddish was what my parents would speak if they didn't want me to hear, and by the time I got on to that, they switched to Polish. Yiddish came into my life when I went to Belgium in 1938. I was fourteen.

That's where I met a wonderful group of people who were into the Lubavitcher way. They had a workshop where they were cutting diamonds and learning at the same time. One guy was reading aloud to the others. I learned how to cut stones there.

Do you remember what they were studying?

Gemara. And Tanya was very strong. They gave me my first Tanya. They also read Larsen, a Danish playwright of existential plays. Everybody in the group had to read *Jean Christophe*, so you would know what growing up and what consciousness were all about.

And during the war?

My family and I were in internment camps in France. A few days before Rosh Hashanah I snuck out of the camp. It was early, around five in the morning, and I went to the butcher. He was killing some goats, getting them ready for the butcher trade. He saw me in my outfit from the camp, and he got scared. He wanted to give me some meat. He figured that's why I came.

No, I explained, I wanted a horn. So he gave me two horns. I took them back, and with a wire hanger I finally drilled through them just before Rosh Hashanah. Everyone was glad I had a *shofar*. There was an old man who wanted to blow, but I said no. I risked my life, I told him, so it should be me who blew the *shofar*. The commander came in as usual with his whip and an automatic.

"What's this noise?" he said.

I said, *"C'est le cornet de notre liberation, monsieur le commandant."*

He said, *"Notre liberation?* Tootle it again." So I gave another blow. On the spot he pulls out a letter and reads the names of the people whose visas were waiting for them in the American embassy in Marseilles. Our family was on the list.

The commander said we could leave the same day. There was a train coming through, and there was a big question about whether we should leave on Yontif or wait until later and risk that he might change his mind. There were people arguing both ways. Papa decided we had to leave. By Yom Kippur we were in Marseilles.

And then to Lubavitch in Brooklyn?

I reached America in 1941 and studied in the Lubavitcher *yeshivah* for a few years. Eventually I got ordained. I was studying at the *yeshivah* of the late Lubavitcher *Rebbe*, and I went to see him occasionally at *yechidus* [the private encounter between *rebbe* and disciple]. Later, I wrote my dissertation analyzing the states of *yechidus* because I was so excited about that process that reaches so deeply inside.

Lubavitch was a very spiritual place. When Pesach came, *bedikat hametz* didn't just mean looking for *hametz* on the outside. You were looking for the leaven, for what was inflated inside your own being. A similar process took place on the other holidays.

The things that are presently being dealt with by transpersonal psychology and humanistic psychology were right there in the *yeshivah*. Sometimes they were assisted with a bottle of schnapps. We did meditation in Lubavitch before the word was bandied about in this country. Experiencing and staying in touch with the inner life was what Lubavitch gave me.

This was during the war. Was the yeshivah *affected by what was happening to the Jews of Europe, or were you off in another world entirely?*

There were a lot of messianic stirrings. In 1943, the late *rebbe* published several newsletters where he said that the *Mashiach* was coming, that the Diaspora was burning. We knew what was going on in Europe, and we believed that it represented the birth pangs of the *Mashiach*. There were all kinds of indications. There was a paper published by Lubavitch, and in the first issue there was a poem, and if you read the acrostic up—and there were arrows to show you the way— it said that the *Mashiach* was coming in 1943, God willing.

Forty-three was a heavy year. Great teachings came down. When the last day of Passover came, which is also known as *Mashiach's* Yontif, I was hanging around the *rebbe's* table, waiting for him to say it already, that he was the *Mashiach*—or whoever. But he was the only plausible candidate.

What, exactly, did you expect would happen?

That the *rebbe* would say, "So and so is the *Mashiach*." And we would go and meet him, bringing a Torah with us.

The intensity of the waiting was so great. Then came the eighteenth of Elul, the Baal Shem's birthday, the last day of the year when we could expect anything. People were wondering, When will he say it? It's got to happen.

He didn't say it. My heart sank. For a while we tried to read the signs a little differently; maybe it would happen next year. Eventually I realized that it wouldn't.

Eventually you also left that world. What made you leave the Lubavitch community?

That's a long story. But one of the things was that doubt was not permitted. I raised some very heavy questions, and when I was told that they were bad questions, and I should put them out of my mind and submit again to the system, I felt it was time for me to graduate.

RELIGIOUS OUTREACH

These days, people describe you in a variety of ways. How do you see your role in bringing people closer to Yiddishkeit?

I'm not trying to become a "holy man." But whatever I'm doing is holy work; I want to do it right. I don't want always to be holy. First of all, it doesn't all depend on me. Sometimes it flows, and sometimes it doesn't, right? In previous times, when it didn't flow you still had to make as if it did. Like—he's a *rebbe* by substance, not by function. I'm a *rebbe* by function, and there are times when somebody else functions a lot better than I do. So the ability to dance in and out of the scene and to make space for the other guy is very important.

I'm limited in what I can do. I have to finance my work by the sweat of my brow. I've never had the help I've needed. I have a *siddur* waiting, and for $20,000 it could be published, and it could open up people to many levels of *davvening*.

Does this lack of support from the mainstream Jewish community make you angry?

I'll tell you, there is something I must be doing to perpetuate that condition. If I want things to be different, there's probably something I should be doing differently.

Still, for many years you've been something of a loner in the Jewish world. That must have been a painful experience.

Listen, if it didn't cost anything it wouldn't be worth anything. It cost a lot.

But it's changing. When the Reconstructionists invited me to be their keynote speaker at a meeting a few years ago, I felt like the *ganif geshnitin fun der tlyia*—when you need the thief, you cut him down from the gallows. I think the Jewish community needs me now. Even the best Jewish teachers are still operating only with the dynamics of the left cerebral hemisphere of the brain, with no notion of what's going on in the right hemisphere—with nonverbal stuff, with energy distribution.

I feel a little less lonely these days. Here and there I have found communities of people who are thinking in these ways.

I think we are *erev* a big change. It's happening all over the place. In a community in Oregon. In northern California. Different places, different communities. Even without much contact between them, new kinds of Jewish groups are emerging. Some of them don't even know that the others exist. Many of them are like *havurah* groups, and yet they have no idea that there is an annual *havurah* conference, or that other people are also thinking this way. This is no time to be territorial or authoritarian, but purely empirical. Let's try things out and see what works so that we can create a kind of avant-garde working together.

What about those Jews who are seeking but who are not part of a community? You're also in touch with them.

I hear from many of them, people who are saying: "My intuition says it's here, in Judaism." I even hear from people who were not born Jewish. What people are asking me is, "How can I acquire that spiritual substance? What practices would you suggest? What attitudes would you recommend?"

When such a person comes to the *yeshivah* and sees the sparks of spiritual energy, he gets turned on. He says, "I'd like to buy into this." And they say to him, "Sure, sure. Start with putting on *tefillin*, keep kosher, keep *Shabbos*, believe this and that." So they unload a whole exoteric trip first before they'll take him into the esoteric way.

But lots of people aren't willing to do that. They find the door locked for them because the esoteric stuff is kept hidden. Instead, what they get is, "Listen, you're a *shaygitz*. How can I tell you the deepest secrets if you're a *shaygitz*?" And that's what the men get. The women don't even get *that* far!

I have a different approach. I believe that some people take on the outer on the basis of the inner. What's important is how to make the soul go up and at the same time be grounded.

A number of years ago I happened to be in Chicago, and I wanted some incense sticks. This was before the days of the head shops, so I called the Vedanta Society, and the swami who answered said, "You Jews are a very spiritual people."

I asked him why he had said this, and he told me that Jews were heavily involved in Eastern religious groups. This made me happy and sad at the same time, because why was it that so many Jews had to go and find their sustenance elsewhere? And then I had to ask myself the same question: How did I get involved in Far Eastern religions? What was it that attracted me, that made me visit ashrams and seek out swamis and yogis and see what their trip was about?

I had a feeling that their technique was something that we needed, something that we had, originally, and had lost to some extent. For example, *pranayama*. For years I had been looking in Jewish sources for material about breathing. After all, so many of our prayers mention it, like "The breath of every living being shall praise Thee," and *"Kol Ha-Neshamah Tehallel Yah"* [Everything that breathes shall praise the lord].

One day I was reading the works of Joseph Gikatilla, a thirteenth-century Jewish mystic and the author of a book called *Shaarei Orah*. As I recall, he writes that the secret of the divine breath is the secret of the divine name, YHVH. You visualize the Y of the divine name when there is no breath in your lungs, and then you breath in. And that sound H is the sound of the second letter. You hold your breath and you push the breath up and down the V, which is the spine, and then you breathe out the sound of the last H. If you do this for a while, he writes, the light will begin to shine inside your body.

Then he said something interesting: "As it is well known to those who practice it. . . ." So I could see that the secret of *pranayama* was available in Judaism and was known, although it wasn't necessarily put into writing.

These days, who are your students?

All kinds. Some of them come to Judaism from drugs and after drugs, and from the Eastern ways, because the Jewish ways have become terribly blocked by bad teachers in Jewish schools and congregations. Because of all the encrusted garbage on top, they couldn't see the high places in Judaism, and nobody showed them. For years, most of their elders had treated Jewish ritual like a dead radio, plugging it in even though no sound was coming out.

But these people are so fantastically hungry and their souls are of such high caliber. I've found that eventually Jews who embark on various quests for truth outside Judaism begin to burp up Jewish stuff from their own and their parents' past lives. This usually brings them back to the purpose of this incarnation.

You're also exposed to plenty of Jews who have a more conventional consciousness. What do you do with them?

Anyone who enters any teaching situation has to start with compassion for the people he teaches. If he doesn't begin with that compassion and love, then he'll come across as the one who knows, and the rest of the people are ignoramuses. There's no way he can communicate to people in that form. So I can't come in and say, "The way you're doing it is all wrong. Throw out the moneychangers from the temple and the pews from the synagogue."

Don't forget that these people have been doing something wonderful. They have continued to keep Jewish institutions alive, even without much that's spiritually nourishing, so that they and their children can celebrate the life events. So I can't come in and tell them that they're doing it all wrong.

I usually start with the *siddur*, and then I help them with breathing and chanting. Chanting, even in English, can make the prayers come alive. Most people have never had the chance.

I talk about the prayers. I point out that, let's say, a psalm of David is a real experience. He was being followed by people who wanted to kill him. Philistines are after him. Finally, he makes it to the place where he is safe and secure, and he gets to eat something. And then he reflects on how God has helped him, and he begins to sing, "The Lord is my Shepherd, I shall not want."

And the way in which he sings it is so full of his experience! What the people have in front of them in their prayer book is black-and-white print. Now to take that print and to move it closer to the experience that King David had, walking through the valley of the shadow of death. . . . Yes, he was afraid. Yes, he had trust. And yes, now he eats, despite the fact that if it were up to his enemies, he wouldn't get anything to eat. "Thou preparest for me a table despite the plans of mine enemies."

Most books are for the mind. The *siddur* is for the heart. So I have to help people get on the other track, the heart track rather than the mind track. Even the printing of the lines has to be done differently, in order to say to people, "Hey, this is for the heart and not for the mind."

The *siddur* is like a coloring book with outlines. People have to fill it in with life, with background, with context. We are not yet talking about mystical stuff. We're just talking about how to use such a resource as a prayer book.

The person with a wonderful secular education shouldn't be made to feel infantilized by the fact that he doesn't know how to recite these things in Hebrew. And I try to use familiar tunes because you can't flood people with too much new stuff.

One time I was working with a group of high school kids who were so full of pepper that they couldn't sit still. I said: "Let's say the *Kedushah* moving our arms like this: *Holy*, with the arms crossed. *Holy*, with the arms lifted. *Holy*, raising them as high as possible and then turning in a half circle, with the arms out, Heaven and earth are full of Thy glory! Holy, Holy, Holy—" and for five minutes the whole place was transformed by giving a channel to the energy that was there. Not asking it to change, but to make a connection.

People have problems with silence. I wish that our people were more used to silence, to working in silence. There's a sense that if there is no program, if the rabbi isn't doing it, if they aren't reading it, then that's the time for chatting.

I try to reawaken people to what's there in their tradition. E. T. wants to phone home. Everybody who saw the movie knows the urgency with which E. T. wanted to phone home. What if we could say: "There's a phone for phoning home, it's in the chapel of your synagogue, go there and use it." But it's a special kind of phone, and you have to be taught how to use it.

Most of us are pretty far removed from our spiritual source. How do you explain that estrangement?

You have to keep in mind that our spiritual home has changed over the years. Judaism, like most religions, has two basic thrusts. One is charismatic and Dionysian, which is fancy language for direct, intuitive, loving, ecstatic. The other thrust is legal, rational, ordered, Apollonian.

Now the legal rational mode originated for us in nineteenth-century Germany. It was that mode that was willing to speak in foreign languages, which is to say, in languages other than Hebrew and Yiddish. In some respects, the nineteenth century did a good job, but they threw a lot of baby out with the bathwater.

When European Jews came to America, they made that impulse into a new form. So—services in English. Sitting in pews, more like other people were doing. The architecture of synagogues and fixed pews make it almost impossible to push the chairs and benches aside and to begin a dance. There's a lot of inhibition.

This inhibition has to do also with the fact that the charismatic leadership did not become rabbis, and the community was not able to develop the charismatic, celebrative part of themselves. What was trained was their minds, their eloquence, their ability to give sermons, to govern congregations. So it's no wonder that half of Judaism is missing from most congregations!

Look: we know God just as we know everything else, in different ways. We know by doing, that's the pragmatic way. We know by feeling, that's the Freudian way of knowledge. We know by knowing, that's the philosopher's way. And we know by intuiting, that's the mystic's way.

But when you divide the world into pragmatist, psychologist, philosopher, and mystic, you've made a kind of division that I don't like. Everybody is a pragmatist when he goes shopping, a feeling person in love. All of us are all of these things. Now when a person begins to realize that he vibrates on all these four frequencies, then I think the first mind-move has been made, and we can start discussing how one knows God on all these four levels.

A Jewish Practitioner of Generic Religion

You mean a lot of different things to different people. How do you define yourself these days?

I see myself as a Jewish practitioner of generic religion. I'm getting to the place in my life where I don't have to worry about whether other people accept my credentials. Even when I went to the Trappists I wore my *yarmulke.* Another time, when I sat in a teepee with Native Americans, somebody said, "Why is he wearing his little hat?"

I turned to Little Joe, the old-timer, the old Pueblo Indian, and I said, "I'm sitting here in the presence of God. To take off the hat would be to deny that. What do you say, Grampa Joe?"

Grampa Joe just looks at me, and he says, "It's your head."

I've also learned from Islam. But I come to Islam as Jew. Once I went to Hebron to take part in a Zhikr, which is that rhythmic dancing and chanting from the Sufi tradition. The Sufis are like the *hasidim* of the Moslem world.

When I got to Hebron, the sheik asked me who I was. And I answered, "I am a *mu'umin.*" A believer.

Then he asks me if I could say the *shahadah.* ["There is no God but Allah, and Muhammad is His Prophet."] "If you say it, then you're a Moslem."

And I said, "No, I'm a Jew, and I'm coming to you as a Jew. Have you ever met a Jew who comes to you like this?"

You see, I'm not just playing Jew because I have to make a living. General religion means to me that there is an element in the universe that doesn't lie. Empiricism tells me that some things work, and some things don't. A lot of stuff in *Yiddishkeit* works very well.

But some of it doesn't work anymore. And the question is, by what means do we decide? I say we decide by empirical means. I don't want it to be my private decision.

How recent are these views? Obviously you've shifted quite a bit since your days in Brooklyn.

I changed a lot during the sixties. Torah had become one of the possible facets. I became aware of alternate worlds, that God could be served by one approach as well as by another, that Judaism is one possible construct of the whole shebang. I learned to wiggle my mind into various other possibilities.

And what is it you want to teach?

The process of relating to God. At one time, religions used to talk about the product. The product was virtuous behavior; the product was faith, hope, charity. People had a notion that there was something to get—a pot of gold at the end of the rainbow.

That fit the old paradigm of the Middle Ages. But there's been a switch now. People are interested in the process. It's alive. When a human being begins to live, that's a process. But most souls haven't been resuscitated, like the slap on the baby that gets the first breath going. Most souls haven't experienced that, and even if they do, they usually stop there. I'm interested in continuing from that moment on in the process.

And within Judaism?

Recently, I've been working with people in davvening and asking the question: How do you *davven* when you're in a *minyan*? Most people still do solo when they're in a *minyan*. They come together from time to time to say *Kadosh Kadosh*, but the rest of the time they're doing solo.

What's it like to *davven* in tandem? In lovemaking, you have a sense of "two-sie" consciousness. If you brought this "two-sie" consciousness to *davvening,* what would it be like? If you shared energy with another person, if you became transparent and as telepathic as possible, what would that be like? And if that could happen with two, could it be expanded to a *minyan*?

In our community, we've been experimenting with *davvening* in groups of two, three, and four. Imagine chanting in a threesome: The first person: *Adonai Melekh*! And the second: *Adonai Malakh*! The third: *Adonai Yimlokh*! And then all of them together: *Laolam va'ed*! And we do this for a long time. With three together, it's very hard for most people to get to a place where it isn't two against one. Are you his ally? Are you my ally? Or are we somehow doing this together?

But the power of the threesome is there, and since we're doing the same words and the same thing, we're tuning our minds to the same frequency. The hope is that if we stay tuned long enough to the same frequency, then we could put our minds in the same place. I think there are such moments, degrees of telepathy achieved as the vibrations come together. The issue of moving from the individual to the *minyan*—that's part of what I like to call *davvenology*.

I see my work as adjusting the machinery. If the machinery isn't calibrated in a certain way, it may not produce, it may not read reality too well. I don't want to give the product of my *davvening*, I want to give the process. I like to help keep people tuned up.

My regret is that my pattern has been so paternal. I have to be the altruistic one, and I don't get much in return. So I'm taking a year off, cultivating Zalman. I've never done that before. I'm going to start with a forty-day retreat at the Lama Foundation. I want to find out what Zalman needs in order to be in decent shape to continue working for a while.

You were involved during the first year of Havurat Shalom in Boston back in 1968–69. Did that experience give you a taste of what it would be like to have spiritual colleagues?

I was a *haver*, one of the *haverim*. Art Green was the *rebbe*. I wasn't there yet. I was asking different questions then, like how to build in an aesthetic, a little silence, a little body movement, things like that.

In those days, I was looking for some kind of electronic indicator, so you could test when the tenth person comes into the room—the *Shekhinah* light would go on so you would know that the divine presence has arrived. I believe that there's a quantum jump that takes place when that happens. If we had such a machine, we could see right away if women should be part of the *minyan*. The light would go on!

And these days, what are your questions?

One of my questions is this: We're moving into a new paradigm, and Judaism has to be able to transform itself in this paradigm shift as it did last time with Yochannan Ben Zakkai in Yavneh after the Romans destroyed the Temple. The Torah was read in the old paradigm as deistic. It was a *shande* to read it like this, so Onkelos in the second century translated it theistically, so that the people, when they hear Torah, shouldn't hear it in a consciousness that's passé. In his Aramaic translation, he edits out any aspect of the corporeal reality of God. He doesn't say, for example, that God descended to Mt. Sinai. Instead, God revealed Himself. Everything that speaks of God in space, or the hand of God, Onkelos makes more abstract.

A new paradigm was beginning. The same thing is true today. The idea that you can pollute the air so long as it's with a kosher pollutant — that consciousness is sick. We need a new consciousness. We can't throw everything away; Reform made that mistake. But we can't keep everything because it's so top-heavy now that it can't work.

THE PSYCHOHALAKHIC PROCESS

One question I would ask about *Shabbos* and work is, what about a rabbi? It seems that we're always working the hardest on *Shabbos*. If I'm washing dishes, only my hands are working. My head and my heart are doing other stuff. Comes *Shabbos* and I do a retreat, I'm operating on all cylinders.

I once saw the Angel of Death. He came very close to me, and I said, "Why now? What do you want from me?" And he said, "This is what you bring on yourself if you don't have *Shabbos*." I think the physiology of stress declares to me that I have to have *Shabbos* everyday for at least an hour in the afternoon. We have to go back and look at what was intended, not like the Reform guys who said, "Come on, enough with this superstitious garbage." So they threw it out. I'm saying that this is wonderful shamanistic wisdom. Let's use it, but in a new way, okay?

I used to say to parents who were upset about their children dropping out: "The reason they drop out completely is that they never saw you drop out on *Shabbos*." The Jewish way is that for 6 days you are a square but you are a hippie for the seventh. Heschel was right when he said that the Jew lives less in space than he does in time. *Shabbos* is the punctuation of time, the signification of time. I haven't seen any other group of people that knows how to experience one day out of the week in such a way as to move so totally out of the everyday into the more mystical realm.

We have a custom in our house that we write each other *Shabbos* letters. Nowhere in Jewish spiritual-direction literature do you find anything like that. But somehow we found that living together, routine takes over in such a terrible way that we never tell each other what really matters.

So before *Shabbos*, we sit down and write each other love letters. After *kiddush* and *motzi* on Friday night, one of the children takes the letters around. And maybe the next generation in their *Shabbos* practice will say, "We received as tradition that on *Shabbos* we give each other letters."

Shabbos is wonderful stuff. It's what everybody's looking for. Give it the benefit of the doubt. Do it and see what works. Now if it works, great. If it doesn't work, what adjustments do you have to make so it will work better? That's what I mean by the psycho*halakhic* process.

Let me give another example. There's a question: How long do you have to wear *tefillin* each day in order to fulfill the obligation? The Talmud says long enough to walk four cubits. In hasidic language, that means it has to happen on all four levels: the level of action, the level of feeling, the level of thought, and the level of essence of being. If only your hands have worn the *tefillin*, it didn't take on the other levels.

So I ask myself: What today would achieve that best? I don't know. Maybe biofeedback. Maybe that's what it's all about, that we should become sensitive to vibrations, to spaces, that normally in our great rush we can't possibly be sensitive to.

The survival of this planet depends on our being able to reach to those regions of wisdom from which to draw on. Bucky Fuller says you can only learn from mistakes. But today the threat is too great. So we have to learn like we never learned in human history before.

As Jews, our piece of that has to be gotten into shape so that people will be able to ask questions like, Is electricity from a nuclear power plant kosher? There are all kinds of questions you can't deal with unless you bring a Jewish sensitivity.

As Jews, we are not surrenderers to God. We are in a covenant relationship to God. That's absolutely essential to understand about *Yiddishkeit*, that there are two parties in the dialogue.

One of these parties is all-mighty and all-wise. However, He doesn't seem to give individuals daily action directives. If I could call up God every morning and ask, "Master of the Universe, what are my orders today?" could you imagine what responsibility would fall off my shoulders? But it doesn't work that way. And so I have to make a decision on how to live, how to fulfill my part of the covenant relationship.

Halakhah is part of that process. I'm now in this place. Someday there will be others in my place. But now I have the responsibility. I have to stop passing the buck. At some point I have to end the discussion and say: "Okay, so what am I going to *do*?"

Projecting Judaism

How do you get these concerns onto the Jewish agenda?

I notice that most of the people who do anything in futurology are Jews. But if you look at the topics with which they are dealing, none have to do with Judaism. I think that a certain amount of money has to be put

aside by Jewish organizations for futurological-thinking type of thinking. If we're really concerned about the future, we can't pay attention
only to deficit financing of hospitals and social services, as important as
those things are.

We also have to maintain our raison d'etre. We have to put something
Jewish out to the world. We can't allow ourselves to be represented by
the *shmegeggie* stuff on the tube that makes us look like wimps.

You know the movie *My Dinner with André*? The actor Wally Shawn
comes out that way, like a wimp. We look bad. This is the age of
television, and what are we doing with it? Moshe Waldoks in Boston is
learning how to do cable and video. But where is the rest of the Jewish
community?

*You have a very visual consciousness. What is it that you'd like to see
on the screen?*

I'd like to do a movie about the life of Rabbi Akiva. It starts in black
and white. People are walking in the night, being pushed along by the
Nazis. There's an older man and a younger man, and the younger one
says: "Teach me what Judaism is all about." And the older man says:
"Under these circumstances, I want to tell you about Rabbi Akiva."

The screen goes boom—wide screen, in color now, and the Hebrew
letters are flying up from a fire to form the word "Akiva." The theme
begins to play, and there's the whole story about Rachel, Rabbi Akiva's
wife, and her father asking, "Whom are you going to marry?"

We see Rachel looking at all the men who have come to wed her. She
really wants Akiva, but not Akiva in shepherd's clothes. So she does this
sort of thing you do with a doll, dressing it up, and she puts Akiva's coat
on his animated image, and *that's* the one she wants.

Whenever there's thought going on, we'll have animations with
balloons. Each time Akiva does a *midrash*, a teaching, the movie goes
back into this mode, like the film version of *Lord of the Rings*, this very
shivery animation. And every so often the Roman soldiers come into it,
and they turn into the Nazis, coming and going in the movie, back into
black and white.

And the finale comes when the young man says to the old man: "But
how can you still believe this stuff?" And they're at the selection, in the
camp. And he tells him about the last part, the martyrdom of Akiva, and
then the fire goes up and the theme plays again. And the credits come on
against the background of an old *yeshivah* where Akiva's words are being
studied, and then a more modern *yeshivah*, and then finally you have the
cutting studio where they study the words of Rabbi Akiva while they're
editing the film.

We're at the end of our interview. If you were an athlete, we'd ask if

you had any words of advice for the young ball player coming along.
What about the young person who is studying Judaism and who wants to
become more serious about it?

He or she should be able to graduate from each level of Judaism. I
think that Jewish schools should have stages: biblical years and biblical
experience, then rabbinic, medieval, modern, postmodern, which is
something that a person might come to at the age of thirty or thirty-five.
Maybe we should have a kind of *bar mitzvah* ceremony to mark each
level of change.

Judaism for adults?

Exactly.

25

MEDITATIONS BETWEEN CONTRACTIONS

In early 1986 I was one of the several members of the National Editorial Board of Tikkun *magazine invited to write short statements to answer a series of questions. The questions were these:*

What kind of tikkun *(healing, repair, and transformation) does the world need?*

What intellectual, spiritual, psychological, and religious resources do we have to bring to that tikkun?

What role can Tikkun *magazine play in this process?*

To insist that we continue to fix, repair, make *tikkun* on what is not patchable is a category error. One can't fix something that has run out of time. Biblical Judaism ran out of time at the destruction of the First Temple. The patch job of the Second Temple could not repair it. Rabban Yohannan ben Zakkai was aware of the paradigm shift that had occurred and instead of asking Vespasian to allow us to keep it he asked for Yavneh and its wise ones.

After Auschwitz we are again in a similar situation: the time ran out for rabbinic Judaism. A contemporary Raban Yohannan ben Zakkai would ask for the Yavneh II to be convened and to bring about the designing and instituting of the Judaism that will be the vital process for us Jews and produce the vitamins needed for the health of the entire planet.

The *tikkun* now called for is not a patch job on the old paradigm. It calls for revisioning the *partzufim*, the interfaces (between the infinite *Ein Sof* and the finite) that we call the names of God, the root metaphors that will give us contemporary roles to play vis-à-vis the current demands of our lives and the eternal Presence. We need to replace the active Father–passive Child, King–Subject, Judge–Defendant with something like mutual and interactive Friend–friend, Lover–lover, Partner–partner.

This is not the task of a single individual, a patriarch or Moses as it was in the time of the biblical paradigm, nor the task of an elite Sanhedrin group as in the time of the rabbinic one. The power base has been broadened since those days.

Today this is the task of the committed aggregate of Israel, including women, including more than one or two generations. It calls for the sharing by people with transparent or at least translucent egos. It calls for sensitivities geared to the new mythic deep structures on which the next paradigm's *aggadah* will be based. It calls for a compassionate understanding – and one based on the state of the art of intuiting where we are in the philogenetic growth process, a balance of right- and left-hemisphere thinking *and* a thorough knowing of the sources of our tradition. Most of all it calls for a vital connection in prayer and meditation communing with the living God in solitude *and* in community.

What follows is a partial list of agenda topics and indications that seem to me a useful direction.

GOD *PARTZUFIM*

In the past we may not have known in a conscious way that the design of the divine *partzuf* called on us to provide the raw materials from the images of our existence. The rabbis have intuited that the "Torah speaks in the language of humans." It is our task to provide the wraps, names, root metaphors, attributes, masks, and personalities (which Luria called the *partzufim*) for the revelatory process in which the Holy One unfolds to us, so that they might (despite all the changes in details) function as process for us as they did for our ancestors.

In fact we need to work consciously to create new language to serve us instead of being victims to its natural inertia. The computer has shown us that we need to make language serve the functions we wish to run. For example:

• God is a verb. We have up to this time used verbs in their active and their passive forms. Our current understanding of process requires that we create an interactive, not passive or active, form of verb. I do not type on this machine, nor is the machine being typed on. The machine and I are intertyping. The flag does not wave in the wind; the wind does not wave the flag. The flag and wind are interwaving.

• The sun does not set or rise. We need to use a more precise form of language if we learned from Copernicus and Newton. Just thinking and saying that this hemisphere is turning to receive the sun makes solar power a natural conclusion. Instead of saying that the sun has gone down we would say that the Earth has turned so that the sun now shines on the Russians. Think of how this would change our thinking about the planet.

• We need an androgynous pronoun that is neither feminine nor masculine and is beyond neuter. This would clean our social relations immensely.

• The *siddur*, our prayer book, needs to be freed from archaic and feudal forms of relating, from its form as a book, in print, and as the result of legislation. The *siddur* needs to open to the new myths that inspire us to become harmonized to the Godding and to become a tool for assisting us to come to global telepathy. At least it must help us to *davven* with the significant persons in our basic reference group. It must provide not only the rubrics telling us when to say *yaaleh veyavo* but also how to attune our consciousness to our recital. The new *siddur* must give us an enlarged repertory from which to improvise the accompaniment for the melody line of our lives.

• Peace! Here is a noun that functions against its own purpose. As long as we think of "having peace," we treat peace as a product, a commodity, and not as an incremental and mutual process. We have such sophistication in destroying lives and we have so little in interpeacing. Here, more than anywhere else, we need an interactive verb and an empirical laboratory to show us how to move from adversary manipulation to interacting peaceably.

• *Pillug*. The polarization between orthodox and heterodox Jews has reached catastrophic proportions. We cannot even hear each other clearly. Our anxiety that someone will coerce us away from our deepest commitments makes us shy of really hearing even the most irenic propositions. We need to apply the highest state of the art to the therapy of the Jewish family. If we manage to heal our split we may have something to share with a world in need of interpeacing.

So we need to do a *tikkun halashon* — a healing of our tongues. It has been long in coming, all the way since Babel.

Concerning Torah in the new paradigm, we must give up the notion of legislation and take on the notion of discovering the laws of nature. We need to discover what works for us instead of legislating what *should* work for us. This calls for an empirical study of *halakhah*, and pilot communities to test, in all self-awareness, the norms we would adopt in our discovery of the *Raton haShem*, the will of the ongoing Godding. (Remember: interverb.)

Kashrut is in need of *tikkun*. We have not paid enough attention to *shemirat haguf*, the protection of the body from harmful substances. We need to expand *Kashrut* thinking to ask such questions as, "Is electricity from a nuclear reactor kosher?" Or, "Is something that is bottled in a one-way bottle more or less kosher than something bottled in a recyclable one?"

One of the most effective ways to interact these days with others in a way that transcends the limits of time and the limits of the space where we find ourselves is the electronic bulletin board. We need a shared and accessible data base for down- and up-loading our how-to Jew-ing. The American Talmud is in the making, The *Jewish Catalog* now in three volumes is the beginning of its *Mishnah*. Such a shared resource may yet help us to heal the schism in our family that looms ahead on the horizon.

Israel. The *tikkun* needed there is immense. We are for the first time in two millennia in possession of land, our own land, and we have become intoxicated by that heady feeling that blinds us to seeing our realities. In the struggle with our cousins, Israelis have not had a chance to learn from the land how she wants to be used. Repeated stints in the army not followed by a cleaning and redirection to civilian life have given the population an increasingly martial attitude even to such aspects of life that call on other ways of coping. The minds are brittle with frustration and anger, and the tone of voice in the streets reminds one of a sergeant's bark. The gentling of Israel's heart and mind is of the highest priority. I am not calling for softness when hardness is needed. I am calling for balance. It will take the *aliyah* to Israel by people who think in this way. I am preparing for our family's *aliyah* in order to help in this. May the infinite interGodding assist us.

26

GAIA AND *MELEKH HAOLAM*

Sometime in the seventies I coined the term *eco-kosher*. I raised questions about one-way bottles that in the classical understanding of kosher are more kosher than two-way bottles, but I argued in contrast eco-kosher would claim that the one-way bottle is less eco-kosher than the two-way bottle and that there is a real question from eco-kosher *halakhah* if the electricity from a Nuke is kosher.

There is reason to think that much of *halakhah* as it concerns *kashrut* is related to an understanding of the cosmos. Much of halakhic thinking relating to *kashrut* is rooted in a pre-Copernican worldview. We have yet to have a reworking of the grid on which the *sevarot,* basic notions of the *halakhah,* are built to come up to date of the nineteenth century-based "science." How much more so when there is an emerging reality map that sees Earth as a living *Gaia.*

This organic view has yet to become the thought of the mainstream. Nevertheless, the growing edge of current cosmological understanding as exemplified by the writings of Elizabeth Satouris, Lynn Margulies, etc., go hand in hand with the thought of Tom Berry, Matthew Fox, and others. Seeing our planet from space has, as Hoyle pointed out, irrevocably changed our point of view.

At this point in our thinking it is abundantly clear that the basic command in the Torah, "Do not destroy her trees," extends even to those trees whose fruit is "only oxygen." Beyond this it extends from the minor

to the major premise, by *kal vahomer* to the entire planet. It begins to
move from the mere *lav*, the Torah's simple prohibition to cut down fruit
trees during a siege to extend to the *bal tash'hit*, the prohibition to
destroy the entire planet. If homicide is a capital crime, how much more
so is being an accessory to planeticide.

The processes of life have three phases, as Sr. Paula Gonzales states,
in which we have (1) growth, (2) use, and (3) recycling, destruction as a
further preparation to growth and use. We constantly look toward the
sustainable use of biodegradeable substances. We travel on spaceship
Earth and everything on it is constantly recycled. We face further
halakhic and ethical eco-*kashrut* questions.

Understanding the processes of life and the food chain of the planet
raises some difficult questions in *kashrut*. How long is *trefa tref*? At
which point can we say that a substance that was not kosher is broken
down again to render the different chemical constituent parts neutral
again? The still-prevailing view has it that once *treif*, we may not take a
forbidden substance and destroy that which makes it forbidden in order
to make it permissible. *Ein mevatlin issur lekhat'hillah.*

I ask at what point in the process does the issur's molecules — let's say
a corpse — become neutral and kosher? The answer to this question has to
do with the intervening processes such as decomposition, being unfit for
human consumption, burning, chemical intervention via acid or lye, the
changing of taste to spoil it *noten taam lifgam*.

To enter into this quandary meaningfully demands that we reexamine
the cosmological underpinnings of *halakhah*. The maps of reality that
the *Tannaim* — who authored the *Mishnah* — used in understanding their
place in the world are different from ours. Their field of observation was
narrower than ours. We, who look at distances in microns and light-
years, need to be freed from handbreadths and cubits.

At first I proposed that we accept as a working hypothesis that once
a *chemical* change is introduced, that is sufficient. However, in household pickling, marinating, cooking, and preparing there occur some
changes in the chemical structure of the food substance. So mere change
is not enough. But if the change is brought about by an agent that is
inorganic and which by its admixture makes the matter unfit for
consumption — let's say lard or butter broken down by sulfuric acid, a
step in the possible production of stearic or lactic acids — then it seems
reasonable to me that we have broken the pattern and may now recycle
the substance as *pareve*.

With food proteins the issue is more complicated. I have since pursued
these questions with food chemists who have a sense of kosher, and here
are some of their suggestions: every food protein has a long history and

contains some features that mark its origin. These markers, whenever and where present in a food originating in what we now assume to be *tref*, might be the ones that keep it in the forbidden zone. But should they have been removed and should the kosher animal or even more, the kosher vegetable product, have identical markers, then we might conclude that the basic chemical structure has been altered enough to again render the product kosher.

For example, amino acids are often greatly refined. At some early levels the markers that inform us whether a product comes from meat or milk sources can be more or less identified. However, at certain further levels of hydrolization, these markers no longer show.

Perhaps traces may remain that will cause allergic reactions in the way that the body's antigens will react to the signature of the protein. But when even these are gone might we not assume that what was once *tref* is now *pareve* again?

I do not think that we yet possess all the data for a decision on these matters. What we *do have* is a basis for halakhists and food scientists to study matters together and to design hypotheses, based on facts and laws to be tested, and from these results further possibilities arise for dialogue, proposals, and decisions.

27

SHARE-FLOW

A vision of the premillenium shift needed

Changing consciousness

COGNITIVE

The brain is formatted and programmed by biological evolution to function in the old paradigm. Our social, financial, and political institutions are based on the old paradigm. Underneath all these, the reality of the emerging paradigm rumbles like a volcano.

In order to reformat ourselves by our intention to evolve in consciousness to be able to function on the emerging reality map, we need to move the center of our survival instinct from the individual to the planetary. This involves making the unused portions of our brain capacity accessible to work in an environment of high complexity and integration. This can be done when we utilize the state of the art of contemplative know-how.

One aspect of the expansion of cognitive capacity is the spiritual eldering work that utilizes those parts of the brain only now ripening for greater effectiveness in accessing global and cosmic awareness.

MORAL-ETHICAL

When we have to relearn to live with attention to renewable resources, our prodigal attitude has to shift to an ascetic one. This asceticism must be this-worldly and appreciative of the sensual. It therefore must focus on the *quality* of experience and be harmonious with the socially responsible context. The scarcity mentality is counterproductive in achieving its aims. More productive is the grateful mentality that produces a greater *share-flow* of goods, services, and communication.

The radio, satellites, and other wireless communications have placed us in a transparent environment. Secrecy and withholding is no longer the guarantee of appropriate ownership and reward for work. Multivalent and multidirectional justice relationships require us to move from the binary, guilty-innocent paradigm to one of rainbow possibilities.

SPIRITUAL

As all species are necessary for the wholeness and the interaction of life on the planet, so are all religions and traditions. Fundamentalism, triumphalism, theological imperialism tend to vulgarize the traditions and interrupt the *share-flow*.

The messianisms of all traditions — Buddhist, Pure Land, Judeo-Christian millenial — contain a teleological urge to wholeness. The mysticisms of all traditions share in their empirical overlays, methods, psychospiritual technologies, and are rooted in teleological "becoming"; they are a response to the summons and attraction of the *Omega Principle*.[1]

PERSONAL

There is deeper and vaster ecstasy available for the individual in participating in the *share-flow*. To share with another takes the ecstasy from arithmetic increment to geometric proportions. Sexuality is awaiting the infusion of spirit and the conversation preparing for this has begun.

SOCIAL

The family structures at the fabric of society are based on models that are no longer functional: multigenerational, near-tribal, oriented to home and hearth, bonded along patriarchal bloodlines. They are also based on

---

[1]That the universe is moving toward the Omega Point when all matter is raised to consciousness.

a shorter life span. The longer life span and the many other forms of association that are emerging now demand a restructuring of covenants for coupling, co-parenting, and intergenerational linking.

ESTHETIC

Entertainment that is based on the Roman circus, furnishing jolts of tension and release, fueled by adrenaline-raised suspense in empathy with violence and terror, needs to be replaced with interactive, collaborative share-flow delights.

Already there are signs of the collaboration of entertainment with spirituality. Poets, playwrights, composers, companions of all the muses, need to be given the environment and the resources to create *"GREEN DRAGON"*[2] *share-flow art.*

My intuition is that as we begin to become better global citizens, we will find ourselves invited to share with other sentient, highly conscious entities beyond our current expectation horizons.

---

[2]See Brian Swimme, *The Universe Is a Green Dragon* (Santa Fe, NM: Bear & Company, 1984).

28

YAVNEH II

YHVH *MELEKH!*

Paradigm shift, epoch change, New Age, Sinai Event, the RAINBOW —
these are all part of seeing ourselves as Jews and planetary citizens. We
realize as such that the way we need to do this is not merely by acting as
individuals — reflecting and deciding. We know that we can't continue
business-as-usual and survive. Change is essential, and we want to make
the changes that are demanded by the aggregated process occurring in
this new environment, our global village.

YHVH *MALAKH!*

This has happened to us before now. When the Second Temple was
destroyed, and with it our sacred technology, we were so disoriented we
no longer knew how to JEW in the new circumstances. Except for
Rabban Yohannan ben Zakkai and the few disciples in his *yeshivah* at
Yavneh, the only group that undertook to handle the shift then were the
new messianists, followers of the Nazarene and his scribes. Their move
was discontinuous. Thank God that the few at Yavneh had the vision, the
guts, and the know-how to lead the rest by following their insight into

"*Et laasot laYHVH — heferu Toratekha!*" ("It is a moment in which we must act for God — by shifting Thy Torah.") Thus they ensured continuity.

YHVH YIMLOKH!

Prayer replaced sacrifice; Sabbath candles and blessings over food replaced worship at the Temple. The changes begun 250 years earlier by the *Anshei Knesset HaGedolah* heightened the schism between the Sadducees (followers of Zaddok, founder of the high-priestly family, prior to the Maccabees) and the New Agers of that time, the Pharisees.

The Holy power was once vested in Moses, a single individual (paralleling the practice of the time, which was monarchy, governance by a single, absolute ruler). Following him and the later prophets, the rabbis too saw the power reside in their forum (paralleling the Senate in Rome). It was a broadening of the power base. In our day the power base shifts again to the total and egalitarian *havurah* of the committed, paralleling our civil representation.

When the Temple was destroyed, a number of shifts occurred. The Holy in the biblical period had been in *space,* a traveling *mishkan,* on *bamot,* that is, high places or altars (*altus* — high in Latin). Later, after a dimension of *time.*

The Holy had been in the world of *action.* From the biblical perspective there was little need or requirement for making verbal statements to accompany sacrifice. After the destruction of the Temple, the rabbis moved the Holy into the world of the *word* — and with it created an entire technology of word *magic,* projecting it on the universe and God. Instead of seeing the Source of creation and revelation in heaven, we came to see it as immanent in us: "*Lo bashamayim*" — but shared only by all the ordained.

Our view of God moved from the deistic projection of the totally transcendent God, who involves Himself in our history and "comes down" on Mt. Sinai, to One "who becomes manifest" (as the *Targum* renders it): "just as the soul fills the body so does the Blessed Holy One fill the world." She is now seen as the *anima mundi.*

There were many aspects to the Yavneh shift. (I hope, *im yirtzeh HaShem*, to spell this out at greater length in a book that has the working title *Yavneh II.*) The most important point is that now, 40 years after the Holocaust, Hiroshima, and the establishment of the State of Israel, we are in a position similar to that of Yavneh — though later in the spiral of history.

Le'olam Va'ed!

The paradigm shift is not only a function of the history of Jews. It has in a most palpable way become the shift for the entire planet. It was the same in the past. But then, though the whole planet was affected by the shifts, we didn't see them as more than a Jewish issue. Today that's no longer true.

Every reality map is affected when a paradigm shift occurs. The people who go through them are compelled to remap their most cherished grids, to redefine their central realities. All life is touched.

Adon Kol Toladot!

Mind moves of such vast proportions aren't made in leisure. They're birthed under irresistible duress by difficult and heavy contractions. We called them the *hevlei mashiach*. We knew in the past and know today that such birth both propels and mirrors momentous change. Luria saw such birthing in *yetziyat Mitzrayim*. But the values and the constructs of past eons can't sustain our present lives. Like a fetus that must become a child in a new and seemingly impossible environment, we are similarly being birthed into a new and difficult time.

For those of us whose minds were blown in the sixties, who had to learn to ground their new visions in the emerging technologies and consciousness, it has become clear that the move is from sacred space and time to the sacredness inherent in *persons*.

Olam, which gave way to *shanah*, now gives way to *nefesh*. The worship and service of God, *avodah,* once mainly bounded by action and speech, is now evolving toward consciousness and thought. The locus of revelation and law is moving from the masculine rabbinic elite to a male-female base of shared power. The planet is not seen as some dead hunk of matter but a cherished organism that demands to be nurtured as our life-sustaining mother.

Tradition in the Service of the Present!
Torat Hayim!

Withal, the Holy tradition isn't something to overthrown but instead understood as the womb that begat our present. It is nonetheless impossible to remain in it and even less possible to return to it.

There is a new attitude toward women and children, and animals too—witness the increased trend toward vegetarianism; and also we see an emerging change of attitude toward the religious strivings of others who are evolving with us, whom in the past we labeled *goyim* and cultivated no more relationship with than was absolutely necessary.

Many who seek God today look for some needed spiritual vitamins in the liturgical and theological medicine chests of others. Among Catholics, people like Merton saw the preciousness of the Buddhist and Taoist teachings and found them valuable in the service of Catholic spirituality. This has come to the point that there are now such recognized hybrids as Christian Yoga and Catholic Zen (both titles of books officially imprimatured). Many of us have also learned from Native Americans, Yogis, Sufis, and Vedantists, in addition to Christians. (Paulist Press also published treasures of our tradition.)

Dialogue-Communication!

In the dialogue with social scientists and people helpers, we have seen cardinal aspects of Torah renewed for us, particularly by the contributions of psychologists. When we read some of the transpersonal psychologists, our Kabbalah opens in new, process-directed ways. What we understood as angelic entities in the past we begin to see as functions and processes operative in our lives.

A new dimension of vision became accessible to all when women, with the lessening of oppression that restricted their communication, began to teach us in the white letters of the Torah the inner that men have missed.

The pace of global destruction goads us to become a *Mamlekhet Kohanim veGoy Kadosh,* "a Kingdom of Priests and Holy nation," as part of the organism of the *Adam Kadmon,* God's vision of global humanity. The atoning and Holy-making (sacrifice) functions of what inheres in us as part of providential endowment needs the interaction with other parts of that *Adam Kadmon.* These are our elemental *Hayot Hakodesh*—beings of sacred life—of the ecological and holistic *Merkabah,* the rest of humanity, the animal, vegetable, and mineral kingdoms.

Not Only are we God's Partners—God is our Partner too!

We are not alone in this enterprise. What we have in the past called *ruach hakodesh,* the spirit of the Holy that we considered the gift of special individuals, that HOLY SPIRIT is now active and can be experienced in our midst. It is part of our social process as we study Torah and meditate in ways that seek to emulate group telepathy.

The *Bat Kol*!

The act of faith required to take the next step is really small. It's only one step of extrapolation from our present self-awareness. We intuit that there are aggregates still higher than our consciousness entering into our process, guiding and helping in ways we can at present reach only through the gates of our imagination.

The process of our renewal pervades everything: politics, economics, philosophy, physics, relationships, generations, and genders, Jew-Goy, Israeli-Palestinian, producer-consumer — all these and too many more to mention are being changed and metamorphosed. The developments are happening in ways that inform us so that we can cooperate in a conscious and ecstatic birth.

Some of us have dreamed the dream together and want to make it more explicit to ourselves and our colleagues. We want to plug our fantastic *neshamah* potential into one synergy of *kavvanah* to enlarge our intuition and to focus it for greater clarity.

So we reasoned that if we could meet, communicate, share, and allow to emerge what we hope for, then our process would fulfill one of the purposes of the pilgrimage Holy days, the *mitzvah* of *hakihel,* to gather in holy spacetime with holy persons.

This is happening in many places and situations. When we look at the brochures of summer offerings by organizations and movements parallel to us, we're amazed to see how massively the Holy *Shekhinah* is agitating the birthing efforts.

We reach out to others who are regenerating as we are and hope to be included in their rebirthing. Still, what is special to us in our tradition is what we will celebrate and share most.

How awesome is this time! It must be that this is the process of God! — an opening of heaven (a paraphrase of Genesis 28:17).

29

PEACE, PARADIGM SHIFT, AND

SHADOW

THE PROBLEM

As this is being written, Reagan and Gorbachev have only just met. They both have yet to feel that the meeting produced real results. Part of their conversation was about arms reduction. This touched only the outermost surface of the conflict. One resorts to arms only when all else has failed. The arms are the effects of causes, deeper and more destructive in essence than the manifestations in hardware. Here is the paradox: our goodwill and sophistication are so terribly out of balance. There is little goodwill for war and much expertness, and conversely there is much goodwill for peace and very little sophistication in waging it. In the state of the art of conflict reduction, one finds very little sophistication. Our know-how in this area is most primitive. We are ignorant of the basic processes and how they invite risk-taking mutualities when it comes to waging peace. Little wonder that the summiteers achieved only a very small measure of conflict reduction at their meeting.

In this essay I hope to explore some grids that will make thinking about these issues a little clearer. My think-tools come from the minds of Kabbalists, historians, Transpersonal psychologists and sociologists, thinkers dealing with the history of the evolution of consciousness (such as Teilhard de Chardin and Ken Wilber, Erich Neuman and Gerald Heard) and those active in the realm of the transformation of the possible human society (such as Jean Houston and Marilyn Ferguson). I take the existence and the function of the shadow seriously and raise the question of the most effective mini-max relationship between our technology and the shadow energizing it and the cost of it.

Karma and Technology

The Bible shows us the beginnings of animal husbandry and agriculture. (The societies we know of as hunters and fruit gatherers are not part of the biblical narrative.) Cain and Abel must have intuited that one cannot hope to enjoy the shifting of the natural process without somehow propitiating the God who is in charge of maintaining the eco-balance.

We don't know why the biblical narrative favors animal husbandry. Our guess is that patriarchs favored the shepherd over the farmer and projected this favor on God, for the narrative has it, "And He turned to Abel and his offering and to Cain and his offering He turned not." The balance that existed before the feat of the domestication was upset, changed, and in need of a God sanction. The adverse effects initiated the change we call shadow. The method judged to be most effective to minimize the adverse effects of the shadow known to work was to offer the heart to God. To them this meant sacrifice, holocaust, slaughter, and fire offering on an altar.

Shadow

Every good effect has its cost. At times the cost gets inflated; then we get large-scale calamities that trouble us. The shadow manifests as the personal unconscious of individuals or as the black sheep in a group. An individual's persona often gets compromised by his shadow. Or a group's persona is scandalized by a person or persons that create a dissonance between the group's presentation of the self and some of its manifestations.

There are as yet no effective ways to be totally rid of the shadow. The shadow does not split off from the person or the group. Kill the shadow, you kill the person. The only way known to work is the shadow's integration in the whole—to take it to heart. Its quantitative effect can also be significantly reduced by absorbing some of its presence into one's awareness. War and conflict are the shadows of peace. The results of the best intentions of an act done in this world are still tainted by some of the inevitable effects of an accumulation Karma. Some of the Karma decays naturally. Some of it can be made less toxic. Alas, we cannot transform it but on a dimension that differs from our usual universe of discourse.

KARMA STOPPERS AND THE TRANSCENDENTAL DIMENSION

Kabbalists refer often to a formula: *Ein hadinim nimtakin ela beshorsham,* the [bitter] decrees cannot be sweetened unless [raised] to their roots. Our attempts to solve problems only on the plane of presumed cause and effect and as happening only in this social and physical universe often result in creating more new and unforeseen problems than they solve.

One needs to reach to the higher worlds of feeling, knowing, and being (*Yetzirah, Briyah*, and *Atzilut*) and beyond to involve an effective Karma stopper. We often speak of this as at-one-ment and connect it in Judaism with Yom Kippur and in Christianity with Good Friday. In reaching the highest and most transcendent pleromatic level one can stop Karma. However, and in this is the rub, one cannot use this as a mere strategy. The human agent must be transformed in the process. Most systems demand co-efficients on the human side such as penitence and restitution in order to make a Karma stopper work.

In the past, sacrifice offered in the holy *place* at a holy *time* by a holy *person* uttering the reconciling and holy *word* assisted the grace of atonement. As we will see, each eon had its own technology for doing so and its own Karmic shadow problems.

How do we think? Once you can show me the way you think I can construct an expert system that will give me, when applied to other data, the likely result of your cogitation. The magisterium and the traditional hermeneutic are the software constructed for thinking through some of the "cosmic" stuff. It is a cosmological tool chest containing the most refined grids that lead one to understand what action directives might be called for at this time in our history.

A civilization's think-tools are often an extension of the various technologies it employed. The collective experiences gained in a group's historic past created mind sets. These we find as the givens, self-evident or revealed, embedded in the sacred documents of humankind. We can look into them for the way in which transcendental truths were intuited by the religious geniuses in each generation. We can see how they, often not fully aware of why and what they were doing, did what they did and derive from them some insights that can be helpful in the present. In doing so we are not forced to accept the contingencies and mind strategies designed by the seers of past epochs as if they were unchanging truths. The most sophisticated ways in which past seers dealt with their issues, the languages they designed to deal with the subtle, transpersonal realms, can be found in mysticism.

The Kabbalah teaches of four worlds, and this compares with the insights of other mystics. They all seem to have had those cosmological inklings that are now paralleled by the transpersonal psychologists. We can now move to scan to the epochs of history as seen by such divergent cosmological theorists as the Kabbalists, Joachim de Fiore, Teilhard de Chardin, and Rav Kuk and the present Lubavitcher Rebbe-Shlita, Rabbi Menachem Mendl Schneerson, and his late, sainted father-in-law, Rabbi Joseph Isaac Schneersohn *ob"m*. This also dovetails with theories of evolving consciousness such as taught by that great savant Gerald F. Heard and those who derive from him.

KABBALAH

Jewish mysticism, or as the latter day Kabbalists like to define their teachings *penimiyut hatorah*, the inner and esoteric part of the Torah, sees itself as the science of the Divine Name often referred to as the Tetragrammaton, YHVH. As the Kabbalah progressed through the ages it taught of four coexisting universes, each one perpendicular to the other.

The world as we know it is the world of *Assiyah* function, doing. This can be a physical realm that runs parallel to the spiritual-astral world of *Assiyah*, which is the abode of the soul aspect called *nefesh* and is the realm of biopsychic energy states. In it everything in the electromagnetic spectrum occurs. This is the world as we know it in the laboratory and it represents creation as God's transitive object to which God relates as to a "thing" and in the "accusative." It is the home of the I-it relationship. Here the effect of the shadow is strong and produces suffering along with any benefits. (For instance, each mile of good highway carries with itself the statistical expectation of highway deaths. So that one would have to consider the death toll as a given along with the convenience of automobile travel.) In other systems one would refer to this universe of discourse as the plane of *Hatha* and *Karma* Yoga (or in Sufism the plane of the *Shariyyah*). In psychology it is the level of behaviorism. In Ken Wilber's model one sees there with the eye of the flesh. War on this plane seeks the total and physical destruction of the enemy.

Perpendicular to it is the dimension/universe of *Yetzirah*. (Formation, the abode of the affective soul aspect call *ruah*, spirit.) God relates to souls in this universe in the genitive. This is the home of the dialogical and the I-Thou relationship. It is the plane on which the emotional-feeling phenomena are known and experienced. Here, the shadow is still greatly present and projected on the other as "enemy" though not as palpable and irreversible as in the world of action. War on this plane means the mobilization of one's emotional energies to hate, loathe, and despise the enemy. Conversely, war here also means the bonding camaraderie with the allies whom one loves as part of one's agape group. Bhakti Yoga and *Tariqat* in Sufism are expressed there, and in psychology one deals here with psychoanalysis. Extending Wilber's model one could say that here one sees with the passionate eye of the heart.

Perpendicular to both of the others is the universe of *briyah*. It is the world of knowing. In it one sees with the eye of the intellect. The *Jnani Yogin* (*Sufi Ma'aruf*) is at home in it. God relates in it to us in the She/He-me relationship. The universe is the dative, the where and when of history. The Humanistic psychologist is here at home (although he will with his/her client also move to other dimensions). Here the shadow exists as nescience. War here is the exclusion of the enemy's point of view from what I consider truth.

Beyond these is the universe of *Atzilut*. Here the divine dimension is at home. It is the world of the Raja Yogin (*Haqiqat* for the Sufi). It is the realm of being. Here one sees with the eye of contemplation. As Meister Eckhart has it: "The Eye with which God sees me is the same eye with which I see God." One is totally intransitive, in the nominative, subject at One with Subject, Self at one with self. In this universe there is no shadow to our knowledge. It is the source of the miraculous, and in it resides the sacred heart of all things. The transpersonal psychologist opened this realm for modern awareness.

EPOCHS

We will now look at epochs in a similar way. Each one of them was possessed by its own consciousness. For easier reference I will utilize the language of New Age astrology and speak of them as the eons of Taurus (4000 B.C.–2000 B.C.), Aries (2000 B.C.E. to 1 C.E. {A.D.}), Pisces (1–present), and Aquarius (our future for the next 2000 years).

There are a number of theories about the passage of time and the consequent changes in consciousness and human tasks.

The rabbis of the Talmud, for instance, speak of a "week" of 7000 years. 2000 years are *Tohu* — chaos, 2000 years Torah — the dispensation of divine revelation, and 2000 years of the messianic era. This time of progress is followed by a millennium of the great Sabbath. (We are in their calendar now in 1986 in the year 5746 *anno mundi*.)

The Kabbalists saw the same in greater detail giving each one of the 1000 years a particular emphasis. They spoke of time as having texture. The texture of the millennia proceeding from the creation of Adam moves along the lines of the lower seven *sefirot* of the Tree of Life. The first was like the first day of creation with its "Let there be Light," a millennium of grace. The second was like the second day of creation "Let there be a firmament . . . to divide the waters," that of the flood and rigor and severity. The third one relative to the mode of compassion ushered in by Abraham and one corresponding to the third day of creation, "Let there be vegetation . . . trees bearing seed" was the one in which the Torah ("a tree of life") was given at Sinai. The fourth one, corresponding with "Let there be luminaries — sun and moon and stars — in the heavens to give light" relative to the mode of *Netzach* — the word means victory and eternity, and has connotations of the imposition of structure via technique — ushered in the talmudic period. This was followed by the fifth millennium of *Hod* — the word means glory, reverberation, and has connotations of esthetics — of the high middle ages and corresponded to the fifth day of creation when the fishes and the fowl were made. We are now in the eighth century of the sixth millennium of *yisod* — foundation, corresponding to the day humans were created and soon are to enter the messianic millennium of the Sabbath of *Malkhut*.

Joachim de Fiore, a Christian Kabbalist, saw the progression in three stages. To him the Trinity was simultaneous only in eternity. In time the divine Persons manifested consecutively. Thus history proceeded from the age of the Father to that of the Son and from then on to the age of the Holy Spirit. We, according to him, are now on the threshold of the age of the Holy Spirit. (NB, the word *spirit* — *ruach* in Hebrew — is in the feminine.)

Evolving Consciousness

In each of these epochs there was a different mindscape in which the daily phenomena were experienced. The *Zeitgeist* manifested its own waves of highs and lows. At about 600 B.C.E. there was a fantastic AHA! blip on the radar of the planetary mind. Isaiah, Ezechiel, Jeremiah — the peripathetic philosophers in Greece, Zaratushtra, Gautama and Mahavira, LaoTzu and Kung Fu Tzu were approximate contemporaries. The visions they shared and expressed according to their ethnic mind, language, and culture vessels attest also to the phenomenon of the hundredth monkey.

Let us then look at these mindscapes albeit in a molar fashion and see what we can learn from this.

TAURUS

Late Stone Age, earliest forms of writing in lapidary scripts, some monuments and artifacts of that time point to the following mindscape.

The gods we knew then were totally different from what we humans were. Most of them were animal shaped to point to the essential difference between us. Such gods as we worshiped were not available to us for communication. The clergy and the gods were both male and female. Often the *hierosgamos* was part of the Temple cult and celebrated by the *hierodules* at special calendar occasions. Some privileged persons served us as clergy and offered for us the necessary, often human, sacrifices from which in response to the intuition that God wants the heart, living, beating hearts were cut out of the victims by flint knives. The technology was one of clay, stone, and wood. Implements were stone axes. The hunt brought captured animals down. Life lived on other life. The steady state was war. The gods themselves warred with one another. Peace was the exception and often only a synonym for abject surrender to the stronger overlord. Cruel vengeance was the order of law. It was both eyes for an eye. The fates acted with caprice. With the infant mortality rate much higher than today, with unwanted children exposed to die, with many women dying in childbed, many men on the battlefield, and a short life span, human life was cheap.

In such times the cost of security and "peace" was constant war. To make sure that one could live one's life, one had to take that of another. Truth was a special privilege granted to the king by the gracious overlord god.

That state of mind lasted for a long time. It, too, had its own high culture. There is an esoteric tradition that the last and highest mind of that age that produced the *Gilgamesh* and the *Enuma Elish* was that amazing being Melchizedek, priest to God most High. He, according to that tradition, handed the mysteries and the priesthood over to Abraham the patriarch.

Here begins the Age of Aries. In Joachim de Fiore's terms it is the age of God, the Father. God is now seen as anthropomorphic instead of as zoomorphic. The new cosmic take led to monotheism. It was a deistic religion. The God, now as Heschel would have it, is seen as having feelings like the ones we have. Anthropopathy if not anthropomorphism reigned. God was served in space. Babilu (Babylon) the gate of the gods, Beth El the house of God, marked locations in which the deistic God appeared to the children of men.

Clergy and Sacrifices

The clergy is now a hereditary guild jealousy guarding its secrets. One communicates with the wholly other, anthropomorphic gods, who want animal sacrifices on their altar. The public *hierosgamos* is not an accepted practice. The worship of the Mother is repressed. Truth has its power base somewhat enlarged and is what the God reveals to a privileged people with whom He covenants. Justice is now limited retribution, one eye for one eye and no more.

War as Steady State

The god is at war with the unspeakable evil of the other. The good Ahurah Mazda is at war with the evil Ahriman. YHVH is at war with Amalek, the arch fiend. Human beings war for God's sake and for the sake of the victory of the good over evil. Holy war is not only a possibility, but it now is divine command. Victory is assured to the loyal warrior of God.

It is now easier to fight because the bow and arrow and the spear have put distance between the warring parties, now ad hoc armies called together when needed and given special commandments limiting war to the enemy and protecting the environment. The catapult and the battering ram reduce fortifications to rubble. At the end of the era we see roads extending from one end of the *oikumenme* to the other. The *pax romana* followed Alexander's expansion.

With the Temple in Jerusalem destroyed, God is no longer tenable as a deistic, anthropomorphic-anthropopathic Other who moves ad-libitum through time and space. God has become the great *anima mundi*. The oversoul of the life of the planet has replaced the territorial overlord. His arena is now time, not space.

The power base has shifted. Instead of the king or the prophet there are senates and sanhedryns of freeman elders, who have gained expertise in the traditions. They want to understand Truth in order to reject falsehood. They are the children of light at war with the spawn of darkness. Shadow still erupts in madness in which brothers kill each other for words. The shadow costs are paid by martyrs and gladiators whose deaths are the mob's entertainment. This new way of cohering security under an imperial overlord is still expensive now that we have our own superpowers.

The changes, now accelerated by swifter means of travel, continued. Communication, enhanced by newly invented ways of writing, replaced syllabic cuneiform and hieroglyphics with easier to use alphabets. The once sacred art of writing now in the hands of the merchants ushers in the eon of Pisces.

Latin became the lingua franca for the next era. This language, whose hegemony lasts to this day, also brought with it a mental rigidity. With Greek it shared the static architecture of thought. This had both good and bad consequences. The good is in becoming refined enough to reach to higher planes of awareness. A firm base for a wide and steady consensus, it advances a civilization. Just as Greek has its grammar as the basis of its philosophy so does Latin have its grammar as the basis of its Law. The bad consequences are that language that does not change when new paradigms come in becomes a prison, restricting growth and renewal.

The Age of Pisces became fascinated by the magic of the words. The sheer power of communication by words, written, spoken and thought, gave the age of Pisces its elegance. Hebrew, Greek and Latin, Sanskrit, Pali, and later Arabic took on cosmic dimensions. Seen as favored by a God who utilized it to create, reveal, and redeem through it, language also brought with it a trance state. Not until Korzibsky did we see behind its hypnotic effect.

The ratio has changed. It is no longer one life to be killed to keep one alive. The ratio has changed from 1 to 1 to 3 alive to one dead. Each sovereign territory commands its own standing army, and its officers are automatically part of the ruling caste.

If the ages seem embedded in an established and firm paradigm of mind and its set, there is a time in between in which the former civilization has passed and the new one has yet to come in. During these fluid times of paradigm shift there is a departure from the legal-rational order to a more empirical experiential mode. This is often identified with gnosticism. The hard linear transmissions of the major traditions become mixed together in an amalgam hated by purists. They often refer to this phenomenon as syncretism. It is a most fruitful time. Religions that are about to emerge or to be transformed and renewed grow in that incubator. Here the shadow is the womb of the birthing of the new.

We are barely coming out of this phase of history. If not inquisition we have brainwashing. Slavery has been replaced by jails for prisoners of conscience.

When we look at the other paradigms, zoomorphic polytheism of Taurus, etc., we see that they were linked with the consciousness of one of the four worlds. Taurus was linked to the world of physical *Assiyah*, Aries to the world of *Yetzirah*, Pisces to the world of *Briyah*, and now as we enter the epoch of Aquarius we enter the consciousness of the world of *Atzilut*. In the Kabbalah this betokens an inordinate break. It points to possibilities that are altogether divine. It also is so much in harmony with what the other epoch contemplatives like De Fiore and De Chardin have taught. We are entering the phase of the divinization of the planet. This is a mindmove of such proportions that we could say that it is totally unprecedented. All the learning accumulated in the past and stored in the collective unconscious must be sifted to be cleared of that which helped us well in the past and may in the present turn out to be a planet-killing atavism, i.e., territorial national sovereignty.

Our problem is exacerbated by the anxiety and the terror of the traditionalists. Their truth and values produced us. We would not have made our progress without their help. They have been excellent custodians of the magisterium of the ages. When they hear traditional processes questioned they, who have given of their time and energy to preserve the past, are from their point of view justified in being concerned. It runs counter to their injunctions to preserve the treasures of the past when they see us as people who tamper with the traditions. To tell them that there is a paradigm shift happening only increases their anxiety. Their move is to strengthen traditional values as if mere intensity and sincerity could make for survival continued without change.

Just as the intellectual move of the Age of Aries was linear logic, so was the intellectual move of the Age of Pisces dialectics. It understood best when placed in adversary positions. The intellectual move of the new paradigm is not yet fully clear. Oscar Ichazo speaks of trialectics. It seems to be able to deal with multidimensional and holistic data without losing the perspective of the necessary details, entities, and processes. We desperately need new mind tools in order to survive the accumulated Karma of our out-of-balance technoeconomies.

To illustrate: Buckminster Fuller pointed out that, biologically programmed, we have always learned by making mistakes and that learning by trial and error is the best way. (He criticized schools peddling information without allowing their students to find out for themselves in the manner in which we were biologically programmed.) However, this time we can no longer afford to learn the great eco-lessons by trial and error. Our technology and communications have connected us globally. A nuclear or bio-technical error can now have disastrous planetary consequences that might result in there not being anyone left who could benefit from the lesson.

The moral energy needed to bring about the changes that will lead to planetary fairness in the sharing of resources cannot be engaged by lower levels of moral development on the Kohlberg scale. Theological homework for cooperating with the paradigm shift cannot be done on lower levels of the faith scale developed by Jim Fowler. To serve as executive government or corporate personnel without having become also spiritually adept would spell out long-term dangers. Looking good on short-term balance sheets might in the longer run be nothing but an undertaker's cosmetic job.

Obsolete Languages

Our languages are hopelessly out of date. We still say "sunrise-sunset" centuries after Copernicus and Newton. Barriers, greater than technological ones, keep us from creating receptors for solar energy. Only when we will have found ways to speak of our hemispheres as turning to face the sun will we be able think solar with any efficiency. We will not escape sexism until we will have created androgynous personal pronouns. Computers have taught us that languages are to assist processes. Our sophistication in the use of such languages will have to make a cultural quantum leap in order for us to be able to wage successful peace.

Once our economy took a weekly Sabbath. Now we push merchandise 7 days a week and 24 hours a day. Such a treatment of our financial lifeblood leads to fevers. Even regarding the economy we need to think organically. Dealing with time as a commodity as if it were an extruded nylon filament to be chopped up into segments has made us blind to the tides of time. It, too, breathes in and out and has periods that bring us close to the brink of war. Kondrateieff and others have studied business cycles. They warn us of treacherous low tides in which we can expect "trough wars." So too in interpersonal relationships we need to heed the 7-, 28-, and 50-year cycles already honored in the Bible.

No wonder our economies still escape our understanding. The shadow costs of the crazy push to sell has flooded us with conspicuous consumption. We push our economies by advertisements forcing the preponderance of the I over the we. This is social cancer, and the Karma of this is apparent. In the present with AIDS and cancer we see that overpopulation has created a need for the planet to rid itself of the redundant population. Only when we balance the ethical with the biological on an empirical level will we be able to survive.

Much of our aggressive programming has had beneficial results in our survival. Perhaps we could now change this to more irenic and cooperative programming. However, to be rid of the biological imperative before we have done our ethical work is suicidal since changing that program may keep us from surviving under lower levels of technology. To continue as we do is also suicidal. Ethics and the biological program have to be harmonized.

It is in this risky place in which we are that I find the teachings of the ancient mystics most helpful. The Kabbalists point to the next phase as one in which we have moved from the deistic and theistic modes to the pantheistic one. (Rabbi Joseph Isaac Schneersohn of Lubavitch, 1888–1950, taught this in one of the most insightful series of discourses in the year 1942, the height of the Holocaust.) The world of *Atzilut* is totally different from the worlds of *Assiyah, Yetzirah,* and *Briyah.* When *Atzilut* manifests all the other old bets are off. The laws of *Atzilut* are not based on differences and distinctions. In *Atzilut* the human is at one with God. Whatever there remains of necessary shadow is much reduced. Religious, political, economic, and mental strategies needed now are different. Property and land can no longer be dealt with as entities owned by conquest or acquisition. Social systems such as the church that depend on hierarchical, feudal models cannot function without having to undergo the most thorough modifications. Biological imperatives have in the past been balanced by ethical ones. Since the separation of church and state, we have lost the compelling force of ethics in our societal structure. We cannot claim transcendental origins for our ethics. We have abandoned cooperative intercultural-racial work with moralists including those from the Third World. Ethics must now become based on holistic notions, patterned after biology-ecology.

This is no longer the time in which the individualistic person is the highest value. True, we had to free him/her from oppression and give the person the greatest scope for development, but the consciousness of larger social aggregates is now needed to network intelligence to act on many dimensions simultaneously, multitasking for our survival.

The computer has shown us how much we control what we do. The DOS, and the software, the hardware, machine environment peripherals and the handshake, the communications protocol, print formatting features all point out the standards that underlie also our interaction as people because we all have smart cable potential as part of our genetic endowment. Most of the time we are unconscious of the structures of our make-up. We do not notice the amount of internal and automatic shifting we do to accommodate input from others with whom we interact.

This also means that the human species need to connect again with other species, plant and animal, on this planet in order to survive. When we needed to be hothoused as individuals in order to become human persons it was important to stress the differences. Now our commonalities are the bridges for our symbiosis. When religious communities needed to develop their identities it was important to push the differences. Today our commonalities lead to a dialogue of a different order. We Jews, who once needed to maintain our distinctiveness, now need to see ourselves as organic parts of the human family — not to disappear and be assimilated but to function in the life process with others, keeping to the tasks assigned to us. For instance: *kosher* was and is for us an important question. It now needs to be taken out from the kitchen and to be put to planetary ecological use. Our witness is needed today as we challenge consumers with such questions as, "Is electricity generated by a nuclear installation *kosher*?"

We need to share the *upaya* of all psychospiritual technologies so that we might reach global telepathy. We need to give up the poker player's secretive and sly attitude in which we give another bum steers. Our lives depend on mutual disclosure.

To live in a period that is azilic as if we still lived in a preazilic space is suicidal. The shadow karma of the present cannot be contained under the old piscean paradigm. We do not yet know how to process life in the new one. Most of all we have no models from the past how one is to live as a descendant of one traditional lineage and make use of the now vitally needed *upaya* of other lineages.

St. Aquarius' Passion

It may not be possible to reduce the shadow to nonexistence. The karmic costs of our technology may still call for some form of bloody sacrifice. It may very well be that we could, if we but learned how to transform the ways of the past so that they may serve us in the future, find it possible to reduce the shadow costs to minima. It may not be possible to eliminate them completely.

Imagine then that we found out that the yearly karmic costs of living with our advanced technology would give us global peace if we were to offer 5,000 victims who would voluntarily embrace death each year. It is not possible that a new priesthood of boddhisattvic Melchizedeks would offer themselves as willing victims? Christians might understand in a completely new light what it means to take up the cross and to follow their Master. Jews who believed in such self-sacrifice under the name *Kiddush HaShem*, the sanctification of God's Name, called their contribution during the Holocaust years by that term.

Many of the points made here will not make sense under the old paradigm. It may not yield more sense to argue this or that point. The best use of these meditations is in the reader's innering via his/her own contemplative skills and methods. They may not come to the same conclusions but the sharing of their meditations with others is the process by which the homework of reconstructing the spiritual, religious, philosophical, transpersonal-sociological-anthropological maps that will enable us to live azilically and globally.

Once we check this out in our contemplation then we find that turning again to the resources of our traditions we see that the holographic prose of the prophets of the past contain the seeds of the visions we seek. "They will not do evil and they will not destroy on all my holy mountain—they will turn their swords into plowshares and their spears into pruning hooks and study war no more—for the Earth shall be filled with the knowledge of the Lord as the water covers the sea."

Following is a chart that helps one to visualize these thoughts.

PARADIGM SHIFTS OCCURRED BEFORE:

BEFORE TAURUS	−600 −2000−1 ARIES	1−2000 PISCES	NOW–FUTURE AQUARIUS
TECHNOLOGIES			
clay	copper	machines	computer
stone	bronze	catapults	psychosocio-
wood	iron	crossbows	technologies
clubs	camels	guns/rockets	
axes	horses	steam	bio
oars	sails	electricity	atomic
hunt	bows/arrows	printing	heart
defend	lances	fixed armies	mind
capture	longer distance	borders of	spirit
life space	ad hoc armies	territory	aggregate
		more abstract	people power
			war or planet
			obsolete

PARADIGM SHIFTS OCCURRED BEFORE:

BEFORE TAURUS	−600 −2000–1 ARIES	1–2000 PISCES	NOW–FUTURE AQUARIUS
RELIGION			
polytheism zoomorphic	monotheism	theism	pantheism God is All
gods	deism	God-anima	
human sacrifice	animal sacrifice	mundi	Energy-consciousness
	father	son	Holy Spirit
	space	time	person
bio-genesis	noogenesis		Christogenesis
life	mind		God
tohu	Torah	Messiah	millennium-Sabbath
gods at war	good/evil	true/false	On what level is it true? To see this vision is to commit yourself to it.
WAR-SHADOW			
Lex Talionis eyes for eye	1 for 1	restitution	healing consoling transforming
caprice	will of God	principle	Whole-Holy-Ing
Enemy	Amalek	Unbeliever	Creative Principle
	Anti-X	Goy	
Population		Mlechcha Kaffir Heretic- Ex-Communicate	
SHALOM-PEACE			
treaty with vassal and overlord	surrender	order imposed by victor	egalitarian dance
	good is what God wills	ethic abstract theologization of ethic. God wills it because it is good	collaborating increment of effective transformation of life equality

(continued)

PARADIGM SHIFTS OCCURRED BEFORE: (continued)

BEFORE TAURUS	−600 −2000–1 ARIES	1–2000 PISCES	NOW–FUTURE AQUARIUS
SHALOM-PEACE			
truth is	truth breaks	order imposed	synergy
gift	through	by ideology	cooperates with
the high	as special		with God
king	dispensation		
Hammurabi	to the whole	truth static	good cosmic
	people	eternal	harmony
GOD WANTS THE HEART			
priest by	priest	Melchizedek	priesthood
guild	hereditary	apostolic	of peacemakers
		succession	
cut out	strong heart	whole heart	broken-open
hearts			heart

30

NEW MYTHS AND REALITY MAPS

With thanks to Rabbi Gershon Winkler

Every creature in the world, but one, is obsessed exclusively with survival. Maslow pointed to the fact that we must fill first the lower-order survival needs before we can deal with the higher-order needs such as meaning and purpose. So we, when no longer hungry or cold, need to make sense out of life in order to live it. For eons we have been preoccupied with the search for the purpose and meaning of life. It is a theme that dominates the length and breadth of every culture, creed, and philosophy. It is the precursor of most major wars, the cause of social upheavals, genocides, and great spiritual and intellectual enlightenment. It is the soul of all folklore, language, and symbology, the very life force of every religion, science, and social organization, from the Vatican to the Elks Club. Each is motivated by a story, a formula, some kind of algebraic equation that puts the pieces of life's mystery into some kind of order acceptable to the respective group.

Story, then, is important. Whether one is religious, agnostic, or atheist, the human animal has a deep psychological need for some kind of story about how life began and how it will culminate and toward what purpose. The need for a story is so great that most people never question the stories they are reared with and seem concerned only that they have a story—any story. And so dedicated are people to their respective group story that they are generally inclined to consider everyone else's story as false or mistaken. Millions have given their lives in the defense of their stories. Millions more have been slain for their refusal to adopt other people's stories.

The saddest thing about it all is this: we have all had the same story all along. Only it had been told in different words, through different symbols, rituals, and ceremonials. And we are only beginning to realize this today as we wean away from the previous, binary mode of consciousness and enter the coming paradigm. As we dialogue with one another, we are beginning to find that our stories are all one story; only the mythical portrayal of the story differs. And so it is inevitable that, if we are to nurture our fledgling consciousness of organic, global collectiveness in the newly emerging age, we will need to shelve the old myths that divide us and create new myths that unite us, which promote this new visioning.

What, then, is myth?

Generally, we perceive myths as lies. Fairy tales. But actually, myths address deep truths. A myth is a story that is true but not factual. Therefore, if I am looking for fact, then the information contained in the myth is false. If I am seeking the underlying meaning of a reality structure, however, then the myth is a great truth.

The difference between fact and myth, then, is but a hairline. It is the same difference as between sign and symbol. A sign is a clear indication and is exhausted by its single meaning. A symbol is a near indication, as if to say, it isn't really there but is as if it were. So powerful is symbol that it exercises a real and potent presence within a system, whether that system is a religion or a nationality. People have given their lives in defense of religious symbols. People have given their lives in defense of national flags as well. So while symbol may seem to bear little if any significance, within a given system it becomes a living reality that surpasses life itself.

Abraham Joshua Heschel was therefore strongly against calling a *mitzvah* (a biblical precept) "symbolic," for within the system that enwombed it, it is actual. In a sense, then, someone converting to a particular religion is "buying into" the system of that religion, and those rituals and artifacts that before had been "symbolic" now become real and sacred.

Kabbalistically, symbol evokes realization on the Image plane of consciousness as sign would on the Actual plane. The difference is that on the Actual plane we are more inclined to base our decision-making processes on fact rather than on symbol, and on the Image plane, symbol, more than fact, can connect us to other dimensions of awareness and meaning beyond the limited givens of physical law. What we do physically can only demonstrate actual performance but not underlying qualities such as intent and love. The wedding ring, for example, is a symbol of intent. We would want to imbue that token band with the symbolic connection of the moment of union, so that whenever something goes wrong in the marriage on the Actual plane, the ring—the symbol—would reconnect the couple to that moment again.

But symbol belongs only to the Image plane. On the Actual plane, it creates barriers between people who image through different symbols. On the Actual plane, symbol becomes easily misused as a measuring stick for judging people, and often a lever for racial as well as sexual prejudice. If I had a negative experience with a member of a particular race or creed, for example, and I meet someone with similar racial features or religious garb, the encounter is likely to evoke uncomfortable sensations and the desire to avoid the person because he or she embodies a symbol of someone I don't like. Rather than seeing an individual human being walking by, I will see and respond to the symbolic quality of that person: his or her race or creed.

On the Image plane, then, symbol is a connector, associating us with a moment or an action, in the physical dimension; or with an emotion or revelatory experience, in the spiritual dimension. It is sort of a bankbook, which enables us to deposit and withdraw from the memory banks of both the conscious and the subconscious. We use symbol to draw from the conscious memory bank when it aids us in commemorating an historic event of religious significance, for example, Passover, Easter, Christmas.

In drawing from the subconscious memory bank, symbol is the impetus that elicits the great, albeit momentary, Aha!—the fleeting realization of a profound truth, the revelatory flash of recognition of something unbound by the strictures of linear reality, of something we know as God, of God simulating Person for that brief but nonetheless eternal moment.

The common denominator between these two banks to which symbol holds the key is the contents of the safe-deposit boxes in both: remembrance, re-kindling, re-cognition, and dis-covering the mystery of the Infinite. Of God. Every religion has this in common. Every philosophy. Science and religion use different terminology and propose differing myths, but both use the same bank, both are mystified by the great unknowable It, whether you call it infinity or the Infinite God, whether your myth is The Big Bang or The Big Genesis.

I can imagine myself in the God-space,
getting the notion of Original Man.
And then, as God I start to simulate Person.
And the *tzimtzum* (constriction) begins.
Because in order to get into the Human-space
there needs to be limitation,
because a human can't
know everything
if it is to be a creature
of self-creating intelligence.
Next, I start
putting out all the biology
and set the evolutionary process in motion,
because I've got all the patience in the world,
for what am I, but God, caught in
infinite and eternal solitary confinement.
Is there another God?
I'll never know.
I'm all that I know, and cannot know
beyond My Allness,
and I assume it is infinite.
But is it?
Well, I went through
all the infinities, searching:
are there any ends?
Then I came upon this notion of Person,
and fell in love with it,
with Person, with Consciousness,
with growth of consciousness.
So first I will make Earth.
Then I will form the Person out of
My Name, *Yud—Heh—Vav—Heh*.
I will make Yud the head,
Hey the shoulders and arms,
Vav the spine, and
Hey the pelvis and legs.
And then I will blow into its nostrils
and it will become conscious.

So goes the story. And different people gave different words to the story, different myths to the same story, the same universal cognition of the same residual God-Knowledge left over in every cell of the human body, every spark of the human consciousness since God Imaged us into Actuality. And each time we experience a realization, a revelation, an Aha!, whether spontaneous or set off by a symbol, we re-cognize, re-member, and dis-cover that Great Cosmic Allness of which we are all equal parts. In that moment of cognition, there is a lightning of Divine Allness that illuminates the consciousness, but soon thereafter the impact of the Aha! fades and a blindness returns between us and the Infinite. From then on, the clarity of both the medium and the message of the Cosmic Flash depends on the myths and symbols that are subsequently developed to communicate and cultivate the revelation.

In the past paradigms, such momentary flashes of Infinity, of dis-covery, were snatched from their eternal dimension and entombed in the world of relativity in the form of religious institution and symbolism. Revelations of cosmic commonality, when etched into stone, often became doctrines of exclusive particularism. It was the myth of a binary world, a world of either/or, of good or evil, of build up or tear down, of Us and Them. Now we are entering an age of alternative, of elasticity, in which God is being liberated from stone engravings and doctrinal codes to become organic again, in turn freeing human consciousness to do the self-growing it was originally intended to do.

And for this latest Flash, as discussed at the beginning of this section, we will need new myths. Organic myths, elastic myths. In creating new myths for a new age we will have to examine the Revelations of our time. Revelations in the coming paradigm will in all likelihood not be found in solitary desert wanderings or transcendental excursions but in the more immediate surroundings of the Planetary Mind and the kinds of happenings it burps up now and then. The message of God the Cosmic Flasher is resonating in Mother Earth, in the very ground we walk on, and the criterion for prophecy, in turn, has been adjusted so that everyone can access it.

Today's symbols, from which tomorrow's myths must emanate, are the actors in the unfolding drama being performed on various sections of the global stage, be it the threat of the bomb or the international solidarity of those striving for disarmament; the rapid development of super- and micro-technology that is bringing together cultures and belief systems that, before, were worlds apart, or the global awareness of genocide and mass starvation in portions of the Third World; the spirit of ecumenism that has spread its messianic canopy across walls and moats once thought impossible to engage, or the ever-growing fanaticism of zealous fundamentalists across every religious denomination, which, in some instances, has led to international terrorism; the miraculous advances of modern medicine in areas such as organ transplants, artificial insemination, and bypass surgery, or the menacing epidemic of a fatal disease called AIDS, against which that same medical technology remains, at this writing, helpless.

Ordinarily, these would be called "signs of the times." But now we need to see them as "symbols of the times." Then, perhaps, we can become open to "dis-covering" and "re-cognizing" and "re-membering" those pieces of the great puzzle we need so badly in order to put today's Humpty Dumpty back together again. Aside from the drama of current events played out on the six o'clock news, we have no other resource for piecing together a new story for the coming paradigm. We don't have myths that work anymore, that connect us to any answers that can address the questions of our time.

We need to look at AIDS, for example, and wonder whether it might be a bottled message washed ashore by Mother Earth, warning us not to get too carried away with the concept of immunity in our zeal to cast down all barriers, to ecumenize and sexualize without bounds, without responsibility, without regard to individualistic integrity. We just went through such a craze in the sixties and seventies, beginning with the sexual revolution and then a headfirst, eyes-shut dive into open-ended egalitarianism as well as undefined declarations of synonymity between the sexes.

In short, we tampered recklessly with immunity across the board and dealt it a fatal blow in the name of brotherhood and harmony, not realizing that immunity, too, has its role in our lives, that while exclusive particularism is certainly not the way of the enlightened, neither is homogenized humanity. That while a puritanically inhibitive sexual morality is not workable, neither is an orgiastic free-for-all morality. That while men and women are equal, they are not the same and need to be honored and related to with consideration to their respective psychology.

Immunity in the body protects us from alien interference with the harmony of our biological functioning. It sort of defends the integrity of our individuality, that although you and I are made of the same stuff, my body will automatically reject your heart or kidney. Recipients of donated organs require temporary suspension of their immune systems.

The sexual revolution may have gone too far, not in stripping sex of the taboos that had inhibited it but in also stripping it of the built-in immunity of individualism so that a great many became faceless slabs of flesh to one another to mount or be mounted, lovelessly, without responsibility or consideration for individual integrity. The feminist revolution may have gone too far not in battling for the inalienable civil rights of women but in also pushing women so hard to become like men that they've all but lost contact with their sense of what Woman is, and, in the process, left a trail of bewildered men who are at a loss as to how to relate to their female counterparts or how to dis-cover the feminine energy within themselves.

The trend toward egalitarianism and cross-denominationalism in religion may have gone too far, not in its noble attempt to foster universal peace and remove belief barriers that had kept people at each other's throats for eons, but in its downplay of the respective values of particular traditions. Everyone has something to offer, to share. And everyone also has something personal, individual; Karmic, if you want, and should be honored as such. This goes for people, genders, and traditions.

Immunity, then, declares that while we are all similar to one another we are also very different and that this needs to be honored. And any attempt at forging a unity between peoples is wholesome only when the diversity between peoples is honored as well. There is a middle way, a balance, and we need to discover it for the overall health of the planet. This is our homework. AIDS might be the difficult Algebra with which we need to wrestle, but in these problems lie solutions that can ease the birthing of the coming paradigm.

Organically, our bodies have this built-in situation that says an attacking enemy must be destroyed. White blood corpuscles come and flush it out and go with it. Comes the sexual revolution and we get into a place where we say nobody is my enemy and everybody is my love partner and I can make it with anybody. When we say, don't repel strange intruders anymore, we get into the issue of AIDS. AIDS is a life thing, a virus, transmitted in life-holding fluids such as semen and saliva, and the indiscriminate exchange of body fluids is like saying to the body: "Stop immunity." It is my sense, then, that AIDS is not just a sexual disease. It is a symbol of a much larger scourge. There is a transmitting going on today for which we have not yet learned to draw lines. I'm afraid that Judaism will get AIDS. Nor do I want to see Christianity get AIDS. I want them to keep having intercourse with one another, to find a level where their social contact will be right for them rather than not have any at all. On the other hand, there are certain things in the body of each that do not mix, which should maintain their respective immunity. We cannot allow AIDS—in religion or sex—to replace the old barriers again. We've come too far, sacrificed too many. We must have faith that there is some kind of middle ground, and we need to sit it out until we find it.

In the old system, when the myths were already presented to us, there was no room for elasticizing a situation, for wrestling with an issue, sticking with it until a middle ground could be found. Everything was prerecorded, spelled out; the script had already been written, signed, and canonized. It was either the one extreme or the other, totally good or totally evil. In our time, however, we have come to see life as process, not fixed, and God as organic, not static. Myth, too,then becomes a process, and by telling the story of that process, we see ourselves as part of that myth.

When Reb Mendl of Vitebsk was in his middle years and close to death he noticed his disciples weeping around what they thought was his deathbed. He smiled faintly and assured them that he wouldn't die yet. The disciples were puzzled. He explained: "When I was a child, I visited the Baalshem, and he told me a story. And as he told it, I realized it was my story. And according to the story I still need to go to Israel."

We are now writing our own stories, creating myths from the symbols of our own times. The story is the same; only the characters have been changed. The dragons we are battling with in today's myths are fierce issues such as AIDS and The Bomb. Part of the story has already been started by the millions who perished in Auschwitz and Hiroshima, compliments of the old story. Their souls have been the Revelation for the New Age: a resounding "Stop! No more!" that has radically altered the consciousness of our time.

The new myth, then, as every myth that came before it, is without an actual beginning. We used to believe that every effect has a cause. Now we understand that every cause has a cause as well and is actually the effect of a yet earlier cause. A figure is only because of its background. The background usually goes unnoticed and seems insignificant. Yet, without the background there cannot be a figure. The biblical word for Genesis, *"b'reishit,"* does not really translate, "In the beginning." A rather more accurate rendition would be: "Once upon *a* beginning." In conclusion, the new story must be ours. It will be an awesome responsibility to develop it, probably the greatest Promethean challenge in thousands of years. But we need to do this one together. And we can begin by shattering the myth that there is only one myth and that all others are false. Then, each of us needs to climb into the story and become an organic part of it in life and in death.

> If I get to know where I belong in the myth
> and the myth has explanations
> that will take me past the death fear,
> I can then die peacefully,
> with a sense of purpose, knowing that
> I am a significant link in a process;
> that what I learned in this lifetime,
> what I was made aware of in this time span,
> will be recycled into the Planetary Mind
> and become transformed
> into a part of the Revelation for the next Age,

another piece to the Great Puzzle.
And it will be my contribution.
My part. My piece. This will suffice.
I am not asking for any higher God-space
When I die, only that my life's Aha!
be ENTERed into the Global Brain as the Aha!
No More than the souls that went up
in Auschwitz and Hiroshima.

So, at my funeral,
I want you to say that this Program,
Zalman.Exe
is now being saved on the hard disk
of the Global Brain.

ACKNOWLEDGMENTS

Grateful acknowledgment is made to the following for permission to reprint previously published material:

Bloch Publishers: "On Mystical-Empirical Jewish Prayer," in *Ancient Roots and Modern Meanings*, ed. Jerry Diller, 1978. Copyright © 1978 Jerry Diller. Reprinted by permission of Bloch Publishers.

COMMENTARY: Excerpts from "The Condition of Jewish Belief," August 1966. Copyright © 1966 American Jewish Committee. Reprinted by permission of COMMENTARY.

Emergence — Journal for Evolving Consciousness: "Reformatting Our Theology," an interview with Rabbi Zalman Schacter and Eve Ilsen by Arifa Goodman. Vol. 3, no. 1, Winter 1988/89. Copyright © 1989 Sufi Order. Reprinted by permission of *Emergence — Journal for Evolving Consciousness*.

Journal of Ecumenical Studies: Excerpts from "Bases and Boundaries of Jewish, Christian, and Moslem Dialogue" 14:407–18, Summer 1977; and excerpts from "Jesus in Jewish-Christian-Muslim Dialogue" 14:407–18, Summer 1977. Copyright © 1978 *Journal of Ecumenical Studies*. "The Dialogical Mentality" 18:11–13, Winter 1981. Copyright © 1981 *Journal of Ecumenical Studies*. Reprinted by permission of the *Journal of Ecumenical Studies*.

Ktav Publishing House, Inc.: "What One Can Say About God," in *A Jewish Child's Book of Why: Questions Children Ask Parents* by Kerry Olitsky, David Kasakove, and Steve Rosman, 1993. Copyright © 1993 Kerry Olitsky, David Kasakove, and Steve Rosman. Reprinted by permission of Ktav Publishing House, Inc.

INDEX

About the Author

Zalman Schachter-Shalomi was ordained as a Lubavitch-trained rabbi and has counseled men and women for more than 35 years. He received his master's degree in psychology from Boston University and a doctorate from Hebrew Union College.

Rabbi Schachter-Shalomi is currently president of Aleph Alliance for Jewish Renewal and Professor Emeritus of Religion in Psychology of Religion and Jewish Mysticism at Temple University, Philadelphia, Pennsylvania. He has published more than 175 articles and translations, and his books include *Spiritual Intimacy: A Study of Counseling in Hasidism*, *Fragments of a Future Scroll*, and *The First Step: A Guide for the New Jewish Spirit*. Rabbi Schachter-Shalomi designs and conducts seminars on spiritual eldering, and he is currently preparing a book on this subject.